Willie Means Well

Willie Means Well

Willie Means Well
(But It Don't Work Out Sometimes)

"THE MEAL"

Willie Means Well

Willie Means Well

Willie Means Well
(But It Don't Work Out Sometimes)

"THE MEAL"

by Willie Earl Means

UNIQUE EUPHONY
Publishing Group

Copyright © 2012
Willie Earl Means 090412
ISBN: Softcover 978-0-9840260-6-7

All rights reserved. No part of this book may be reproduced or transmitted in any form by any means, electronic or mechanical, including photocopying, recording, or by any information storage or retrieval system, without permission in writing from the Publisher.

This book was printed in the United States of America

To order additional copies of this book, contact:
Unique Euphony Publishing Group
706-577-3197
www.uniqueeuphony.com
inquiries@uniqueeuphony.com
Interior Layout by Barbara M. Pierce
Cover Design by Kirk Knox

Willie Means Well

Willie Means Well
(But It Don't Work Out Sometime)
THE MEAL

Table of Content

Willie Means Well.....11
Negative Mood.....39
Willie's Girls.....71
What Is Real.....89
Overwhelmed and Overdue.....102
A Letter To the President and Other Editorials.....
Weekends Should Last Forever.....195
From Outdoor Toilet to Indoor Plumbing.....198
What Is Real (Here's to Reality).....200
Murder at Nine Twenty Fourth Avenue.....208
I May Have Found Netra – Lil Lover.....214
You Took My Love from Me (A Thought for Janice, Pay).....216
Janice (Pay).....218
Willie Means (My Grief).....232
Intertwined.....234
Chicago (1703 West Walnut Street).....236
Snow (For Those of You Who Do Not Know, Chicago Always Gets Some Snow – 1967).....244
Roxanne.....247
On The Move.....248
The Man at the Top of the Stairs.....250
Journeying.....253

Willie Means Well

1307 South Saint Louis....256.
Lexington (2800 Block).....262
Lexington 1968 – Summer 1970....263.
Ouija....269
Marshall High School (Track and Field.....281)

Out of the Frying Pan and Into the Fire – summer 1971 through spring 1974 - (The Cabrini Green Housing Project) Death Walks the Street.....292

King.....295
JoAnn and I (Our Grief).....299
Death Walks the Cabrini.....305
A Whirlwind Romance (Reform, Alabama).....307
Hazelnut.....315
Elizabeth.....342
Thanksgivings (2011).....357
Death in the Family (December 19, 2011).....370
Denice – 'Dee'
    (Denice Elaine Hale Hardaway Means).....372
Sweet Melissa.....373
Who Am I? Damned If I Know.....374
What Is Real – Here's To Reality....375.
Mary.....377
Psychology.....386
The Study of the Human Mind.....387
A Fight With My Sister.....389
Mary, Mary.....411
    I'll be back
Mary, Mary.....417
The Ouija Board....419.
What Is Real – Ouija ll.....423
Mr. Ouija and Me.....429

Willie Means Well

Here's To Reality.....431
You Abandoned Me.....433
My Rose Bloomed Anew (Dedication For Naomi).....442
Well! Here's To Another Day in the Live of Willie Means.....446
Actuality! (Here's To Reality).....450
Little Spider.....454
A Ride In The Snow.....460
New Years 2009.....474
Oh By The Way (My Life In A Nutshell).....476
Just A Chance.....477
The End (I Am A Fucking Dinosaur).....479

Willie Means Well

Willie Means Well

"Morning all and I truly am thankful for a new day!!! Is there anyone out there who ever thought that his or her house could be haunted? Well, I do believe that I have an unwanted guess! Have not did anything bad but it does scare me. I do pray and asks GOD for protection but besides that, what would you do 'Facebook'?
K. Josey M. Johnson, my daughter, 5th Generation in the Family Lineage of Ms Virginia Pack McSwain

Katina 'Josey' Marie Johnson is my daughter. My first born... I nicked named her Josey because her mother had been pregnant and we just knew it was going to be a boy. We were going to name the child Joey but things got out of hand one night when, as usual, her mother wanted to follow me and refused to listen to anybody. I remember 'Big Bud', the man who was responsible for our moving to Chicago, had come over to see Momma. I do not recall if they were going to try to get back together but all these years later, I feel my conduct that night might have played a part in Big Bud changing his mind.

    We had moved back to Lexington. We were in the two-story building that had a church in the basement. We had the apartment on the first floor and a man named Frazier lived on the second floor. Very nosey individual and I will tell you of an incident with him later. As I said in my initial offering, when it came to living in places that had unusual activity, we had more than our share because of our background and the way we had been raised. The Pastor of the Church in the basement and his wife had lived in the apartment we now lived in and I guess she did not want to leave even after she had died. I know I had my share of sightings in that house but what really got me was I was the only one able to sleep in the back bedroom. That bedroom was very haunted. I remember our first night in the house after moving in and everybody going to bed tired. With my dog King, I braved many things; even things unexplainable to many. When I finally lay down, I had the room neat and clothes tied in bundles stacked in the closet. I called King in to me and left the door cracked so he could get in and out. At this time, he was totally turned into a watchdog. You will read about King later how he and I met each other and him almost biting me in the neck. When we lived on Lexington in 1968, your dog had to know how to fight because boys and teenagers in the gang enjoyed dog fighting. Your dog needed to know how to protect itself because normally at night you let the dog out by its self... With all the dogs running around, your dog was bound to get into a fight. King had one hear chewed from a run in with a German shepherd named 'Killer Duke'. Therefore, I fought King at times so the guys would know he was mine and they could see their dog might get hurt if the dog jumped on King.

    That night when I went to sleep, King apparently saw something I would not want to see anyway. Oh, my pet name for King was 'Old Man'. I am sure many of you know what I am talking about when I talk of being in deep sleep and coming only half-awake when something tries to wake you. I remember it was almost like a dream. I heard someone walking in the kitchen and then my bedroom door came open. It was dark in the bedroom but the darkness I saw through the door in the kitchen was darker. I did not see anyone come in the door but I could swear I heard Old Man growling. Old Man was sitting up and looking towards the closet, and when I said, *"Old Man"* he turned his head to me and licked me. I was drowsy and I thought I saw the curtains move that was hanging to cover the closet door. I remember I said, *"I don't see anything King!"* Then I patted the bed and King jumped up on the bed with his head facing the closet. I rubbed his head and went back to sleep.

    When I woke up, the door to the bedroom was open and I could hear Momma in the kitchen cooking. Old Man sat up from the floor and I rubbed his head and squeezed his mouth. He growled and nipped at my hand and put his two from paws up on the bed for me to rub his chest. When I sat up to rub his chest, I looked at the closet, and the clothes had tumbled out on the floor. What made me angry right away was the bundles had been untied as if someone was looking for something particular.

"Momma! Who has been in here messing with these clothes?"

"Ain't nobody up but me and I haven't been in there. I saw King up on your bed through the door and I asked him what he was doing up on your bed. Sometimes I believe that dog understands everything we say. He eased off the bed before I could tell him it was all right. What is wrong?

"Look at these clothes. Momma I had this room straighten out last night and the clothes tied in bundles and stacked in the closet. Now the clothes are on the floor. Last night King was growling at something but I did not see anything."

"Well, you know I done told you that animals see spirits too. In addition, I will ask Reverend Hays if he ever had a problem in that room. He told me his wife didn't want anyone living in her house so maybe she was trying to see what you had."

Now normally, this would seem odd to the everyday person, but me. Even today, I shiver when I think of some of the things that have happened to me in the past and my momma was pulled into it. Before we left Bessemer, Alabama in December 1966, we lived at 920 Fourth Avenue in Jonesboro across from Bessemer Stadium. Now you talk about someone who loved Church! I was crazy, madly in love with Church when I was ten years old and had been since I was baptized at eight years old. I already knew all the books in the Bible and I preferred to be in Church rather than out playing with my friends. The problems I was having came to me at night while sleeping DREAMS!

Mother told me I was being attacked by demons and she, Mother Brown (who was a Prophet and told Mother I was going to be a Preacher someday), and others in the Church had Prayed for me and anointed me with 'Holy Oil'. Since it was only a three room house we lived in, my sisters slept on one side of the room and my oldest brother, when he was home, and I slept in a curtained off section of the room. I do not recall what my brother had done but Mother had put him out and he was living with a friend named 'Bowlegs'. I think I had bad dreams for several nights in a row when this particular night in my dreams I was being attacked by a demon and it looked like the dragon in this orange book that the Jehovah Witness' use to pass out to people. This dragon had me cornered and was reaching to eat me as I was yelling and screaming for Momma. Of a sudden, the dragon stopped, looked off to the left, wish in actuality was towards the front room where Momma slept with my baby brother Marzett, and turned and rushed into the bathroom which was also in the middle room with us. Sure enough, the light came on and Momma told me I was standing at the head of the bed screaming and pointing towards the bathroom. Even today Momma swear that when she looked towards the bathroom she saw the tail end of something, with the tail shaped like a pitchfork, going into the bathroom. Momma picked up my Bible and went over, said *"In the name of JESUS"* and opened the bathroom door. I probably do not have to tell you it was empty. Well, my sisters were awake, Momma allowed Joyce to sleep with me the rest of the night, and we were allowed to keep the light on. There was always something happening in that middle room. It was that same middle room where my Sister and I first saw the little boy and girl who eventually led me to find the knife a woman had been killed with who lived in the house before us.

So you see, when Momma made the statement reminding me about animals seeing spirits, it was no surprise to me.

"Well Momma. Tell Reverend Hayes to let his wife know we need somewhere to live and we are not bothering her. Tell him to let her know I will be sleeping in this back bedroom and I hope she do not bother me because I be very tired when I come home."

Momma looked at me and told me she would pass the message on and asked me not to be scaring my sisters with what had happened. Later in that same bedroom, my friend Jimmy Ray was over one day while I was gone and Momma explained to me what happened to him when he decided to take a nap.

"Jimmy Ray came over and he looked so tired. I don't know if he had been drinking or he had been up

a long time," Momma explained. *I told him he looked like he needed some sleep and he said -'Momma Means I been trying to help William 'em work on his car and I told him I wanted to come over here. I believe they got mad at me cause I wanted to come over here. That was early this morning and you see it's after four o'clock now.'*

"T told him you was out of town on a track meet so he could lay down in your room and get some sleep," Momma continued. *Well, he was back there about twenty minutes and all of a sudden, he came running from back there, and he stood in that door, and kept looking at the back door. I asked him what was wrong."*

"Jimmy Ray, what's wrong with you?"

"Ya'll hear anybody come out the church and walk in that gangway?"

"No. I've been sitting here doing this baby's hair and everything has been quiet."

"Momma Means, I might have been dreaming but I seen the church door open but I didn't see nobody come out the church. Then I was looking at

the gangway and I could tell somebody was coming but I could not see anybody. Of a sudden, I was seeing out the backdoor and I could tell whatever it was had came up on the porch and was coming to the door. The screen door opened and that is when my eyes must have come open because I realized I was looking at the ceiling. Momma, all I wanted to do was get out of that bedroom because I knew whatever it was, it was coming in that bedroom."

"Well, my son, look like you had done saw something because even when you were staring back, I could see you was really frightened. Buster sleeps in there but he always go the sleep with King in there with him. You let that couch out and gone back to sleep isn't anything going to come in here.

I was a Junior Deacon at Concord Pentecostal Missionary Baptist Church during that time and between my track and field and church, there was definitely a war going on in me. I loved Reverend Clark and he was the closest thing to a father I had in a long time. Momma had boyfriends over the years, but Reverend Clark taught me so much. Some will dispute this, but until the day I die I will always believe Reverend Clark laid a curse on me and even though I tried to overcome it, it came back and dominated my life; even now. Reverend Clark was intimate with several women in the church to include my mother. His wife niece Linda and I called ourselves *'going with each other'*. They might call it dating today, or being a couple, but back in the day, it was *'going with each other.'* I guess the best way to state it was *"Linda had my nose wide open!"* I told her everything. Then, to top it off, Reverend Clark was with my mother one day when one of the women from church came by to get me to do something at the church. While we were walking to the church, she asked me how to get to the back of our building. I remember my girlfriend Margaret's mother was looking out the window and heard the woman ask me how to get to the back of the building. She asked me what I was doing and I told her going to the church to help the woman. When we got to this vacant lot, I told the woman she could get to the back of our building that way. She asked me to show her and I did and Reverend Clark's car was parked in the rear. I guess that sometimes you can be so honest you can be stupid as I was. Then Linda dropped a bomb on me and told me she had told her momma and daddy everything we had been talking about because she was tired of hurting her auntie. That Sunday after church, it all came out in the open and after all was said and done, I will always recall Reverend Clark not taking his eyes off me. That night before bed, Momma called me and told me she should whip me for what I had done.

"I thought you learned a long time ago to stay out of grown people business. I guess the LORD works in mysterious ways. Your Pastor told me to tell you that someday you will marry a woman older than you will and she will rule your life and make you miserable. I thought about whipping you but at your age I don't want to have to physically punish you again."

Joseys' momma and I have to know each other very well in that bedroom. I was 19 and Joann was 20. During those days, we never could get enough of each other. I know whenever we had to leave each other for the evening, I could not wait for school and track practice to be over so I could go by and see her. She had *Little Man* by Harvey and at first, her family tried to keep us from seeing each other. Even my Mother tried to keep us apart once she realized we had gone beyond laughing and talking and sneaking a kiss every once in a while. Joann was spending a lot of time with us while we still lived in the Cabrini Green Housing Projects. Everybody suspected we were having sex but no one could catch us until one day I stayed home from work and she came over from her sister house in one of the other projects. I was 18 and she was 19 when we both realized we wanted more of each other than just kissing. Our first attempt at sex was standing outside the door at her mother and her sisters were watching the baby for her. I have heard people say, *"Love is so much sweeter when you are stealing it!"* Well, not telling you to get in any trouble, but try it and I will bet you will enjoy it a great deal. My goodness, standing up against that wall and feeling myself inside of her felt good. I was scared but I was not going to turn down the opportunity I had been waiting on since I first met her in 1967. I could actually hear her sisters talking through the door and I heard one tell their mother that Joann was in the hallway with Buster. Next thing I knew the baby was coming up the hall in his walker and crying. Joann sisters started yelling at her to get her baby, and if she had heard the baby crying.

"Oh God Buster I got to get Lil Man", she stated as we both were breathing heavily and moving up and down against the wall.

"A couple of more minutes, A few more minutes," I moaned as I could feel myself beginning to have an orgasm.

"Buster, Stop! I've got to get my baby!" I do not know how she did it, but just as I was getting my release, she rose up on the tip of her toes, at the same time took her hand, and pulled me out of her. The stuff went everywhere. I turned away to stuff my penis back in my pants and she put her panties back on and turned and opened the door and picked up the

baby just as her mother was coming up the hall.

"Joann! What you doing letting that baby cry like that. If you can't see Buster and take care of your baby too, then you don't need to be seeing him or nobody!"

"Momma, Punk, and Carolyn were playing with Lil Man and I was just seeing Buster out the door."

I told Ms. Johnson I was sorry and did not mean to keep Joann from her baby.

"Well it's late anyway and time for you to go home."

Joann had Lil Man in her arms and she pushed me out the door and came out behind me. Soon as she closed the door, she began to laugh.

"Damn Joann, I don't see what you laughing about. You know your momma gone call my momma and tell her something that's going to get me in trouble."

"I'm sorry Buster. However, I thought you were going to run out the door. You still scare of my momma. She ain't gone bite you. That is all she is *going to do is fuss. That is why I am thinking about getting my own place. You call me when you get home so I'll know that you got there alright."*

Ms Johnson had recently returned from Monroe, Louisiana and lived out West near Division. I walked to Division and caught the bus and all the way home, I could feel my sperm cells wetting my shorts and running down my thighs. By the time the bus came to my stop, I did not want to stand up because I knew my pants were wet.

That was my sweet, little Joann whom I met the summer of 1967 when we moved to 1307 South Saint Louis on the Westside of Chicago. She and Joyce were the same age and they played together. However, Joann had a way of standing off to her, and just watched us when the boys started playing with the girls. In fact, I believe that blasted Bernard Davis, also-known-as (AKA) Man, stole a few kisses from her even then. I jumped on him when I got the chance and always made another excuse but Johnny knew why I would be jumping on him. It even led to a fight between Johnny and I because we were co-leaders of our little gang and Johnny told me I was too afraid to talk to his sister so do not be jumping on Man if he did.

I will talk about our little posse on Saint Louis later. I started a short story in Ms Lundergan's English Class while in tenth grade at John Marshall High School on the Westside of Chicago. I really got a thrill when Ms Lundergan showed it to the *Drama Teacher* and they asked me to do more because they thought it would make a good play. The short story was about my time living on Saint Louis and meeting Johnny and his family. (insert here the fb contact with Ms Lundergan)

Right now, I want to finish telling you about my daughter Josey Marie. As I pointed out, she is fifth-generation from Ms Virginia Pack McSwain. Looking back through the years, I recall something happening to the head of each family that stood out, was unexplainable, and made your, as the old people use to say, *'HAIR CRAWL'*.

I did not know much about my Great Grandmother, Ms Virginia Pack McSwain. I do know that like all the females in the *Pack Family Clan*, she was strong, as most Black Females had to be since slavery time. It was not just the Pack Family Clan, but, coming up in the South, you would consider a Black Family 'Rich' if there were a Daddy involved. What I knew about Great Grandmother I learned listening as my mother told stories to my sisters about being proud of the family for making it through the *Great Depression*. I know the Family roots are in Cuba, Alabama very near Meridian, Mississippi. Momma told of the Family having land, animals, and timber. Like many families during the Depression, sometimes several grown-ups would be in one household to make 'ends meet'. From listening to the stories momma told, I guess the Pack Family Clan lived well off the land they had. I guess the family not struggling and doing all right during that time is what got Great Grandmother killed. The way momma explained it, one of the uncles wanted to sell off the timber and when Great Grandmother would not allow it, he got her out the way.

"I remember we had eaten dinner and Momma was combing Madea's hair. It was in the summer time and we had the windows open so the evening breeze would blow through the house. We were sitting around listening to Momma explain to Madea why she would not let her brother sell any of the timber or the land. Madea had just told Momma she was right when the wind blew the curtains and Momma asked who that was stuck their hand inside the window. We all turned to look at the window and my daddy jumped up and rushed out the front door. Madea ran towards the back door but neither one of them saw anybody outside. Daddy even got a lantern and looked on the ground outside the window but found no footprints. Momma said that sure was strange and she know she saw a hand come in that window.

We all went to bed and I knew something was wrong right away the next morning when I realized it was daylight and most of us were still in the bed. I remember Madea was walking through the housing and Praying and Daddy was trying to tell her

Willie Means Well

everything was going to be all right. I asked what was wrong and my sister told me they could not get Momma awake. Now that was strange because nobody beat Momma up. Momma would be up, that wood stove would be burning, and she would have breakfast ready by the time we had finished our morning chores. Since we had animals, the animals had to be fed and let out to Pasteur before we ate. In fact, we all had our morning we had to go to the chicken yard and gather the eggs. On my morning, Madea would always have Daddy get her some switches and then tell me, "Roe Lee, go get those eggs." Now I liked eating like everybody else but I always tried to switch chores when it was time for me to get the eggs. I did not want to go in that chicken yard and get chicken 'do, do' on my shoes. Therefore, on my morning to get the eggs, I would start the day with a whipping. Just because I was, a girl Madea did not have mercy on me. Even during school time, on those days I would go to school with whelps on my arms and legs.

The doctor came out to see Momma and he gave

her some medicine and told Madea and Daddy she just needed some rest. They gave Momma that medicine but after a few days, Momma could not keep anything in her stomach. She got so weak they had to lift her out the bed. A man that Daddy knew told of a doctor in Mobile, Alabama that they should let check Momma out. Momma was taken to the man and I was allowed to go along. The doctor saw Momma right away and I was sitting looking through the door. He did not do anything but scrape the silver off a dime into something he poured in a cup and they got Momma's mouth open and got her to swallow some of the stuff. I never will forget Momma started moving as she could not breathe and put both hands up to her throat and tried to cough. Of a sudden, this thing came up in Momma's throat, you could actually see her neck extend, and it made a long croaking sound like a frog and then went back down. When it went back down, Momma just flocked down in the bed and did not move. That man looked at Daddy and Madea and told them it was too late. He told them somebody had put 'voodoo' on Momma *and it was too late. He said had they gotten her to him a week earlier he could had saved her. Momma only lived two weeks after that and I will always believe it was my great uncle who killed her for that land."*

I was going to take this: one-Ms Virginia Pack McSwain, two-Ms Mary Bell Pack Knight, three-Ms Rosie Lee Pack Means, four-Willie Earl Means, *yours truly,* and five-Katina Josey Marie Johnson but since I am sitting here listening to voices coming out of my computer speakers, and I am not on the internet, I will jump to me, four. I have already told you a little of myself so it should not surprise you for me to be telling you this. I was raised to believe the entire Bible, *From Genesis to Revelations.* This means I also believe in Spiritual Gifts. My son Ike was born February 4. I tell people I frustrated and aggravated his mother until she went into labor because I figure he was trying to hold out for my birthday. I am the Valentine's Day Baby and it is bad enough that I have to share my birthday with my sister's oldest daughter Roxanne. I have always looked for the connection between Joyce and my birthday. She was born February 1 and I February 14, one year and thirteen days apart. I believe there is some kind of bond but I cannot find a *'formal'* term for it. There are times I go into this period when everything is fitting just right. I recently explained to Ike, for lack of a better term, we are in a *'Peak Period'!* This is a time I have been trying to get Ike to understand to pay close attention to and he probably could somehow benefit from it. Me! I am 56 now and do not really look to get any breaks in life unless I create them somehow. If I did not explain it to you earlier, I know that I am living under a curse placed on me by someone I loved very dearly then, *1970,* and now *2011,* and will the rest of my life, Reverend George Clark. He was my Pastor at *Concord Pentecostal Missionary Baptist Church* in Chicago. I was caught up with his wife's niece Linda Lou and told her everything Reverend Clark was doing. I do not believe he intended to but he was angry with me when he spoke the words that stuck me with this curse. My first wife *Hazelnut* was caught up in the damn curse and she probably thought it was something she did that broke our marriage. It was not.

I played with an Ouija board when I was a junior in high school. Later realized the damn thing is not a toy but is very real. From my dabbling with the board, I also studied *witchcraft, demonism, Satanism, spiritualism, and Extra Sensory Perception, better* known as *'ESP'*. Along with me learning the Bible, and even sneaked and read my Mothers' copy of *"The Fifth and Sixth Book Of Moses',* I have seen, felt, heard, smelled, and tasted when spirits, ghosts, h'ants and other stuff I cannot explain, is around or happening.

My daughter Josey was born while I was away at Kansas Wesleyan University in Salina, Kansas. I was only there a couple of months when Red Cross called and said my Mother had a heart attack. My roommate, Henry, and I divided the things we had purchased together and he drove me to the bus station. Henry and I started out on Lexington together in 1968 and we became good friends. Track and Field at John Marshall and Wright College, we had plans to work our way onto the football team at Kansas Wesleyan and try to get scholarships. I truly believed it would have worked. Henry was a good quarterback and with my speed, I could run down anything he would throw my way when we would do our own workout when the football team would practice. Henry said he had word that the coach was asking who we were but then I had to leave. Guess what! My Mother answered the door when I got to the house at three in the morning. I stood there looking at her in surprise and stated the obvious *"Momma, I thought you were in the hospital with a heart attack."*

"Well, the doctor said it was a stress attack and I was doing too much. I tried to get Red Cross to call back but they said once the message had been sent they could not get it back. Come on in and give your Momma a hug."

Needless to say, I was upset. I had turned down scholarships to other schools because I did not understand them and I was trying to make up for it by going to Kansas Wesleyan.

"I know school is important to you but you also got a beautiful little daughter now and you need to be here helping to take care of her."

"Momma, Joann, and I have already talked about me being in school and she knows what we are going to do."

"Well, we all need to sit down and come to an understanding. Some of them want to say it is Harvey's baby but Joann swears the baby is yours."

"Well, I will go over when I get up. I just want to get some sleep right now."

That bus ride from Salina, Kansas to Chicago was not that long. What had me stressed out was dealing with people trying to rob me. Damn if I did not fall sleep with this woman sitting beside me and I woke to the feel of someone trying to go in my shirt pocket. The woman had moved to another seat and some guy was sitting next to me. I popped the switchblade I had in my jacket pocket and just looked at him and he got up and moved to another seat. Damn if the woman did not come back and start talking to me getting off in Saint Louis and having a drink with her at her place. She almost got me. She was not bad looking but I have always liked big legs in a dress or a skirt. This babe had on one of those short skirts that inched just high enough when she sat down to get your imagination going. When the bus stopped in Saint Louis, I went to the bathroom and when I returned, she and the person were gone. It was after one in the morning and I stepped outside before the bus loaded again. I am standing there leaning up against the wall and this convertible pulls up with music blaring and two females in the front and two in the back.

"Hey baby! Want to go for a ride?"

They were rocking to the music and making the car jump by pumping the brakes. Interestingly enough, there was another person standing outside and he gave me a quick negative signal so I gave him or her wave of my hand and returned to the bus.

I did not get to Joann until around seven that evening. We talked on the phone and I told her William, her brother and my brother-in-law, was coming to give me a ride over there. She wanted me to take a taxi but I told her we could save that money. When I finally got to her place, I was in for a treat.

Ms Johnson answered the door for us when we got there. Brother-in-law had wanted to take me out north to his place but I told him Joann was already mad so I had better get over there. I must admit I was a little intimidated by Ms Johnson but she surprised me.

"Well, well, it's the new daddy. Come on in here and see your baby. Can't anybody deny that baby is yours? She got your forehead and looks just like you," Ms Johnson stated. *"She should be awake. She's been sleeping most of the day."*

Joann's brothers and sisters teased at me as they showed me to her bedroom. When I opened the door, all the feelings of not seeing her for a couple of months flooded over me and I smiled and hugged her.

NEGATIVE MOOD!

16 March 2011

I will get back to Josey Marie. Would you believe I have been up since around one-thirty this morning, which is about the norm for me since surgery November 30, and I was still late for my physical therapy appointment at 9a.m...? Therapist and his staff, Wayne and the Posse, are good people and after I explained to him that the shoulder has been hurting me something fierce since Saturday, he allowed me to reschedule for tomorrow. I am three and a half months out from this doctor putting something in my left shoulder and the damn thing still hurts like crazy. I have almost gotten my range-of-motion all the way back but there is no strength in the shoulder. I just turned 56 and since that is seven years since I turned 49, I figure my body is going through another physical change. I wonder does anybody pay attention to such things any more. I HURT! I hurt and I came home to lock myself into my room before I allow anyone to agitate me and I

Willie Means Well

lose it and let myself go on them. I can truly say when I get in these fucked-up moods; I find it better to isolate myself. There are times I realize the Army really fucked me both mentally and physically. They only talked to us while I attended noncommissioned officer school in Kransberg Castle in West Germany. However, those instructors were Special Forces and all of them, except Staff Sergeant Gove, had been to Vietnam. After listening to Sergeant First Class 'T' and how good he got with piano wire, or Sergeant First Class 'Y', and how he preferred a machete on patrol, you knew how to execute the usage of their preferred weapons. Sometimes I find myself wishing for an opportunity to be in a dark room with these Veterans Administrator Representatives who make it hard for Veterans to get the disability benefits they deserve. Not all of us are combat wounded but we did our time and we have the right to have our needs taken care of if something happened while we were serving. I joined the Army with 20/20 Vision and a very healthy back. In March 1977, the Army still used the old 500 physical training test. My first score was 491. The second was 493. I finished Basic Training with a 497. Later the physical training test was changed to 300, which included 'The Push-up, Sit-ups, and the two mile run. When I was discharged in March 1985, I had maxed the push-ups and sit-ups. I never liked distant running so I never maxed the run. After all the training in Artillery, I needed glasses while in the military. After refusing to play flag football and the Battery Commander was told I was participating in track and field with this German Club, he had the First Sergeant put me in charge of extra duty for three nights in a row. The word I received, I was to be in charge of extra duty until I agreed to play flag football. I was told nobody was keeping me from practicing with my track club but I had to do the extra duty before I could leave. Extra duty would not start until six in the evening and not end until eight. After three days, I agreed to play football. We practiced and we were on our third game before I was injured. I had ran back two kick-offs for touchdowns. I had caught two passes for touchdowns. I had run a touchdown from scrimmage. I was on my way to another kick-off touchdown when this person did not even try to get the flag but slammed into my right knee and knocked me out-of-bounds. I rolled over trying to get him but I felt this pain in my right knee. When I looked down at the knee, to this day, I could swear the kneecap was sitting on the left side of my leg. The Battery Commander, who was also the quarterback, ran up, snatched my hands away from the knee, and pushed it back in place. The person was penalized and put out the game, they got me up, and I was able to jog the pain. Next day while playing a team from the Infantry Unit in the Brigade, I was on my way to my second kick-off return when I made a cut inside and the knee popped out of socket again. This time, however, I was not able to put weight on my right leg and they carried me to the aid station. I remember they gave me something for the pain and an icepack to keep on the knee. That night I woke up in pain and when I looked at the knee, it looked like the size of a 16-inch softball. I was transported to 197th General Hospital emergency sick call in Frankfurt. We were there all night and the captain who checked me out said I just had a knee spring and it would get better. We returned to Friedberg and that evening I went to track practice. The coach and my teammates were glad to see me. Another soldier on the team had told everyone why I had not been to practice. They really made me feel good telling me how sorry they were that I had to put up with such bullshit. I remember Eva Maria Crouch worked out with me that day and told me she was not letting me out of her sight. I laughed and teased her about missing me. Eva had a Volkswagen Rabbit and used to come and pick me and another person up for practice. The first time I got in the car with her I let the window down and she looked at me, waved her finger back and forward, and told me *"Nain, Nain!"* She told me to let the window back up and we headed to the Autobahn. When we got on the Autobahn, Eva got in that outside lane, locked her elbows, and floored the gas pedal. Frankfurt is approximately 38 miles from Friedberg and we made it there in like ten to 15 minutes. I kept my mouth shut all the time because I definitely did not want to distract her.

Oops! Took a quick break to warm my coffee and peeped out at my babies, my dogs. Ever since King in Chicago in 1968, when I get a dog I name him King. In addition, of course, his pet name *"Old Man"*. Well, opened the door and spoke to him and his mate, *'BG' aka Black Gal,* and then got a baked chicken out the refrigerator, cut it in half and gave it to them.. I did cut some of the white meat off and cut it up for the heathen cats out front. Thought about how I would have loved to give the chicken to someone hungry. While all these conflicts are going on, I will bet we have Elderly and others eating cat and dog food again. I love our Military. However, I feel it is not being utilized correctly. When I joined in March 1977, I made three hundred forty-eight dollars a month. I believe they come in making almost two thousand a month now. I am glad for them. However, I have heard so many soldiers say they want to go back where they are fighting because they make all kinds of money. I do not see any glory in our People dying when we have the capability to

Willie Means Well

be in and out of an area in a month. If Americans knew what our Military had, they would scream bloody murder for officials to allow this stuff to go on. However, like Vietnam, you have everybody and their brothers and sisters making money off those conflicts.

Anyway, Eva and I had done some sprints and we walked over to a wall to do some stretching. We were laughing, talking, and stretching each other out when we started to do some leg swings on our right legs. One repetition was all it took and I found myself on the floor on my back and wondering what had happened. Eva called my name and then yelled for coach. I tried to get up but she and some of the others would not let me up. When coach came over, Eva started speaking in German. Coach kneeled beside me and slowly moved my kneecap around. Even before coach said anything, my teammates began to make sounds that let me knew they saw what was wrong. They all helped me up and had me sit in a chair and coach got on the telephone. Eva jogged off with Bab and every once in a while I saw her looking at me. After about 15 minutes, a guy came in that I later learned was a specialist in sports injuries. He checked my knees and he and coach, I believe coach name was *'Kuenta'*, walked off talking. I saw the guy get on the phone for a while then he got off, shook coach hand and left. Coach came to me and told me the team sponsors had such confidence in me that they wanted to do surgery on my knee and repair the damage. This surprised me and made me feel good at the same time. About a month earlier, I had showed up for practice but left my shoes. Coach got on the phone and in 15 minutes a guy showed up and they gave me a pair of *'Adidas TRX'* running shoes. Through high school and a couple of years of college, that was my first pair of real running shoes. The surgery never happened however. When I explained to my chain-of-command what the track team wanted to do, I was told no. I was told the Army had doctors and I still belonged to the United States Army. Kuenta was a teacher at this girl college in Friedberg and I went to see him and explained the Army's stance. He told me they were being stupid. I left and never saw any of the team members again. I was told by a Lieutenant Colonel the captain at the hospital did not know what he was doing and it led to knee surgery May 29, 1981. They gave me a *Spinal Tap* to do the knee surgery and I have had back problems since. I recently filed for compensation for my back injury, but I was turned down. I appealed their decision and even wrote the President. So you see, as I said, *'THEY FUCK YOU UP AND THEN DO NOT WANT TO TAKE CARE OF THEIR FUCK UP!!!*

I searched for years for Walter Lewis Ford, Jr. Ford took me under his arm and taught me artillery when I got to West Germany in July 1977. Of course he sent me to get a *box of deflections* from the Maintenance Sergeant and I like a stupid, dumb little *'CRUIT',* went looking for the deflections. Anybody that deals with Artillery will tell you that deflections are the direction we tell the guns to shoot. After going from one maintenance bay to the next and next, a Motor Sergeant snatched me around and chewed me out up one side and down the other. He then told me to get the hell out of his bay and go tell whoever sent me to "shovel it up their ass!"

You will not believe how low I felt and I fought hard to keep back the tears. As I passed the maintenance bay for Bravo Battery, the guys started laughing. When I got half way, back to the track we were working in, my mind remembered what deflections were. Ford was standing out front of the track when we locked eyes and he turned and went to the rear of the track and jumped in. I was hurt, I was pissed, I cursed him and told him to come outside the track, and I would beat his ass. The Section Chief finally jumped out the track, grabbed me by the shirt, and pulled me to the front of the track.

"Listen Private E-2 Means. You need to shut your mouth and get yourself together. You're new in the section and jokes are always played on new recruits. You will apologize to Private First Class Ford and we will then get on with being a Section. You understand me Private.

"Yes Sergeant. However, I don't think its right. I come over here to do a job and those guys round *there laughed like crazy and this one Sergeant snatched me and chewed me out. All because I was doing what I thought was a real request."*

"Well, like I said, we do it to everyone and Ford was elected to welcome you into the Section."

We walked back to the rear of the track and Ford was called outside for me to apologize to him. I remember he listened in silence then told me *"Willie, you're in Germany now. You're away from home like the rest of us, so sometimes you have to do crazy stuff to break up the monotony.*

Ford taught me well. When he rotated to the states a year before I did, I went downtown Friedberg and go smashing drunk. There was this thing that if an American personnel go drunk and passed out downtown, you would be picked up by the German Police or the Military Patrol and your name would come up on what they called *'The Blotter'*. I did not give a shit. I remember downing a fifth of Jack Daniel Black Label and there is no telling what I drank downtown. I do know that I later found out the reason why I did not get on the blotter was because a bowling buddy of mine was on patrol that night and they put me in their jeep and returned me to the barracks. The guy who was on the bowling team told me he found me at a table passed out with this lady. He said it was one of the bars where Soldiers hung out and the owner would not let anybody bother me.

When Ford rotated to the States, it was more than 30 years before I found him again. I believe it was the military part of *'Classmates.com'* that help me locate him. It took me a while to pick up his voice but then he began telling me of all the ladies he had dated. As I listened to the different nationalities, I knew it was Ford. That boy knew he loved him some women. Only catch, they had to be out of his Race. Ford was White and Black mixed. Perhaps in another book I will tell you of some of our escapades. It was less than a year after I found Ford again, and he was dead. He told me he was trying to get The Veterans Administration to start his disability because the Army knew he had a disease and drinking made it worst. In Germany we were issued ration cards for the *'Class Six Store and the Commissary'* (this is *where we purchased our alcohol and cigarettes).* You got four half of gallons of alcohol and four cartons of cigarettes each month. Ford and I, along with the guys in our *Fire Direction Center (FDC)* put some alcohol away while we were in Germany. Somebody would always have a half gallon of Rum. Somebody would always have a half gallon of Seagram 7. Somebody would always have a fifth of Jack Daniel. In addition, before I learned to hate the taste, I would always have a half gallon of Vodka.

Ford was not just smart, he was super-smart, and he showed it when it came time for us to train for nuclear missions. The boy could work some mathematics. There also were the times we *'popped strawberry mescaline'* and we would take on the computer to see if we could beat it completing *'Fire Missions'.* The guys in the gun sections said they loved Ford and me. When we were in the field training, the gun sections rarely had to re-bag powder or shells because Ford and I would help them fire up the rounds. The lieutenant and the section chief learned real quick not to leave Ford and I in the

FDC along because instead of the lieutenant's 'Battery one round' in the *fire-for-effect phase,* Ford and I would give them 'battery three rounds, or battery four rounds. We did not really have much paperwork to do but getting rid of the rounds made it a whole lot easy to put a zero for rounds remaining than trying to find each and every round that did not get fired.

As I look back today, I realize I probably acted too quickly when I joined the Army. Even the recruiter responded in surprise when he saw I had some college. After I took the entrance examination, he told me I was in luck. He told me my scores were high enough to work in any field. He told me after basic training and advance individual training, he could guarantee me an assignment at Fort Sheridan, Illinois. This was right up the highway from Chicago and I am sure many would have jumped on this assignment. Me, I was not interested in staying Stateside. I wanted to go to Germany so I could continue my track and field career. He then told me they had openings in Artillery in Europe and I told him I would go for the Artillery. The man looked at me as if I was crazy and asked was I sure; I did not want to change my mind. At that time, I had Josey with Joann but a female bowling friend of mine, Donna Katherine White, had graduated Austin in 1974 and joined the Navy in 1975. I was proud of her and wanted her to be proud of me. In addition, I knew in the military, I had a chance of finding her again. I never did however. When Donna left for the Navy, she wrote me telling me she was having training somewhere in Florida. I in turn wrote her back expressing my feelings for her and talking of marriage. Donna returned my letter to me, opened, with a letter from her written on a piece of brown paper bag. Boy did she bless me out. I felt so bad and after that, all I wanted to do was get out of Chicago. The opportunity came when I relocated with my father in Reform, Alabama in June 1976, however, with everything closing at 9p.m... I was back in Chicago in February and joined the Army in March. I wrote Donna again and this time her letter was so much better. It even had a promise of us meeting up eventually oversea somewhere and sees about starting a life together. I always wondered what happened to her. That was more than 36 years ago and I never heard from her again. In addition, of course, she has ever been in my memories.

    You know I started this way back when telling you of my daughter Josey Marie. I shall eventually get to finish telling you of her and who or whatever else I have talked about since beginning this. However, allow me this also, because today is the first day of spring, March 20, 2011, and looking back, so much began in March. My high school, I recall we had Indoor City Track and Field at the University Of Chicago on 55th Street out South. I lettered in track and field three years at Marshall and each year the coach would not give me my letter because I would not come to the banquet at the end of the season. I made the banquet my Senior Year but then I received a little silver pin shaped in the form of a winged foot. I accepted the thing but I wanted my large 'M' that I could sport on my jacket that showed I was part of the track team. I remember something else from my senior year that involved track and field. We were waiting at Coach Poole's house on a Saturday Morning getting ready to leave for a track meet out-of-town. I would always get me a comic book, sure wish I had them now. I recently saw an issue of a Spiderman Comic Book that sold for over a million dollars. The very same issue I recall reading one morning on the way to another track and field meet. I would get me a comic book, get over in a corner by myself, and really shut out everything around me getting my mind ready for the track meet. I do not recall what really happened but the guys were laughing in the kitchen and then they called me. When I got in the kitchen, they told me one of the junior guys on the team wanted to ask me a question. They asked me to step outside the kitchen door and a kid name Moore came up to me and said something. Before I could stop myself, I left the fingers and palm of my hand printed on the side of his face. Everybody got quiet and I remember Moore did not cry or try to get back at me. He just looked at me, turned, and walked off to himself. I felt so low realizing the varsity guys had gotten that kid to confront me with whatever it was. I still feel bad about it today and wherever Moore is, I want him to know that I have apologized a thousand times for striking him that morning.

    I had to make a store run to get a newspaper and other stuff and on the way home *'Benny and the Jets' by Elton John* was on the radio. The song brought a smile to my face because my memories took me back to six of us in this young woman name Vicky's Pinto on the way to see Wright College play a basketball game. Vicky was dating Bobby Polk, a track teammate, and she allowed us to ride to the game with her. Wright had a basketball coach named Ed Badger, he coached the team to a thirty-two and two record in 1974, and we ended the same record in 1975. He coached well enough that he got a holler from the Chicago Bulls. I almost played for the guy. One night during intramural activities, I was having one of those games where every time I put up a shot I scored. We had played three or four games when the intramural coach when and got Ed Badger. I saw them come back into the gym but I did not realize they were checking me out until the next day at track practice when the track coach called me into his office and asked me had I been playing any basketball lately.

March 28, 2011
(Doctor Day)

Do not worry; I will get back to whatever I was talking about the last time I was here. Today I returned to the doctor for him to check my shoulder again. Told him how the damn thing still hurts me like crazy and there is still no strength in the shoulder or the arm. You know that damn doctor gave me a steroid shot to get rid of the pain, and told me he wanted the therapist to push on strengthening the small muscles in the shoulder before concentrating on the larger muscles. Told him I could tell he knew what he was doing because I swear it seem like the needle went right into the area where the pain seem to be generating from. You know what his response was. *"This ain't my first rodeo!"* In other words, he done did it so much, he know what he is doing. Isn't it amazing; it takes pain to cure pain. Believe you me; I thought I had torn a hole in the bed grabbing it so hard with my fingernails.

Back on the highway headed home, I realized I

had dozed off right away when I heard my wife say something, I looked at the clock, and realized thirty minutes had passed. We were on I-285 South. The rain was coming down and it created a hazy effect on both sides of the highway. Now I was never in Vietnam but suddenly to me it seems the road was the Mekong River that flows down the middle of the Mekong Delta. As we moved along a story came to mind from an old artillery friend of mine who was on a gunboat in the Navy during that time. Wright said one day while they were patrolling with three other gunboats they got a distress call from an Army patrol near them that said they were being pushed into the Mekong and about to be overrun. Wright said communication flags went up on all four boats that signaled they all got the call and all were ready to respond.

"Man when we got that call we had to be less than a quarter mile from them. I was gunner on the lead boat and our radio guy returned the call that we were in the area. Man the 'Chief' opened that thing up and you could feel that boat lift out of the water.

It's as we were floating on air and we were ready to 'GET SOME!' We came around the bend in the river and there were some guys' waist deep in the river and firing at the trees and bushes along the bank. They saw us about the same time and later the guys told us all they could think to do was dive under the water. That probably saved their lives because we were on them and opened fire towards the areas we saw them firing... Now you see how much damage one of the fifty-caliber machine gun do mounted on the artillery pieces. Well, we were armed with what they called 'Quad-fifties'; four fifty-caliber machine guns firing at the same time. Man, we made a pass up and then we came back down. All four boats unloaded on about a quarter mile stretch. We turned around and came back to pick up the Army guys and they were just staring as they could not believe in what they were seeing. Those quad-fifties had leveled that area so low you would think a logging crew came through there. I don't know what kind of festival they were having or why so many North Vietnamese Regulars were in that area, but we later

Willie Means Well

learned we had a kill count of over three thousand. We knew where we were at on the Mekong but we never did find out why those Army Boys were that far north. We did hear those people in Cambodia raised holy hell about us crossing into their territory."

Wright was all right. He was just another guy who served his Country and saw too much for young minds to comprehend in that damn war that we lost. I forced myself to stay awake because I did not want an incident on the highway with my wife and son in the car. As I said, I was not in Vietnam buy my Artillery Unit was full of Vietnam Veterans when I got to Friedberg, West Germany in July 1977. Then along with being around the *Special Forces* types at *Kransberg Castle,* sometime the mind will play tricks on you. At one time, I must have been on 12 or 13 pills every morning until it landed me in the Veteran Administration (VA) Hospital in Tuskegee, Alabama. I attacked my wife while we were sleeping. I was dreaming. I was on patrol in Vietnam and I was taking out a guard before we hit this village. I remember I had put my hand over his mouth and snatched him back and was delivering a blow to his throat when I heard this soft kind of whimper. In the dream, I was afraid I had not made my kill and was preparing to strike again when the guy looked at me and said, *"Bill."* I hesitated because I wanted to know how this joker knew my name and my eyes blurred and I blinked to clear them. When I opened my eyes, I was kneeling straddle of my wife and had my right hand raised ready to strike her, and man, you talking about jumping up. I turned the lights on and I could see where I had hit her in the throat. I got her up and made sure she could swallow well. I could not apologize enough. I remember pacing back and forward, she kept telling me it was a bad dream, and it probably could not happen again. I was scared. I told her to lie back down and I would come to bed when I settled down. I sat listening until I heard her sleep breathing then I grabbed a blanket and got in the *'fetus position'* on the floor. I had to be knocked out, because when I woke the next morning, she was on the floor beside me, and had covered us with a sheet. I went to the VA Clinic that morning and explained what had happened, and the doctor explained sometimes that someone could imprint something in your mind so strong that you could live it yourself in a dream. I guess that must have happened and it got me a week stay in VA Hospital. I will never forget that week and I remind myself of being locked behind closed doors when I get agitated about the VA. Each night there was a plus three hundred pound guy right outside my door. The first night I got up and looked out the door he looked at me and asked what I needed. I told him I was thinking of going to the bathroom but I could see his *'Clone'* down the hall from him. Now before I put all this weight on, I believe I weighed maybe one hundred eighty-pounds or less. You know I lay back in that bed and tried to figure out how I could get both those guys. I told myself I knew I could get the first one but then the other one and the rest of the staff would then make me pay dearly for what I had done. I told myself I did not have to use the bathroom and slept the night away.

Willie Means Well

APRIL 4, 2011

Well, once again, here I am. I am not apologizing; this is the style I have come to like. By jumping around, I can tell you of things that I deem important or worth talking about. This all started because I wanted to explain why Josie Marie has abilities she do not understand, simply because she is in the linage of my great-grandmother Ms Virginia Pack McSwain.

Today, however, I am recalling what happened on this black day in Memphis, Tennessee in 1968. The slaying of Dr. Martin Luther King, Jr. Would you believes that another person who tried to bring equity for the Black Race. Today, they have the word *'Minority'* out there so all these places can get money from the federal government to help the less fortunate. Before minority, so many places stood to lose federal funding because they made it so hard for Blacks to get any kind of loan. However, by adding the word minority, it made them eligible because they could show where they were still helping the less fortunate. Just not providing any help for Blacks.

That evening when the news flashed that Doctor King had been killed, it was like a magnate pulling people out into the streets. It was not long before they made their way towards Roosevelt Road on the Westside of Chicago. Roosevelt Road was lined with store after store with any kind of merchandized you needed. Looking back now, I realize it was a mistake to crash those stores and burn them. Where as it once was a nice shopping area that kept you from heading all the way downtown to shop, after the riots, there were nothing left but burned out buildings that help create more crime in that area.

The Chicago vice-Lords and the Roman Saints were the strong powers on the Westside of Chicago when the rioting began that night. I was thirteen, my friend Johnny had just turned fifteen, and we made our way to Roosevelt Road behind the adults. People were milling up and down Roosevelt Road and of a sudden, you began to hear glass breaking as people began to toss bricks through the storefront windows.

The owners were long gone. I guess they knew what could possibly happen and it did. As windows shattered, people would rush into the stores and grab anything they could. I remember Johnny running out a store with a twenty-inch bicycle and soon as he got to the sidewalk, someone pushed him down and took the bike. We both were tried to run back into the store but somebody started whistling and this man grabbed us and stopped us from going in the store. Now Johnny and I were the co-leaders of our little gang called the *'Chain Gang'* and we yelled at the man to take his hands off us. The man looked at us, laughed, and asked us was he going to have to whip both of us. We looked at the man and told him we wanted to get back inside and get us a bicycle. Man told us when we hear whistling that was the sign to set the building on fire. Just as he finished explaining, someone ran up and tossed a firebomb into the store and look like less than a minute and fire was shooting through the smashed out area where the window had been. Johnny and I then looked at the man and told him thanks. Then the guy called us by name and told us who our older brothers were. To this day, I still do not know who he was. He ran off into the crowd of people, and Johnny and I ran down and helped pillage another store. That night moved so fast and we both got a few things before the police finally came in force and fought the crowd while the fire department worked on getting the fires out.

April 21, 2011

Well, here I am, back again. Still fighting writer's block but felt like sharing some more about me. Just had another therapy session on my shoulder and I want everyone to know that *the physical therapist at Occupational Medicine in Columbus, Georgia is really a very nice individual. Mr. Wayne and his assistants are nice and I appreciate them listening to me complain about the pain I am going through from this shoulder surgery I had in November. THANKS WAYNE!*

What put me in sort of a writing mood was seeing two of my co-workers *'LIP-SMACK'* today. Bad enough this young woman had on a dress with no stockings yesterday and she has just enough hair on her legs that makes her extremely sexy. I told the guy lip smacking would not work for me because she would have to push her tongue between my lips just a little and that would allow me to suck her tongue into my mouth. Guy looked at me and shouted, *"Mr. Means!"* I looked at him and walked off laughing

with surging thoughts of how I trained myself through the years to please my partner before satisfying myself sexually. I took a pain pill when I returned from therapy, and I took a leg cramp pill. Therefore, you see I am feeling good and stupid because I asked my wife would she mine if I took a swallow of her beer and she said, *"Now Bill, you know I do not mine you taking some of that beer."* In addition, you know she really does not mine. She would give me her last breath of life if she thought she was helping me. What really frustrates me is our sex life. I am not exaggerating when I say that after a quarter of a century, I call myself *'One Shot Willie!'* I have always enjoyed a healthy sex life with my partners to the tune of two or three times during the night, day, or whenever the mood would hit us. You know, especially, a little *'Afternoon Delight!'*
"Gonna find my Baby gonna hold her tight gonna grab a little Afternoon Delight" ...Why wait until the middle of a cold, dark night? That would be *Circuit 1976, and* the beautiful Summer Time in Reform, Alabama for me. I had finally gotten tired of the

killings and other stuff that went on behind closed doors or out in the streets for that matter. Being a Youngman of nineteen in 1974, I got a job at United Parcel Services (UPS) while attending Wright College on the North side of Chicago. When getting off at 3:45a.m. I would cruise Madison Avenue and watch the girls work their trade. As a matter of fact, it was a big leg lady in a mini-skirt who danced across the street in front of my car that sent me to the doctor for the first time to receive those magical twin shots, also called *'Silver Bullets'*, after a brief tryst, in a darken blocked off area. Even today, I do not know what the hell *"Ten for two"* mean, but being between that lady's big thighs sure was enjoyable.

Willie's Girls
April 28, 2011
(The Day after Yesterday)

A killer storm rolled through the area last night. I am thankful to GOD that my family, along with our possessions, environment, and animals and I are well today. Yes, I am jumping ship again and swimming around in circles trying to get my bearings. Rambling through stuff, I came across some music I recorded off my YouTube Site. Playing the music on my cassette player is not giving me the greatest sound but I have always loved to hear music as I remember it off the radio. I like to associate songs with my memories. Majority of the time the memories are pleasant but sometimes the memories are sad to me. *"...Gone party till the lights go out; nothing but a PARTY!"* Netra Brooks was my *Lil Lover*. She was only sixteen when I met her during my taxi driving days in Columbus. Beautiful, cream colored, dark eyed young lady with legs that you wish you could get between. Yes, I have been married more than a quarter of a century but when you pick up feelings for someone, you cannot help which way your heart lean. Netra's mother was a beauty also. When Netra introduced me to Mary, I realized I had met her already. One day I got a call to pick-up at this club on Schatulga Road. The fare was a lovely lady in shorts and a sleeveless top. I could see she was wearing a red bra because the straps came from under the top. I could also see she was wearing red undies when she bent over to pick up something off the ground before she got in the taxi. Mary was downright sexy and Netra had her physical attributes. My Lil Lover was one of those girls who came from a good family but wanted the *Bad Boys*. Perhaps I will get a chance to tell you more about Netra when I share her poem later. What I will share right now is my looking at her in shock one day when she got in the taxi in a blue jean mini-skirt. She got in like a lady and before I could stop it, the words *"Damn Lil Lover!"* slipped out my mouth. She just looked at me and asked did that mean she was looking ok. I told her excuse me but she was looking damn good. She told me thanks and then added, *"You know you gone get the pussy someday. It's just not your time yet!"* The little Heifer then had the nerves to stare at me all the way to her destination. When she got ready to get out, she put her hand on my thigh, looked me in the eyes, and said, *"I hope I didn't shock you. I do intend to have you between my legs but it's not your time yet."*

May 22, 2011

In the immortal words of that POOR GUY that we love so dearly in the movies, *"I'll be back!"* I will say this for him. *"He only did what many a guy do or want to do when his woman is pregnant. I believe many women have a hard time at childbearing because she feels, or someone has told her, that it is not good to have sex once you get pregnant. Not all these so-called gentlewomen realize by denying their man sex, she has gave him a free pass to seek sex elsewhere. As for me, I was not stupid enough to lie on my woman's stomach, but there is nothing wrong with having her lie on her side and pull one leg up so you can get to the 'GOOD SPOT!'* If he was cut-off or his wife had a bad time of it, like throwing up all the time, he definitely had my vote to get it somewhere else. In addition, I bet you every guy wish he had someone like that maid who saw what he needed and provided. Women can be so temperamental when it comes to that special garden between their legs. Gardens need plowing and

Willie Means Well

cultivating to remain subtitle, soft, and yielding. In addition, I know a lot of you are saying what if the situation was changed. Something happened to the man and he cannot GET-IT-UP or PERFORM on demand. Let me tell you something! He has fingers, toes, hands, and best of all, A TONGUE, if he truly wants to keep his woman from letting another man get what is his. Hope I did not just shock a lot of you. Love is a great feeling. It is even better when you achieve physically what the bodies are capable of having once you reach satisfaction.

So interesting about my *'Lil Lover'* that I met her during the tender time of her teenage years when she was really discovering sex. As she told me of her sex-capades, I realize she had not really been introduced to *'Love-making'*. As one young lady told me who had a baby. *"He was young and at first I thought I was having the thrill of my life having sex with him. However, he always satisfied himself and all I got out of it was pregnant. Hey, I was a Cheerleader and one day after school this teacher was helping me with my lessons and I really do not know how it started but when it was over all I could think of was I wanted him to do it again. It was the first time I had an orgasm and that also started me dating older men because I knew that it was something in it for me. Not just laying there and let the guy moan and grunt as he is going up and down between your legs."*

WOW! Makes me wonder whatever happened to Sonya. I believe she went on to become a nurse. I may be wrong. However, I believe a woman can tell when you are having a conversation with her and of certain; you both want it to be more than talk. So many times, I have had a lady rub my thigh; put her arm through mine and rub my shoulder; or simply take my hand in hers and look me in the eye. Over this quarter of a Century that I have been married, I have always found the strength to back out because I really tried to hold true to my wife. I will admit that with *Lil Lover,* it came close one day when she called for me to pick her up and I was already close to her house. I realize just how close we had gotten when I pulled into her driveway and she came to the door and invited me in. This had never happened before but once inside she told me she did not want me sitting in the hot sun. I do not know what Nettie had in mind but she was very relaxed and I could feel this feeling coming from her.

"Mr. Willie, you've never been in my house before, has you? Before I could answer, she continued. *"Come on. Momma's not here and I don't think she would mine me showing you the place.*

She started downstairs and showed me the living room, the kitchen, and their den was one of those that you stepped down. By the way, something I forgot to tell you. She had a towel wrapped around her because I came before she got in the bathtub. She came to the stairs to go upstairs and she stopped, turned, and looked at me and said, *"Our bedrooms are up here. Mine may be a little messy but I want you to see the whole house."*

I do not know if she was trying to see just how much she could trust she or me had certain other intentions. I was forty then so that would make it 1995. She did not know my age but she had confided in me that a guy she was seeing sometimes was forty and that was her current age limit to date a man. The little Heifer even had the nerves to turn, look at me, and ask, *"I'm not making you nervous am I Mr. Willie? You came so fast and I was getting ready to do my bath."* I told her she was not making me nervous and I remember she had already told me it was not my time yet. That little heifer, she looked at me, smiled, put her hand in the center of my chest, and said, *"Momma said I didn't have to worry about you because you are a gentleman."* She was getting ready to turn seventeen and believe you me; I was pulling up training from my military days to control my excitement and not letting it get to my physical attribute below my waist and between my legs. Even today, I do not know if she were playing with me because as I see her walk up those stairs pulling me behind her by my hand, she was dripping with sexuality. She showed me her mother's room and as we were headed towards her room, my military hearing picked up the sound of a door opening downstairs. When we got to her room, she turned, looked me in the eyes and said, *"Don't be shocked now."* I knew I was not going to be shocked because I was not going to go into that bedroom. Those stairs were carpeted but I could hear someone coming up them. She opened the door and asked me to come in but I decided to be the gentleman she said her mother named me.

"Hey, thanks for showing me the house but I will sit downstairs and wait for you," I said to her, making contact with my eyes and flicking them a couple of times towards the stairs. She was very smart and caught the eye movement and stepped towards me and looked in the direction I flicked my eyes.

"Ok, that will be fine. Momma should be home soon. Tell her I didn't want you sitting out in the sun so I invited you in and showed you the house."

At that time, Mary stepped into the hall and she was very calm.

"Hey Mr. Willie what's Netra doing; showing you this dirty house?"

Now I told you Mary was one good looking

lady. She had on some pants that came just below the knees and a white blouse that was opened a couple of buttons at the top. That woman had one of the finest thick heads of hair that any man would want to get his hands.

"Hello Ms. Brooks. Yeah, she was showing me the house. I told her to hurry a little because I didn't want the neighbors thinking bad things."

"Oh. Netra didn't tell you we are surrounded by our relatives. I seen you when you pulled up but I was doing one of my cousin's hair. You're welcome to come over here anytime."

So, what do you think she had planned had her mother not come when she did? I do not know what has happened to my *Lil Lover*. I stopped driving taxi in December '01 and I have not seen her since. My wife came to me with an obituary one day and showed me a picture of a lady that looked just like Mary Brooks. God knows I hope that even today it was not her. The last I saw of *Lil Lover* was when I told you I allowed her to drive from Macon, Georgia back to Columbus, Georgia one night. That was ten years ago. I so wish they were both alive. Perhaps this book will sale and it will somehow find its' way into one of their hands and I will hear from them. GOD BLESS THEM BOTH!!!

Wow! Took a quick break because I felt myself getting tired and my shoulder really bothers me from where I have had a second surgery on it. It's so funny about working in the *'Mental Health Field.'* You can do everything right to give the patients *'dignity and respect',* but someone else would come along and do that one thing wrong that makes the patient explode and go into *'Crisis'.* While working with *Bridge way*, at West Central Georgia Regional Hospital (WCGRH) in Columbus, Georgia, one Sunday afternoon after arriving to work, this adolescent was on visitation with his mother. As soon as I heard that child was on visitation, I knew there was going to be a problem getting him back inside. When that child's mother got ready to leave, he made it very clear that she was not going out that door without him. I think that kid was 16 or 17 and he started fighting when staff was told to bring him back on the Unit.

Everything was going well until I found myself holding his legs by myself. That kid kicked out with one of his legs and it slung my arm back with enough force that I first had to have two screws put in the shoulder to hold something together. Later I had to have a second surgery to have the joint along with something replaced in the same shoulder. That is why now, even after six months of having the surgery, my shoulder still hurts like the dickens and I can only type about 15 minutes at a time before the shoulder really hurts and bother me. By the way, would you believe West Central terminated me because the doctor would not release me when they wanted him to? I thought I had a legal case against the hospital but the attorneys I checked with in Columbus told me the hospital was State and the State could terminate me if they desired. I do have an attorney in Atlanta working for me and in the end I really hope something come up from where that hospital has mistreated employees and terminated them over the years that a *'Class Action Lawsuit'* can be brought against them.

Willie Means Well

While taking my break, I walked outside to try to clear my head. The sun is bright and the temperature is already getting up here in Cataula. As I was walking from one entrance of the driveway towards' the other entrance, a dark colored snake about three feet but slim, started to cross the road but turned and went back into the grass. It probably felt the vibrations from my walking. I looked to see where the cats were and of the five, momma cat, the three boys, and one girl from her first litter, I only saw the female stretched in the yard enjoying the sun. My wife said I should not have fed them the *'SLUMP!'* You ever see that movie where Cuba Gooding, Jr. goes to Alaska because his biological mother has passed. He has a couple of wild times with his mother's dog pack. A young lady finally began to show him how to work with the dogs and she shows him how to feed the dogs this foodstuff called *'SLUMP'*. Well, momma cat has had another litter of kittens and has brought them to the house from the woods. Even though the neighbors are tolerant of the cats, we know we have to find a way to catch all of them and have them *'FIXED'*. I have always been a dog person and I always try to keep me a dog-named King in honor of the dog I had back in Chicago. Sometimes I think that crazy dog and his mate, *Black Gal-aka-BG,* really try to talk back to me when I am addressing them. Anyway, you know animals can tell if you are going to hurt them. Well, those kitten, three of them, will take off when I get ready to feed them, but the other one, as my wife calls the *'Runt',* just gets down and stare at you with his or hers pretty little eyes. Once I get this house secured, I plan to have a semi-private fence put up so the cats and dogs can run free.

    I was telling you how I feed them a concoction called Slump that I copied of that movie. Well, I went to the *'Dollar General Store'* because I saw some *'Jack Mackerel'* in there for one dollar a can. Growing up in Bessemer, Alabama, I learned to prefer Jack Mackerel to Salmon. Momma probably bought this because it was not expensive. If you're Momma and Sisters and Brothers know how to cook, many times you will be able to enjoy delicious meals because they know how to flavor the food just right. I also found some could cat food five for two dollars. I mixed the Mackerel, a can of food, and some dry cat food together and when I put it down, the cats tore into it like crazy. The first day I put it all in one pan but after seeing how the big cats reacted to the kittens, I started separating them. Even the house cat, *Gracie Lu,* with her finicky butt, tore into hers and licked the plate. When I was feeding the cats outside, I saw King and BG looking like, *"What is that daddy giving those little things now?"* That is one reason why I want to save the house. I do not want to have to have my animals put to sleep again. It happened when we moved off Corinth Drive in Columbus and I sure felt bad knowing my sons knew those dogs I had gotten for them had to be put to sleep. I also want to keep the house for my son Bobby. He can do what he wants to do with the house but when my wife and I are gone, we will know that he has a roof over his head. He is my *'Gentle Giant'* and I feel he has already gone through enough in his young life. People can be mean and cruel and we as Christians are supposed to allow the LORD JESUS to take care of those who mistreat us. My Baby has done great and I PRAY the day when life gives him the break and send all good his way.

I just took another break and went to the store. Now that I am back, I remember what it was I wanted to share with you that pushed me to writing today. I also had to take one of my pain pills to stop this shoulder from hurting and I can get some more typing in. I want to catch up on the CRAZY, SILLY things our President is now doing but right now I want to talk about my mother. As I have shared, Momma gave us this *'Gift of Sight'* but I guess when you get away from your upbringing and live in a large city like Chicago, as you grow older, you forget about things you learned as a child.

"The days of our years are threescore (60) years and ten (10); and if by reason of strength they be fourscore (80) years, yet is their strength labor and sorrow; for it is soon cut off, and we fly away" PSALMS 90th Chapter and the 10th Verse

Willie Means Well

Momma is eighty now. If our LORD AND SAVIOR JESUS CHRIST grants it, Momma will turn eighty-one in September. I am PRAYING that Momma make it to the Century mark. Momma is definitely a child of our Savior. A week ago, my sister found Momma on the ground outside. The doctor said Momma had been on the ground for hours. I spoke to Momma and she told me she went outside the night before to bring one of the little boys back in so Dot, my baby sister would not be upset. However, Momma fell somehow and broke two ribs on each side. My oldest sister, Roxanne, said when they found Momma, there were six or more cats sitting around her so no snake got close to her. I wanted to tell Big Sister those cats were ready to dine had Momma laid there and died.

What I want to address is they have Momma on a psychiatric ward and supposed to have her on a medication that is supposed to slow dementia and Alzheimer disease. My baby sister was telling me the doctor said the medication would stop Momma from seeing people she claims she is talking to and trying

Willie Means Well

to help. I tried to tell my sister that she realizes Momma was not seeing things in her mind but she probably was seeing spirits for real.

What Is Real

Bessemer, Alabama

2731 Eight Avenue North

Four double-tenant houses sitting in a hollow
Filled by families with love, no one they bothered
Ms. Rosie McNeil and Mary Lucille
Jake and Laura lived in sorrow
Ms. Ada Baker, my "Big Momma"
Daddy and Momma, we were humble
Mr. Frank and Mom, Ed, Des, and tee
They shared a whole house with Pickaninny
Cannonball and Ethel with their children
Bay Bundy and Gundy, Gundy, Chicka-Bo was my Honey
Mr. Hooker completed the list
Ed and I med his granddaughter, a pretty little miss
Nothing but fun for us when the weekends would arrive
Life was strong and innocent, and everybody was alive

Willie Means Well

I remember my daddy worked in the mines. Momma used to get up and fix him lunch when he got a break. Daddy would sit me on his hip and rock me up and down while he cut onion up in some black-eye peas. If my Daddy did not like his job, you would never have known it. He always had a smile for me and he would sing this song. *"I'm way down in jail on my knees. They feed me off of cornbread and peas."* Daddy also played a harmonica. One of his friends played a guitar and another one played a bass that stood on the floor. My daddy drank and so did his friends. When they had drunk so much, they would begin to tell SCARY stories. The one I remember most was the story of a man's face in a courthouse window, in Carrollton, Alabama, that would not go away. I would hide under the bed because he would make me leave the room when they got to talking about such stuff.

There was a freed slave who was passing through Carrollton, Alabama. Someone had been burning courthouses and other public buildings in the area. The freed slave was accused of committing these crimes. The freed slave, it was said, begged and pleaded for his life and repeatedly told the people in the town he was innocent. There was no trail. The freed slave was carried outside of town and a rope was tossed across a tree. The freed slave told the lynch mob to prove his innocence; they would never get him out of the town. The story is told that after they hung the freed slave, the lynch mob congratulated each other and headed back into town only to find a crowd gathered in front of the courthouse. Pushing through the crowd to the front, the lynch mob saw a reflection of the freed slave's face in one of the courthouse windows. The story is told that they took the window out, but the freed slave's reflection came in another window. After numerous attempts to get the face out of the windows, they decided to leave it alone and come up with their own story as to why the freed slave reflection was in the window. They said the freed slave was looking out the window as the lynch mob gathered and lightening flashed and etched the free slave's reflection in the window.

Willie Means Well

In 1976, I left Chicago and went to Reform, Alabama to find my daddy, and I did. One day, while out and enjoying just being together again, we pulled up in a parking lot in Carrollton, Alabama. Daddy got out and began to roll a Prince Albert cigarette. *"Buster, you remember when me and my friends used to talk about that man's face in the window?"* My reply was, "Daddy! I'm a grown man now, and don't be trying to scare me with that children's stuff."

"Yeah, I figured you thought we were just telling stories. Look up at that window in the top."

Well, the sun was at an angle that caused you to put your hand up to shade your eyes. At first, my eyes began to water and I had to wipe them. When I looked again and my eyes focused, I began to back away from the image that was cast in the window. You could plainly see the face of a person with a hat on. There was indescribable agony where the eyes and mouth were. You could also see the rope leading from his neck. That chilled me for the reminder of that day and years that followed. While stationed at

Fort Benning, Georgia on Kelly Hill with the *197th Infantry Brigade (Mechanized) (Heavy) (Separate)* in 1984, I took Larry 'Sleezy' Spruell, Nolan 'Lord Munchies' Solomon, and DeWayne 'King Dog (KD)' Ward to Reform to get away from the clubs in Columbus, Georgia. Along with Bernice 'Bern-Yay' Jackson, and Ike 'Bum Brother' Howard, we called ourselves 'The Inner Circle'. Sometimes we would allow a couple of the other guys to hang out with us but us six were the 'Crew'. We had almost a different club to go to each night of the week. In 1984, the age to buy beer and wine in the clubs was dropped to nineteen and the clubs stayed full of college kids. One particular club we really enjoyed, the waitress, and the barmaids knew Howard and I personally, was the 'Zodiac'. I'll tell you what. I have met some fine females in my time but I met a young lady name Susie at the Zodiac and I nicked named her 'Susie Q' after the girl the group sang about in the movie 'Apocalypse now'. "...Oh Susie Q, Baby I love you, oh Susie Q!"

    Howard had just returned from temporary duty

(TDY) to Fort McCoy, Wisconsin and we were hitting all of our clubs that week. The other guys hung with us Friday and Saturday nights but Howard and I had been going strong every night since my return from training at Eglin Air Force Base in Florida the first week of November 1983. By the way, I can only call him what he was, and that was a PARTYING FOOL! I had 'Winter Environmental Training at Fort Drum, New York in March of 1984 and Howard had the Fort McCoy training. Other than being away from each other those two times, we partied every night until the beginning of Thanksgiving Week 1984. That is when we both left the Noncommissioned Officers Club (NCO) on a Sunday night and jumped in our cars to race to Phenix City, Alabama to see who would get to Richardson Lounge first. Howard took off down South Lumpkin Road and I headed up Fort Benning Road. Don't know what made me do it but I stopped at the Circle Grocery and got a bottle of sleeping pills and returned to the barracks, got me two Colt 45s from the beer machine, wrote two goodbye *letters and downed the damn things. Ask me why? I HAVE NOT THE SLIGHTEST IDEA! I had my dumb ass on B-4 in Martin Army Community Hospital for Thanksgiving. That should have broken up our little group partying all the time. Buuuullll Shit! I got my ass out the hospital the day after Thanksgiving and damn if Howard and I were not in the NCO Club that night. Howard was pouring down Crown Royal and me Jack Daniel Black Label. That's why I call him a partying fool. He damn near killed me. My partying started at Fort Benjamin Harrison, Indiana to the National Training Center at Fort Itwin, California, to Camp Carroll, Waegan, South Korea and finally ended at Fort Benning, Georgia. Perhaps I will give explicit details when I do "Once a Soldier".*

Well, anyway. The night we were at the Zodiac. Howard and I were drunk. To be honest, Howard may have been slightly tipsy but I was, '*I don't give a damn drunk!*' I first saw Susie Q when I went to the back of the club to use the toilet. There she was sitting up on the deck in a pink, sweater mini dress. My eyes went straight to those sexy, big legs of hers and when I raised my eyes to her face, she smirked at me. I said, *"DAMN!",* and went into the bathroom. This Brother came in behind me and told me to join the line. She had been sitting there for at least an hour and had not danced with anyone.

When I came out the bathroom, I made my way straight to her table.

"Excuse, me Ms. Lady, Would you like to dance?"

Damn Heifer put her hand up to her face and told me she was waiting for someone. I was a gentleman. I might have been drunk, but I was a gentleman, AT THAT MOMENT!

I made my way back to my table and had the waitress bring me another Jack Daniel. My drink came and I had just took a sip out of it when Ms. Fine, ass Susie Q walk up to my table, grab my hand and tell me, not ask me, *"come on let's dance."*

Howard is looking like, *"Means, where the hell you find her at?"* I laugh and allow her to pull me to the floor. The dance everybody was doing then called for you to easy your legs out to the side, rotating from the waist down and then thrust your pelvic in the direction of your dance partner. It was almost like sex without touching. Howard and I had both spent time in Germany and we loved us some *mean German tailoring*. The slacks I had on really accentuated my lower extremities and I noticed this guy dancing next to us kept glancing at Susie Q. After the dance, Susie Q came to our table and asked us to join her and her girlfriend at their table. I was getting ready to say no when Howard gave me *THE LOOK* that said *"You better not be cheating me out of anything tonight Means!"* Howard and I had a thing that we really loved ladies in the healthcare field. When we came across two that we liked, we would take them to an early breakfast at the Days Inn Restaurant and grab a room if everything worked out for us. So Susie Q got my drink for me, we returned to her table, and she introduced her friend to Howard. When the girl looked up, I almost laughed but took my drink from Susie Q and took a swallow. The girl was a little on the overweight size but she had Howard laughing right away. I saw Susie Q look towards the front and the guy who had been checking her out on the dance floor was headed out the door with the girl he had been dancing. Susie Q excused herself and walked to the front of the club and out the door. I cannot remember the young lady name but she told us that Susie had come to the club to meet that guy. Howard looked at me and I just picked up my drink, drained it, and went to the bar to get another. The barmaid started teasing at me and said *"I guess we want be going home tonight either. That girl looks good in that pink dress, don't she?"* I just smiled and got my drink and returned to the table. Susie Q had returned and Howard told me *"the ladies were going to let us treat them to breakfast."* I looked at Howard and told him I was ready to go to the barracks.

"*Oh, you don't want to go to breakfast with us,"* Susie Q spoke up. "*I guess you're one of those guys who don't like a woman to talk to no other man if she is dating you."*

I looked at Howard and told him, ok, let's go to breakfast. Howard looked at me and he told the ladies we would follow them to the Days Inn Restaurant on Macon Road. By now, Mr. Jack Daniel had control and Howard asked me to be nice. When we got to the restaurant, the ladies slid into one side of the booth and Howard and I slid into the other side. When the waitress came and took our order for coffee, we told her we just wanted coffee for now. I slid my hands under the table and started softly singing a cadence song we sing when we are doing physical training (*PT*). By the way, before my episode with the pills and beer, on many PT mornings, the company would be in formation when Howard and I would be just getting in to the barracks. They would start clapping and cheering and yelling we had better hurry. Howard and I would always make it. The First Sergeant called me in his office one morning after we had finished running and showed me he already had *Article 15s* in his desk for Howard and me as soon as we missed formation. All they needed was the Company Commander's signature. He then looked at me and said, *"Sooner or later 'Sweet Willie' (and the name has stuck all these years later) you two guys are going to fuck up."* Shit, I was thinking, *"Then, DAMN! Why don't you get me some help? That damn partying fool is going to kill me!"*

My hands touched Susie Q's knees under the table and she looked at me but at the same time eased her legs open. To me that was an invitation to go exploring and I did. Young lady had some really soft thighs and that has always been my weakness when it comes to a woman. She eased her legs open and I was enjoying myself. When I really touched pay dirt, Susie Q reached up, began to twirl her finger in her hair, and said, *"I really can't believe you are doing this to me right at this table."* I don't know what Howard and the other young lady was discussing, but her head snapped around and looked at Susie Q then looked at the way I was leaning on the table. She jumped up, made the statement *"Susie, come and go to the lady's room with me!'* At the same time, she pulled Susie Q up and this of course pulled my fingers from where they were delightfully enjoying themselves. Howard turned to me and said,

"Means! Don't you know that girl knows what you are doing to her friend?" As I said, Mr. Jack Daniel had taken over and I didn't even glance at Howard, I was enjoying the smell on my fingers. Howard made the statement, *"Wait until I tell the guys. Means was finger-fucking the girl right at the table in the restaurant."*

OVERWHELMED
And
OVERDUE
14 June 2011

I have always given my Sons the basics of things I see they may have an interest in and I back-off and allow them to do what they will with the knowledge. As I have said, and told many, it was my being good in track and field that allowed me to be decent in any sport I wanted to play. However, come to think of it. Having good hands and eye coordination started with the games, we played back in Bessemer in the early Sixties. A game of Jacks, spinning a top, or playing with a Yoyo all played a part in teaching me how to hit a baseball, and have hands quick enough to catch a football well. From my track and field days in High School and College, I made one big mistake. When I came to my fork in life, one leading to following my upbringing and becoming a Preacher, and the other leading to wanting to excel in track and field, I did not know

Willie Means Well

how to combine the two.

Willie Means Well

Fourth of July
2011

Well I am back again for now. Wanted to write several hours ago but had to take a pain pill for the shoulder. In fact, I should say some several hours ago. Now that I recall, I woke right after midnight and could not return to sleep. I was hurting in my chest as well as the shoulder. On top of that, I was trying to get a cramp in my legs. I want to write but the pain is demanding that I do another pill but it will knock me out again. I feel my attorney and doctor know each other and I am not getting what I should right now.

I have had three of the last four days off and between stressing over this house and animal and the pain I am experiencing; I just cannot focus to write. I have probably lost my publisher because I told them I would have this book to them back in April. Well, at least I will do this much:

PATRIOTISM

One who loves his or her Country!

If I could just stay focused long enough to get this letter to My President done, I believe I could get a few pages out of the way.

Willie Means Well

Monday July 18, 2011

I worked last night to help third shift. When I was supervisor of third shift, I tried to teach my workers teamwork so we would not only watch over the consumers, but each other. I am going to stray once again from my letter to the president and tell of a few happenings over the years while working, as many call it, *"The Graveyard Shift!"*

I came home totally out of it, left arm, and shoulder hurting as if it did not want to be part of the body any longer. My doctor who did the shoulder surgery November 30, 2010, has allowed *Risk Management and Workers' Compensation* to bully him into saying I can do things that are not true. My therapist had me working with one-pound weights and as I seem to adapt to the weight, the therapist moved me up to two pounds. It only took working with those two pounds a few minutes when the therapist came took the weight and told me it was too much. I reported this to my doctor and he showed concern. However, like a week after I saw the doctor,

I get a letter from Risk Management saying the doctor told them I could lift between twenty-five and thirty pounds. I later asked my doctor had I offended him in some way. When I explained why I asked him, I must admit, he did not show anger, but told me he was going to request a *"Functional Capability Examine" (FCE),* to show my true capability. The test was done last Thursday and here it is four days later and you would think I just had the surgery. In other words, *"I HURT LIKE HELL!"* Even the guy who did the testing wanted to know what was wrong with those people sending me to him when I could not do almost anything without hurting from it. I have been trying to stay off the pain pills but I am so afraid that the surgery on the shoulder, (second surgery, and same area) is going to affect the surgery done on my neck and then I have to have the neck surgery done again. I know this is possible because it happened to my wife. She had neck surgery from an injury while working with New Horizon and later rotator-cuff surgery when she got hurt working at West Central Georgia Regional Hospital. That is right, we both worked at the place and we both wound up having surgery. Would you believe some of my coworkers at the hospital told me the Unit Director wanted to know how I was always getting hurt? It made me angry. Hell, I would walk on that Unit after shift change and some days did not get to sit and take a break until those clients had snacks and had settled down some. One of the male nurses told me they expected me to take a goody powder and keep work like the one many of the workers did. I really wish there were an attorney smart enough to bring about a class action lawsuit against that place.

    Anyway, the first hour or so of working last night was not bad. Then I heard this person screaming. From my military days, I learned to trust my ears at night over my eyes. As I zoned in my hearing and focused on the apartments, I realized the sound was coming from behind me in the area of the railroad tracks. On top of this, I could swear the sound seem to be focusing in on where ever I looked. I like to pull a van down to where ever I am going to work. That way I can see whatever movement goes on until all the consumers call it a night. I climbed back into the van but caught myself constantly checking the mirrors. Then the thought came creeping into my mind about the ghostly experience I had on Britt Avenue and Tenth Street during my taxi driving days. I had to fall back on my military discipline from my pulling guard days and make myself get out of that van and walk and keep listening out for any possible problems with the consumers. Something else that came to mind was my wife telling me of the soldier who had killed a female and buried her in a shallow grave off Cusseta Road that ran into Sand Hill on Fort Benning. It was during the *Stocking Strangling Days* in Columbus, Georgia and this guy had told the media he was going to kill a lady every week until they caught the guy killing the old white ladies. Part of the properties owned by the guy who owns the complex we have our consumers living in once was a small club. My wife said until they found that lady body off Cusseta Road in that shallow grave, it had almost became unbearable in the area from the stench.

Last night really had the hairs on my body electrified. I had just heard on the radio from one of the Christian Teacher saying you could not see demons or angels but you could be exposed to their presence when they would indwell in a person. All I have to say about that is he needs to talk to my mother who along with the rest of us *See, Feel, and Hear Spirits.* I would gladly give my share of this gift to anyone who wants it. As if I am always telling anyone who wants to discuss the Bible, *"You cannot pull out parts of the Bible to justify your beliefs or church. You have to take the Bible from Genesis to Revelation and realize that it is all real."* Being raised Sanctified, I definitely believe in *Spiritual Gifts* and I have had more than my share of hair-raising experiences.

In February 2002, I was hired to work on the Adolescent Unit, which at the time was in Building 7, at West Central Georgia Regional Hospital (WCGRH). The charge nurse for third shift and her sidekick were a *trip*. Right off Jump Street they begin to lay demands on me and telling me what I was supposed to do because I was a new hire. Guess I rather began to make enemies my first night. Her sidekick was a health service technician (HST) like me and was a decent person when she was not around that nurse. She showed me through the building and a television room where she would come and watch television on her break. I should have known soon as we walked through the doors on the other side that I should stay from over there. I became sad and depressed and found myself trying to see through the darkness that seems to hang in the corners. What I was also looking for was a toilet I could use without the possibility of being disturbed and I found one behind the HST desk. I was glad when we exited that side of the building and got back to the other side. I asked the HST had somebody got hurt over there or something and she wanted to know why I would ask that. That first night I went to the toilet on that side before taking my break in the television room. It did not take long, as soon as I closed the door to the toilet and sat on the stool, I know I heard and felt someone messing with the doorknob. I made the statement, *"I will be out soon!"* It got quiet and when I came out there was no one there. I shut the door to the toilet and went to the television room. I was sitting watching television and I heard the footsteps coming to the door so I changed the television to another program. The steps stopped in front of the door but no one came in. I could actually see under the door as someone was standing there. I got up and opened the door but no one was there. In my mind, I said *"OoK!"* and finished my break. I decided to use the toilet again before I left and the door was standing open and the light off. I am sure you know what I am talking about when I say looking into the darkness, I know someone should have been there but there was no one. That first night was enough for me and I would not go over there by myself for a while. I had to go over one morning to the room where they stored the clients' clothing. Have you ever been in a room where it seems the light just does not penetrate the darkness in the corners? That morning, I had this kid with me and I could notice his being nervous. I finally asked what was wrong and he told me this was the room where, and he called a name, but I cannot remember it, hung herself. I looked at him and said, *"WHAT!"* In addition, he said one of the young ladies had hung themselves in that room. That next night I had the opportunity to spend some time and talk to the assistant nurse. She later told me I was stupid and did not pay attention to things. I later realized she was letting me know that she was married to the *Stocking Strangling Accused, Carlton Gary*. All I can say is she was a very sweet and religious lady. She filled me in on some stuff about the unit and that female HST, since the charge nurse was not there, actually loosened up and verified what Ms. Gary was telling me. They later used a bunched of bull-crap charges to get rid of Ms. Gary. I knew then they were a clique and if you did not march to the beat of their drum, they got rid of you. I was an HST and I knew many things they did were not right. They had this Black Kid that mother was afraid of him. He was a big kid and when it was times to rotate the kid out, his mother agreed to send the kid to an area in North Georgia where there really was the possibility of him getting killed. I talked to the mother and in a roundabout way told of her a similar place I believe it was in South Georgia near Florida that would had been a lot safer.

    I had been on that unit maybe a month and I was very paranoid about being anywhere in that building by myself. The charge nurse and her sidekick had started the word around that they had never worked with a man as scared as I was. I later rather helped sit up the situation that got both of them put in their places. I was sitting in the kitchen on my break and I caught a glimpse of someone walking in the hall coming towards the kitchen. I had seen similar things during my month there but I would look for ways to logicalize it. This particular night, I had gotten up and was peeping through the window to see if I could see the person when I got the feeling that someone was standing right beside me. On top of knowing someone was there, I could hear someone exhale and a puff of smoke appeared in the air right in front of me. I stared, then turned and walked out door and returned to the unit. Ms Gary and another female HST looked at me and wanted to know why I was back since I still had at least twenty minutes on my break. When I explained to them what had happened they both looked at me and told me they would have come from over there too. We began to talk and I told them how the charge nurse and her sidekick were treating me. Ms. Gary and the HST whispered to each other then Ms Gary told me to ask the Charge Nurse about the time she went into the kitchen trying to catch whoever had been taking stuff from our refrigerator. Apparently, the charge nurse came back telling everybody that the pots and pans started coming out of the cabinets by themselves and stacked themselves in the sink. They said she had run back to the unit and they thought she was going to have a heart attack.

    That Unit was very strange. In 2005, they closed the Unit and dispersed the staff to the Adult Units. I was assigned to Unit 10 and worked with three great Lead HSTs that taught me how to be a Lead HST. It was Henry Johnson who told me I had not imagined that toilet door being opened. Henry said when they had adults on that units, staff had come to realize that something was wrong when every time someone came out of that toilet and closed the door, when you looked up the door was open again. He also verified that the girl had hung herself in that room and they could not keep anyone in that room any more but everybody they put in there complained that somebody kept messing with their stuff.

Through the years, I wondered if the buildings that housed the children became haunted or were it the children themselves that brought about the haunting. When I started on adolescent, the charge nurse had me on one-on-one duty several nights' straights. She said she wanted to give me the time to ready the policies and learn my duties. Ms. Gary told me I should have reported her because she was not treating me fairly. She was supposed to rotate me with other staff.

Sometimes, those first days, they would come and play cards with me to keep me awake.

Sometimes, I was just there trying to peer into the darkness to make sure the kid was all right. The kid was a practicing witch and he gave many of us the creeps. You could look in to check on him and you would think he was sleep but when you looked again, he would sometimes be sitting in the middle of his bed just staring at you. What really got you was when you might go in and checks but when you walked out the door, he would be standing at the door and staring at you. When we moved that kid on, no one was able to sleep in that room. Not even another kid who we got later that was a practicing warlock. They all began to talk in their sleep and told of dreams where they just knew something was coming for them. One kid told of hearing his name called and something began shaking his bed when he would not answer. Ms. Gary said the kid came running out the room and told the charge nurse something was shaking his bed and calling his name. The charge nurse told the kid she was a Christian and he needed to go back to bed. I was told the kid sat by the door on the floor the remainder of the night and the next day they put him in another room.

The reason why I wondered was the kids making this stuff happen was we had to move into building six while they worked on building seven. The very first night the pay phone rang at five minutes after one. We took the phone off the hook and sat the receiver on top of the telephone. The phone would ring off the hook. This went on for the first week and I called and talked to my mother about it. What amazed me even to this day is my mother wanted to know, if there a unit out there that kept people who had hurt people. I explained to her there was and I told her about the hospital being built over or near an old Indian burying ground. Here is what my mother told me.

"Willie Earl. You all have got spirits trapped out there and they are trying to communicate with anyone they can. They are trying to get off those grounds but they are not able to go pass that front gate."

"Momma, how do you know this?" As you can see, now, I even overlooked the way we had been raised. I already suspected the phone ranging had something to do with spirits. During one of our HST meetings, I asked some of the HSTs who had worked on Unit 6 did they have a problem with the phone ringing around one in the morning. Several of them looked at me and told me they had never had problems with any of the phones on that unit. I told them what was happening and they told me they were glad they would be turning that building into a shopping mall for the clients when the Adolescent Unit moved back into building seven. Come to think of it. My wife worked security with the hospital for a short time. My wife told me that before shift change, she was required to go and sign a sheet in each building showing they had checked the building. My wife said, *"I'm telling you Bill! When I get to building six, I have to get my nerves under control. Majority of the time the lights will not come on and you be trying to hold a flashlight while getting the sign in sheet out of the plastic protector and all the while you just know if you turn around somebody is going to be there with you. Then, on top of that, you* can be still and you hear the sound of someone walking. The footsteps always seem to be coming towards you but you never see anyone!" My wife said she talked to some of the security staff that had been there for a while but they would always start laughing and joking about other stuff.

"Willie Earl. I don't think those spirits are strong enough to hurt you, but, I want you to take a pair of your shoes that you use for work and do exactly what I tell you to do."

Even I get skeptic at times, but when Momma is trying to help me with something, I try to be compliant. Momma told me things to do to my shoes and I did it. When I returned to work that night, I got busy and did not realize it was almost three in the morning before one of the nurses said they must had finally fixed the phone because it had not ranged. I looked at the phone and then realized the phone had not ranged and the receiver was on the hook. We got peace from that phone for over a month. Then my son had gotten a job at Winn Dixie and he needed some black sneakers as part of his uniform. He asked if he could wear my black sneakers, and I told him sure. I was in the bed resting but woke up looking for the shoes when it was time for me to get ready for work. My wife told me I had let my son wear the shoes to work. I put on another pair of shoes and went to work. At five after one, the pay phone rang and I and the other HST looked at each other and I looked down at my shoes. Both nurses came to the HST desk and told me, *"Go answer it Mr. Means!"*

I made the statement, *"You know what? I am going to answer it. This has to have a logical reason behind it. Besides, we didn't take it off the hook."*

I walked over to the phone and snatched it off the hook!

"Hello!"

There was silence on the other end, and then a sexless voice spoke, *"hello. I was trying to call the forensic unit. Do you have the number to the forensic unit?"*

I held the phone away, looked at it, and then said, *"Yes. I can get the number for you. Hold on for a minute."* The nurses and the HST wanted to know who it was and I told them I couldn't tell if it was male or female because the voice sounded strange. When I returned to the phone, I gave the number, the voice said thanks, and I hung up. I picked the phone back up and held my hand over there earpiece until it stopped making the beeping sound. I put the receiver on top of the phone and turned to walk away. I got half way back to the HST desk and the phone rang again. I looked at the HST and the two nurses stopped talking and looked at me. I turned and went back to the phone. I eased the phone up to my ear and before I could say hello, a voice spoke. *"And Don't Be Answering This Phone Again!"* The phone went dead. I stood there holding the phone and one of the nurses came over, took the phone, and put it up to her ear.

"Ain't nobody on here now Mr. Means. What happened? You look like your complexion got lighter!"

"That same sexless voice just told me not to be answering the phone no more."

"Mr. Means, you know you lying!"

Willie Means Well

"No I am not. It just told me not to answer the phone again and I don't plan to either."

"Mr. Means, why did you look at the floor when the phone rang?"

"I was looking at my shoes. My mother had told me something to do to my shoes and I didn't wear them tonight because my son wore them to work. For over a month that phone has not rang and here tonight, as soon as I don't have them on, the phone rang again. I'll be glad when we get out of this building."

It was not long after that we did move back into building seven. Arrogant fools had taken the HST desk out. Talking about maybe the reason the clients hung out at the desk so much was because they wanted staff interacting with them. They closed Adolescent in 2005 but I was not there when they finally got off the last child. I had been out for more than a month with my heart giving me problems. I really had concern for those children. Adolescent was one of the Units making money but they used the excuse the unit was spending too much money to close it. You try not to get attach to those children, but you cannot help it when you see them transformed from when they entered the Unit and what they become as they give in and allow staff to assist them and show them staff really is concern with helping them. Would you believe, we already had a child that was about five feet six inches and weighed over 270 pounds when they sent us one that had just turned 14, was over six feet, and weighed over 270 pounds also? The two of them got together and decided they were going to run the unit. We only had one Lead HST for the entire Adolescent Unit while the other Units at the hospital had at least two each shift. Being senior HST for third shift, sometimes we would holdover on first shift, and got a taste of those two trying to control the Unit. One morning one of the female adolescent started throwing stuff and fighting with the female staff. When staff on the male side went over to assist, these two adolescent males came to me and told me, *"You don't know how to work on first shift. You suppose to take all of us over there and you are supposed to help."*

When I just looked at them and told those staff had everything, they looked at each other and stated, *"Let's rise up!"* They then headed for the hall door and were getting ready to put their strength against the door to force it open. I do not remember how I did it because at that time I only weighed about one hundred-eighty pounds. The kid that was five feet six and 270 found himself lying on the floor three feet from the door. When the other one saw him lying on the floor, he dashed pass me and yelled he was going to his room and he was sorry. I looked at the one on the floor and shouted, *"NOW GET IN YOUR ROOM!"* I had to stop from laughing because I could see the fear and surprise on his face as he scrambled and crawled to get to his room not bothering to try to get to his feet. They both slammed their doors and I heard another child say, *"Wow! Mr. Means grabbed him by the shoulders and threw him pass the HST desk."* As I said, I do not remember what happened. I lost it for a couple of minutes because I knew those two had several of the male staff intimidated. The next morning, the kid over six feet came to me with another adolescent and asked to shake my hand. When I reached out to shake his hand, he certainly had my arm and asked what I would do if he tried to break my arm. When I looked at him and told him they would both wake up in the hospital, the other kid jumped back and the kid released my arm and told me he was just playing. I later found out that was how they had intimidated the other male staff. They got hold of the staff then would force them to the floor and refused to get up until other staff would have forcefully remove them off the staff on the floor. Much as I hated it, two days later the sheriff came, handcuffed the tall kid, and took him away. They let the sheriff on the unit so all the male clients could see the kid get his hands cuffed behind his back and be led away. For the remainder of that morning all the guys remained in their rooms with the doors cracked. When they closed the unit in 2005, the other 270 pounder was the last kid to be placed. Damn kid had come to love me and I really helped him remain out of trouble. Last, I heard he had been turned out on the streets in Macon, Georgia.

    When I returned from being sick, I worked with the adult patients on Unit 10. My experience with the adults left me with four levels reinforced in my neck. One of the adolescents came back as an adult patient and this one weighed in over six feet four and 300 pounds. When the man first saw me, he ran up and wanted to hug me but I told him we would shake like gentlemen. For two days the guy did not let anyone cost me any problems. Have to admit he was not violent. He would just tell them how I was one of the nicest workers there and they should appreciate me more. I really did not have any problems. We were on smoke break and the guy was lying on the ground at my feet and smoking a cigarette. He had told me he was expecting a telephone call from his sister. When the call came, he went in to get the phone. Next thing I knew all hell was breaking out in side and I could hear the guy yelling at everybody. I got everybody inside and into their rooms and the guy was turning over furniture, kicking the clothe hamper and throwing chairs across the room. Now state policy tells as long as they are not really threatening anyone, let them destroy the furniture. I was just shaking my head in sorrow and wondering what had happened when the guy grabbed a picture and physically pulled it from the brick wall. The screws extending from the rear of the pictures had to be at least two inches and pointy. He started rushing the other patient's rooms and slamming the screws into the doors. When I tried to talk to him and get the pictures from him, he told me I had better get out of his way. To this day, I never got the straight of what happened. He was trying to kick the fire extinguisher off the wall and when he could not, he headed for another clothe hamper. I rushed and moved the hamper and I found myself on the floor with the guy, people screaming, and the stress bell going off. I remember hearing a female yell for me to stop choking him and me felt hands and arms pulling me off the guy. I later found out it was one of the patients who had been a police officer. They got the guy down for a shot and the Nurse Supervisor sent me to the emergency. In the end, it led to my neck surgery and I have never seen the guy again. I found out later what set him off was he had just found out he no longer was allowed any contact with any of his family members. I felt so bad. I never returned to that damn unit. They started a Crisis Stabilization Unit for children and adolescents and I was selected for one of the HST Lead positions on second shift. We started out on Unit 3 and low and behold if that damn building was not haunted by one of the children who had been killed by an accident outside the hospital main gate. Then another female had hung herself grieving over the other girl. I remember my Nurse Manager told me she was in that building all hours of the night and early morning by herself. She said she walked in the protection of the LORD and did not fear any spirits that might be in the building. Many of us did not have her faith and always doubled up when we did mostly everything in that building. I was assigned the task of inspecting the building weekly and I always walked and PRAYED wherever I had to go in that building. The spirits were there and I felt them all the time. On occasion, I might be checking the children after bedtime and so many times, I would see spirits sitting on the beds, standing in corners and even looking out the windows. I remember one female staff reported she had her head down doing paperwork one night and she glanced up when she heard the bathroom door open. She said just as the door was closing she saw a female. She said she jumped up and went to the bathroom, snatched the door open and started telling the female that she knew she was suppose to ask permission to get up. The lady said she stopped mid-sentence when she realized there was no one in the bathroom. She said one of the nurses came out and wanted to know what was wrong and when she explained, they both checked the children and everybody was sleeping. Later one of the HST working on the unit when the child was killed outside the gate asked the lady what the girl had was wearing. When she told her cut off blue jeans and a blue tee shirt, she said the HST told her that is what the young lady loved to wear when she got in from school.

Willie Means Well

The place is really full of spirits. Working third shift we had to take the census and other paper work to the hospital supervisor by 2a.m... Like I said, I always walked and PRAYED when I was either inside or when I was outside. Before I left Adolescent, I recall one of the workers who saw the movie *Gothika*. Poor guy really meant well but the mental health field is not an easy field to work in. He did not make it. He told me about that damn movie and how the lights would flicker any time a spirit was around. Now I had been taking those papers to the supervisor for over two years and never really had a physical occurrence happen. Like I have said, I can feel and know when a spirit is around. It unnerves me and many times, I really feel my hair crawl on my head. The first night after that man told me about that movie I was approaching to pass the forensic unit and damn if the lights did not blink. I started saying a protection Psalm aloud and the lights blinked a couple more times and stopped. There is a large pond that sits in the middle of the campus and a walking trail goes around the pond. Now I learned from my mother at an early age, listening to stories of things that happened to the family when they were still in Cuba, Alabama that you do not stare at churches in the dark especially when you are alone. Well, that same night as I was passing the forensic unit, I saw something moved out of my peripheral vision. I turned my head to the left and just as I looked, a lady vanished. Man I tell you I got cold chills and my head went to hurting me something fierce. Would you believe when I got in the building and was giving the supervisor the paperwork she made the statement, *"What's wrong with you Mr. Means? You look like you just seen a ghost."* She laughed and I just looked at her. I went to the break room and loaded up on snacks the staff had asked me to bring back and I left PRAYING ALL THE WAY!

    In April 2001, my wife and I had a brief split. We had been married 16 years by then and she had always told me, *"If you leave me, you will have to leave Columbus or go to jail!"* Sounds a little selfish, right? Well, I did not leave Columbus and I did not go to jail. However, guess what? Damn if she did not lie and I wound up in that damn hospital for eight days. My mother and some family were there the next day to get me out but this damn doctor told me she was sorry but law said she had to keep me three days or something. What I want to share with you is my mother and the receptions got to know each other and my mother said while they were sitting in the lobby talking the receptions interrupted her and pointed out this lady walking the pass by the pond that went behind the Chapel. Mother said she was watching the lady and she walked behind this small tree. Mother said she and the receptionists were still having a conversation when she realized the lady had not come from behind the tree. Mother said she looked at the receptionists and asked, *"What happened to her? I know she can't be sitting behind that little tree."* Mother said the lady looked at her, smiled, and stated, *"She's gone." Many times I have sat here and watched her walk that passes but when she gets to that little tree she vanishes."*

Mother said it had to be only about one in the afternoon and for a spirit to be that strong, something really bad had to happen to her to be strong enough to manifest herself in the middle of the day that way. All I know is it must had been her that scared the dickens out of me that night. As a matter of fact, thinking of it, she would fit the category of a *'Haunt'*. Haunts like to scare you and I know she scared me. On another occasion, I was walking up to building ten and a lady came walking from the building and passed me. I spoke but she just walked by and did not say anything. When I got to the door, turned and looked, the lady was nowhere in sight. I walked back out from the door and looked but logic was telling me that she could not had gotten away that quick. Then I realized I had not heard the door close anyway. Go figure!

    After my second surgery from an injury I got at that hospital, would you believe those UNGRATEFUL MOTHERFUCKERS terminated me. Told me had the doctor released me when he originally said he would, I could had kept my job. That damn hospital did many workers wrong. What really pisses me off is that you cannot get an attorney to suit their asses. I have now had a second surgery on the same shoulder and believe you me, I Pray for my former coworkers out there but I find myself many times wishing the WRATH OF GOD on them when I hurt.

Today is July 26. I hope that when I have at it again, I will be writing my letter to the president.

July 31, 2011
(Things are really heating up all over!)

Well, managed to break contact with *'Unusual Happenings'*, but I do believe I will return there before this one is over. I have been putting this off for a long time but I really want to get this letter to the President done. If you noticed I said, *'to the President, and not my President!'* There is a reason, and I am sure Ms. Helen *'Lundragon'* Lundergan, will probably get on me for it. I also believe this is what really will sell the book for me.

Willie Means Well

*A Letter to the President,
Of the United States of America*
Dear Mr. President Obama. This is former United States Army Sergeant (E-5) Means, Willie Earl. I have written you several times requesting help with problems I have been having with getting the Veterans Administration to admit I am owed more disability for some of the other stuff that happened to me while in the military. I figure letters from LOW JOES like me have about the same chance of getting to you as a snowball in hell have of not melting. I hope that by the time this letter reaches you in one of my books, that debacle in Washington over raising the "Debt Ceiling" will be outdated. I want to remind you a little of whom I am. Like I said, I know you are screened from everything so one unhappy, former, Army Sergeant, complaining about the shot of you on stage with your back to "Old Glory", our Nation's Symbol of COURAGE, HONOR, FAITHFULNESS, RESPECT, DECENCY, PRIDE, JOY, AND THE GREATEST TO ME, FREEDOM! Before you were elected to lead this

Willie Means Well

Country, is still a very low thing to do to the American People. I seen where one group titled, I believe, "African American Veterans for Obama", pledged their support. If you have not figured it out by now, all these groups jumped in line because they wanted to ensure it showed where Blacks gave a high level of support for you even had you not been elected. I voted for you but these days I could never look myself in the eyes again if I had voted republican. The republicans had began to show distain at the Poor, the Working Poor, and even those who think they are back in the Middle-class. Oh, and before I forget, they were smart enough to take on the titled, "Born Again Christians", to fool those entire WASP (White, Anglo-Saxon Protestant) Elderly Voters and their offsprings belonging to those Mega-Churches. So very funny that once those people were in power, they reached out to punish Organizations like the N.A.A.C.P. and other Black Programs that supported the Demontracs over the years. However, all those mega-churches, especially in Texas, openly pray, even today, for God to do something with YOU! That guy James Dotson, who had been head of "Focus on the Family, was so outspoken that he resigned to keep pressure off him and that organization. Anybody with a grade school education can see that the Republican Party is now nothing more than another attempt to return Blacks to slavery. Those so-called "tea-party" people are nothing more than another name for the "klu Klux Klan". Now, I guess what I am trying to say to you right here is, "go to the American People and be truthful about your former religion preference, and then apologize for having your back turned to Old Glory.

 I knew you were going to be President when they stated you had an Ivy League Education. Not just an Ivy League Education, but from Harvard, itself. Many do not know or understand the power of Groups who are associated with the Ivy League. You may be Black, but you still belong to them and you brought great honor to that school being elected President. I, myself, am 56 years old and still need Precalculus Algebra for a degree, actually a double degree, one in Psychology, and one in Human Services. My transcript shows that I have met the requirement for these degrees from Troy University. They will probably give me a hard time of it but hopefully in the end they will honor my studies. The student loans set me back something fierce. I would seriously encourage anyone applying for such help to read the fine print.

You know, I wrote to another gentleman who held that office, former President Ronald Regan. So many want to rant and rave about what he did. All he did was show his racism and tried to help kill off the lower echelon of the population in America. We are still suffering from the foolishness of giving the Wealthiest in America all these tax breaks. There really was a great TRIGGLE DOWN EFFECT! It was so great that all those rich people sent American jobs to other countries so they would not have to pay decent salaries to the American People. Then our Government turns around and allows them to bring the merchandize back into the country and continue to get rich. Sounds familiar? "The Rich Get Richer and The Poor Gets Poorer!" Ralph Nader if I recall correctly. Actually, Mr. Sold-his's-Country-Out Nader. You can check if you need to but you will see and understand Nader had to have sided with the republicans and stole votes that Al Gore would had benefited from and never would had gone through that mess in Florida with that other Bush. You need to call for an import tax so heavy that it would make up the part of unemployment the Government has to pay for those put out of work by the rich out-sourcing those jobs.

Perhaps I am not making much sense but you need to talk to us and tell us what I am telling you. Let the American People see where the blame really lies with this Country tittering on the edge of destruction. This is all of our Country... not just the rich. Regan showed he was only for the white and rich when Reverend Jesse Jackson returned that Black fighter pilot from Libya. Regan was all smiles and grins until they brought the pilot's wife on stage and he saw she was White. So very sad! Regan would not shake the lady's hand nor say anything else to the pilot. I wonder why people look over incidents like this. We are human and we all bleed red when cut. During slavery, the white master had his choice of beautiful, fine Black Females when he so desired. With more than a hundred years pass since the Civil War, a Black Man still gets heat from marrying a woman of another race. GO FIGURE!

By the way, never trust Higher-ups in the Air Force with any secrets. If you check, you will find numerous things have been leaked by those guys. Even during Vietnam, I was told by guys the Army Commanders also use to be high above the battle zone in a helicopter, out of harm's way, dictating the battle on the ground. If you like all music like me, perhaps you have heard the song titled "Sky Pilot". I was told the song is in reference to those commanders in their helicopters.

Another incident during that damn conflict that never should have made national attention was Meeting Li. Once again, I was told it was guys in a helicopter gun-ship that got between those men and that village. How many times did it make the news that a man from that platoon had been mutilated by the Vietcong before the guys from the platoon went all out to destroy that village? Everyone, even today, wants American Military to fight a 'Gentlemen's War' when they are dealing with those utilizing barbaric tactics. So you will get a look at the kind of person I am when it comes to protecting this Country, had I been there, I would had knocked that helicopter out the sky with a M-79 and had those guys complete their mission. This is where I say, "FUCK EVERYONE WHO HAS NEVER BEEN IN THE SHOES OF COMBAT BUT WANT TO DICTATE AS TO HOW THE WAR IS FOUGHT!" I would like to say I am sorry, but I truthfully am not. When the Commander-In-Chief, You included, Sir, have no military training, allow the Pentagon to do their job and stay out of the way. Are you aware that our Military has the capability to end those conflicts in Iraq, Afghanistan, and any other little country who wants to step up and blow their noses at the United States? From my Artillery Days, we trained on a system that was very powerful. Over the years, I

Willie Means Well

had convinced myself that no such system was available. It was just something to frighten the Soviet Bloc Countries. Then while former President Clinton was in office, the Chinese guy was caught trying to slip that very blue print for that system to China. China has over three billion people I think and that system was engineered for such.

Guess I will also include former President Jimmy Carter. It was he who empowered these "Mice that Roar" to step up and challenge the United States. The Israelis taught the United States how to deal with terrorist. When that situation went down in Pakistan in 1979 that got this Nation in one of the worst embarrassment in our history, it could had all ended in less that twenty-four hours. While at the Defense Information School (DINFOS), a joint service school, in 1980, I met a Marine who told me how we were half way over there to get our people back when President Carter had them recalled. You see, within the first twenty-four to forty-eight hours, the aggressive group is jumping and shooting at shadows. Had some folks throwing ice and peanuts

Willie Means Well

at me on a flight from Chicago to Atlanta when they heard me and another military person discussing the issue. Stewardess had the nerves to tell us "serve you right. You need to think about what you are saying."

    Mr. President, I wonder if you even realize just how powerful you are. I once had someone in Military Intelligent (MI) tell me that there are just as many floors under CIA Headquarters as above ground. I am telling you this because you need to turn those protecting you loses and allow them to do the job they are paid to do. I guess the really strong last democratic president we had was JFK. You can damn well bet Sarah Palin would have her ass in one of those cells along with many from the Republican Party. They could all share a floor with the agent who allowed those two people to get in at the event you was having. Many laughed about it but they could have just as easy been sitting you up to assassinate you. I even heard a former CIA Agent complain because you apparently bowed to one of those people in the Middle East. You see, I would gladly burn this world up before a foreign power

Willie Means Well

took over America. Were I President, you would see what I mean. You have the ability and you need to put it in play. I am not sure, but I believe former President Bush, Sr. had something to do with the CIA if not the Director. You did not take that route but you can be just as powerful. YOU MUST SHOW THEM THAT YOU CAN PLAY ON THEIR LEVEL ALSO! By the way, get that Trump guy too. That guy Putin in Russia attained the rank of Colonel in the KGB (Komitet gosudarstvennol bezopasnosti (Soviet) State Security Committee. He went on to become President of Russia and he put many of those wealthy people in jail. He knew what he was doing. You did a nice job with Wall Street but you should not have stopped until you had the head of many of the corporations. If I know it, I am sure all of you who call yourselves running this Country know it. They shout words that they feel will frighten the Nation. Words like socialist make people think of Russia and even Nazi Germany but that is not where we were or is headed. The Poor wants to eat just like everybody else. They are not trying to get steaks and

Willie Means Well

potatoes like the rich. Probably some beans and soup and some kind of bread will be enough to hold us together.

    One last thing I want to share that will prove they just do not want a Black Man or person President. Denzel Washington made many good movies but he did not get an award until he lowered himself to their level and played a crooked police officer. Why? Because they only want to make money, money and more money, anyway they can. Halle Berry did many nice movies but did not get an award until she took her clothes off and got in the bed with the White man in Monster Ball or some title like that. I like to tell people and I write letters to the newspapers telling everyone who will listen "The job did not change just the person. The job of that person is to take care of not just the rich or the poor, but the WHOLE COUNTRY!

Thank You Sir!

Willie Earl Means

P.S. If I by chance get an invite, I do not do beer unless it is Coors. Not the 'Silver Bullet' stuff but

Willie Means Well

THE MOUNTAIN GROWN STUFF FROM COLORADO. *Or, you can simply allow me to sip Jack Black on the rocks then put me to bed in one of the spare rooms in the White House (probably what has them so confused, THE WHITE HOUSE!).*

Finally got it done. Now will share some of the letters I have written over the years to the newspapers. Go ahead, and vote me into the Presidency. I bet I will have this Country back at the top of the World in two years because I will kick the world's ass and make them get back in line behind THE UNITED STATES OF AMERICA!

P.S.S. If I had the chance to sit with you in person, I would tell you of my view of "The Russian House" when it comes to dealing with all these Maximum Security Prisons. However, as I said, we would have to be sitting together so no one else could hear.

Willie Means Well

Saturday, June 24, 2006

8:14 AM

(No Subject)

I was glad to see your printing of the letters about the way our Military people are treated. As the writer said, "WAR IS HELL". For all combat arms personnel active and former, the situations in Iraq and Afghanistan have to be extremely frustration. To know our Military has the capability to end both situations in one week but once again is being used like two children playing with army men is very sad. We should have taken those oil fields while we were over there during "Desert Storm". You cut off all foodstuff to those troubled areas and I'll bet the people will come to realize very quick they can't drink or eat that oil and they will be more than happy to utilize those same barbaric ways to get rid of those small entities that are causing all the problems. Our Military are not dealing with ladies and gentlemen. Everybody wants our Military to be civilized. If those people want to be barbaric, then turn our Military

Willie Means Well

loose and let them end these ***"So Called Wars".***

Friday, February 9, 2007

11:33 AM

The Draft!

Rich man, poor man, beggar man, thief... doctor, lawyer, Indian Chief. I wonder how many people recall this childhood game. Unbelievably this how the draft worked and this is how it would be effective if it were reinstated. The draft got everyone regardless of your wealth. Mer. Bush has promised his wealthy associates that there will be no draft. This mean their children will not possibly face what the All-Volunteer Military is going through now. Well the draft needs to start up again. In fact, let's see how long the U.S. will be fighting in any conflicts with the wealthy children on the line in these foreign lands. Something is wrong with our Society. Congress and the Pentagon should have been at each other when Congress made the statement that Pentagon did not have the authority to promise benefits to Retirees. We need to go to a minimum and maximum salary for those people in Congress and kick them out of office and into a Federal Prison when we find out that they have violated their trust of office.

Thursday, May 31, 2007
1:18 PM
It has become a joke!

A classmate once told me that they would eat a Social Worker alive if one became President. I don't think so and I believe we need one to get this Country back on track. The other morning on "Rise-N-Shine", representatives from both major Parties was talking about the upcoming election. I feel Mrs., Clinton is best for this Country. People keep calling Iraq a war. IT IS NOT! If it were a war, our Military would go from one end of that country to the other in a weeks' time. Our Military could have done the same thing in Vietnam but too many people were making money from that conflict. Every Democratic President makes the same mistake: they put their hands on our Military. PUT THE SAFETY OF THIS COUNTRY IN THE HANDS OF THE PENTAGON AND LET THEM DEAL WITH ALL THE OTHER ENTITIES THAT DO NOT PERTAIN TO SOCIAL ISSUES. Just think! Mrs. Clinton could

Willie Means Well

focus on the People problems and get this Country back together. All these people say they are 'born again Christians; Add it all up and see how much money they have. Like the stat points out, 1 percent of the population has over 90 percent of the wealth in this Country.

Sunday, July 15, 2007
10:59 AM
R.E.Mfs.

While stationed at Fort Irwin, California in 1981, Our General had the Public Affairs Office re-do our weekly newspaper (The Combined Arms Monitor) because an officer from one of the line-units wrote a letter-to-the-editor titled 'R.E.Mfs. I didn't know until the Colonel explained it to me what the officer was calling us. Well, all these years later, I really wish the 'R.E.Mfs.' Assigned to the Military now would wake-up and realize our military people are not trained for the JUNK they are facing in Iraq. Our 'Special People' in the other place is a different story. However, I don't see any glory in having our people die in something that can end in less than a week if our Commanders were allowed to do their jobs. If you will take a moment and think about it, we did not have to enter our 'Ground Forces' into the first conflict over there. We only did it to silence the critics. We have the technology to hit those people

Willie Means Well

wherever they try to hide.

Willie Means Well

Wednesday, October 17, 2007
9:07 AM
America!

Such racism! Such hate! Why people? Are we so afraid that someone will get the opportunity to live? All these comments about the health care bill for children. The children are our future. Not Black children! Not White children! All children. When will it end? It must end. I've come to realize that you still have so many thinking God is their color. On the other hand, those whose god is green. I truthfully believe until we get someone who truly put people first (not Black; not White), but people, we are going to remain on this pass of hatred and racism. Why do candidates need so much money for a "War Chest", when bidding for the Prudency of this Country? Remember that "GUY" who did the 'fireside chats' with America? He talked to the People. That's what we need right now. Someone who will look at this Country as a WHOLE and pull it together. Buy so many children needing health care that should tell

Willie Means Well

you that 'Welfare-to-Work' did not work. A minimum wage job but no way to take care of yourself or family. Today, certain hospitals will fix the immediate problem if you come to the emergency room. However, they will send you on to another hospital if you don't have insurance. So many are able to go on vacation outside the Country, but complain when other people need helping hands. Ninety percent of the wealth held by one percent of the population. Let's not begrudge them, but show them there is enough for everyone. In addition! That 'trickle down stuff does not work"

Willie Means Well

Tuesday, February 19, 2008
12:46PM

Presidents!

President Day! When is the last time we had a good one? I wrote a letter about what Obama needed to do if he wanted the support of the American People. What I wanted people to realize was the man was running for President but seemly had no respect for our National Symbol "Old Glory". From Ebony Magazine to 'BET' Television, so many are airing advertisements supporting this guy. He even made statements about what Ronald Reagan had done for 'The American People'. Ronald Regan only made the rich richer and came up with the ridiculous idea that when rich people had overage in riches they would share it with the less fortunate. WHAT A JOKE! When I flew from Chicago on my way to being stationed at Fort Benning in 1983, a couple of people threw ice at me on the plane because I pointed out that Jimmy Carter didn't keep his word about the Iran hostage situation. He stated we would

Willie Means Well

go in full-force if we lost one American life. I think we had an entire crew perish but we backed-off. I realize now that people care less about moral attitude and the only thing important is getting all the money they can. Even if it means looking the other way when people lie and disrespect what our Country supposes to represent.

I sent this to a number of newspapers and Ebony. I think we are on our way to becoming "Morales America".

Willie Means Well

Sunday, February 24, 2008
9:51AM

Whose side are you on?

I wonder whose side are you really on. I want to tell you that I am a 52-year-old Black Male living in Georgia. I saw your article on Oprah and Obama in your magazine. Just sort of scanned until I saw this has crossed over onto 'BET' also. You know, that "SELL-OUT" Ralph Nader helped the Democratic Party's Al Gore loose by splitting the vote. Now I truthfully feel everyone who gets behind Obama will help achieve the same result. I'll bet Republican Party Members are enjoying what Oprah has done by jumping on the band-wagon and swaying a lot of support Obama's way. People talk about change. America is not going to support someone who was photographed disrespecting our flag. You have many who don't understand what he did but every Veteran from the Military understands. That was a slap in the face to all our Military. If Obama wants to be elected, have him apologize to the American People

Willie Means Well

and to our Military. Next, let Obama promise the American People that he is going to take care of this Country by first keeping his hands off the Military. Give Pentagon its budget and then make everything else fall in after the Social Programs. Have him remind the People about our Elderly only being able to afford cat and dog food starting with the Reagan Administration and it has only gotten worst. Leave the Military along and allow them to end all debacles that the Republican has gotten us into. Have Obama show the American People that he will put America back on 'TOP' IN THE WORLD and stop allowing the rest of the world to make us march to the beat of their drum. One final thing! Denzel Washington did not win a major award until he played the crooked cop. Halle Berry did not win until she played the part of a Black Woman giving her all to a White Man. don't you see! Obama has to show that he will be able to move around the world of not just Black America but White America too. In addition! Remember. We are no longer even number two in population.

Willie Means Well

August 13, 2011
This and That

A quick split from my letters to say something about the mood I am currently in. If I talk **TOO MUCH** about sexual stuff, I do not know if my publisher will still publish for me. I was working on a book about my escapades when the first representative of the publishing company told me, *"We will not publish porn."* I did not consider it pornography since these days most major magazines publish sexcapades in name brand magazines but only add the work *'Red'* in the title somehow; i.e.."*Avon Red"*. At 56 for me and 57 for my wife, it is normally me who 99 percent of the time initiate sex. I even admit that these days I mostly satisfy myself and feel embarrassed once I am done for allowing myself to give in and have sex with her in the first place. I have had my share of decent love making and it really does hurt and embarrass me when I perform to the standard of the nickname, *'One Shot Willie'*, I have given myself. I entered this relationship back in November 1984 one-quarter-inch from having nine to work with. Now after all these years of *"one pop it's time to stop",* I think I may have three left. Anyway, came this way, because I tricked her into giving in to me this morning when I just wanted to see if I could. I came home yesterday and went straight to bed. Not watch television; not talk to the boys to see how their day went; at *6pm,* I was in the fetus position under the cover, totally drained and frustrated with coworkers. I have always believed in mission accomplish before allowing myself to take a break. These days more and more the slogan *"How can you sore with eagles when you work with turkeys"* keep popping up in my mind. The mental health field is already stressful enough without dealing with coworkers who are more interested in playing with each other, *a little feely, feely here and a feely, feely there!"* I am a case manager who tries and make sure the transportation is working well and safe. When you work with people who only want to get the key and jump in, and go this makes it hard to keep the

Willie Means Well

vehicles operating correctly because nobody tells you when something is wrong. The only way you know when a vehicle is 5,000 miles over the oil, change is when you have to drive it for some reason and you look and see the mileage. Well, had my fill of it yesterday, tossed the keys on the desk at shift change, and walked out. I do believe when I left them then went and picked the vehicle up from the automotive shop. The Site Director and her Sister, The Columbus Director, were both out of town trying to enjoy some time with their families and the supervisors seem more interested in touching each other and playing around rather than doing something constructive. I returned and apologized later but my supervisors were gone. I guess at 56 the games they want to play I have been there and done that. I hear, as I said, lots of touching going on. One of my coworkers so damn fine and love to wear dresses with no slips. When I got a silhouette shot of her with the sun outlining her body, I knew I was going to have my hands on her thighs before the week was out. Damn fine ass Honey layer some

Willie Means Well

information on me that made me turns and run the other way. When a couple of the guys queried me about it, one told me he did not see things as I did so he jumped in with both feet. Me! I could just see myself really, have a hot and heavy lovemaking session with her then go in the bathroom, look in the mirror, and be white as snow. That is how strong my religious belief is. Would you believe for a while that seem to make her try harder. A couple of times I found myself looking up at the sky and pleading for permission. Our Big Daddy upstairs did not respond but you can bet the other one tried to tell me it was all right.

In all honesty, we have our benefits but we are just a group of 'Working Poor' trying to make it. They would not believe this, but I sometimes want to come in on my days off just to share their company.

Willie Means Well

American Work gave me a chance
I heard Ms Ann say, "There's My Man!"
We met each other in '95
New Horizon's Family Enrichment we arrived
Charlotte, my boss is very nice
They think she is soft but she has nerves like ice
There is Ms Gwen so sweet and lovely
An 'LPN' so jolly, so bubbly
Paula is nice, and she will work with you
Trying to take advantage of her will leave you blue
Jeff, Greg, Gloria, Tricia and two new
Tonya is from Alabama I would like a clone or two
Bass, Quick, Bedell, a guy name Willie Means
Priscilla, Jada, Debra, Comeka the girls are keen
Sabrina, Daniel, Kingsley, Jackie,
Marlene, Kalima, Kelvina, and Michael
Providing coverage and care
We are the ones always there
Third, First, and Second
To the Mental Health Field, you are Welcome!

Willie Means Well

Tuesday, April **14**, 2009
4:27 PM

When the City die!

I just returned from Chicago, and if anyone needs scaring straight about the possible future of Columbus, they need to see what I saw, and what I mostly felt. Chicago is not home but I was raised there. One thing about that city was the streets were always in descent condition. However, two streets that are major through fares in that city, Western and Chicago Avenues, are now so broken up with pot holes and other rough spots, I don't see how any vehicle can remain mechanically sound after being driven on the streets. I wondered about the recent calamity with the former governor that led to his impeachment but after seeing and feeling the condition of those two major roads, I can only be led to the conclusion that the city or the political figures no longer really care about the people. Someone once pointed out if you want to know about the

Willie Means Well

advancement of a civilization just check out the road systems. People get tired of being over taxed but in some situations, they need to put everything behind them and give support to anything that is for the betterment of the people. It does not take a genius to realize that the one percent of the nation that holds more than ninety percent of the wealth is trying at every turn to get back to lining their already bulging pockets. The Working Poor is still baring the burden of the biggest taxation of this Country and it is sickening to see those people get on television and talk about what they want commotion instead of supporting the budget outlined by the President. The rich have gotten richer and they want more. The money needed for those streets in Chicago, I'll bet it was available but by the time everybody got their own pet project allocated there was nothing left. Chicago is ten times the size of Columbus but you can bet the same thing is happening.

Willie Means Well

Monday, May 25, 2009
8:19AM

Shake up the Country!

Returning home this morning after dropping my son at work, I realized today is Memorial Day and school is out. For people today, many hate this and many think it's good. I feel the entire Country need to make this the 'NORM' and head back to the "Good Old Days" when it comes to education and other stuff. I'm 54 but I recall being out of school the first week in May. We had "May Day" and we were out by the eighth and had a long summer vacation.

Today, we have those with such crazy ideas running everything from education to the military. It's no longer "politically correct" to talk of Communist Influence. However, I take issues with people wanting their children to stay in school year round. Remember congress telling the military the military was not authorized to promise members of the Armed Forces retirement benefits? I was stationed at Fort Irwin, California in spring 1982 when congress

Willie Means Well

stated they had it on good information that we no longer needed an Airborne Division because you could not jump a Division at one time. I had escort duty with a reporter from the San Bernardino Sun that Spring morning when the sky over 'Bicycle Lake' was filled with airplanes and parachutes. We lost some soldiers but the information congress received was proven wrong. This Country need to get back to its' basics. I take issues with people who measure the aptitude of our students with those of students from countries we have kicked the stuffing's out of. I'm telling you, we use to have Memorial Day, The Fourth of July, and Labor Day for our summer vacation. We have lost so much and we are losing more. It's time for a recall, a shake up, or whatever we need to do to get the United States of America back at the front of everything and give the Country back to the People. Kick out those who are getting rich and wealthy at the expense of the American People.

Willie Means Well

Thursday, June 18, 2009
12:26PM

Look at those CZARS

The President seems to be playing a strong chess game with the Legislature. Every time you turn on the television you have some republican complaining about what they did and what the President is now doing. The President has "Castled" and now continues to maneuver his pieces into striking positions. That President has an Ivy League Education. Eventually, people will realize what kind of force is behind the President. One of my Sociology Professors at Troy got upset when a student told him that compared to the Ivy League, all the other schools get in line to-do the bidding of the Harvard's, the Yale's, etc. The President has fortified his position and control with these CZARs. The Republican Party has gotten super rich off the taxpayers and now they scream every time the President do something to give the Working Poor a break. Look at what Putin did in Russia with the

Willie Means Well

wealthy. It's about time to shut-up and help get this Country back out front. In addition, when all those Congress People are ready to declare war on North Korea, The Middle East, and other countries that oppose our way of life, then we can really look forward to a time when our Country really will have peace and rest. The Infantry might be the Queen of Battle, but the Artillery is still the King. With the technology we have, none of our Military people need to be dying in these little conflicts.

Willie Means Well

Thursday, July 16, 2009
12:27PM

Commander-In-Chief

I recently wrote Mr. Obama to ask for help with a situation with the VA. I once received a letter from Congressman Phil G. and felt he was just going along with what the VA wanted. After watching "Rise & Shine" on the morning of 7/16, I wish I had waited to add my opinion about the FIELD GRADE OFFICER (would you believe a Major) who refuse to honor Mr. Obama as the President. I am sure there are some things that we will not be aware of, but this situation should be like a clap of thunder in the ears of everyone in this man's chain-of-command all the way to the Pentagon. You can bet many junior military people will be affected by this situation. I wonder if the guy remembers this: I AM AN AMERICAN FIGHTING MAN! I SERVE IN THE FORCES, WHICH GUARD MY COUNTRY AND OUR WAY OF LIFE! I AM PREPARED TO GIVE

Willie Means Well

MY LIFE IN ITS' DEFENSE! I was still driving taxi when 'Desert Storm' went down. I use to listen to African American Soldiers discussing with each other how they felt about going to fight other Black people. I would listen and then asked what did being Black people have to do with fighting for the rights of your Country. In the end, it would always be 'PROUD TO BE AN AMERICAN-SIR! This man should not be let off with an insignificant punishment. I don't say make a public example of the man but his punishment should send a message through the military ranks.

Monday, December 21, 2009
6:52AM

Veterans!

It was good to see the article on homeless female Veterans. It is true that we are a capitalist society and people want to put making money first in everything. There should not be one homeless Veteran in America... male or female. Once again, lines have been drawn in Congress because of a bill that would provide health care in the end to many. You have so many congressmen getting so much money from these big corporations that they will not support something for the People that will stop the STUFFING of their personal pockets. I'll bet that throughout this Country you have empty facilities that can be converted into shelters and medical clinics to provide care for not just the homeless but the down and out also. GREED has run rampant in this Country for so long that the rich don't want to see their way of getting wealthier stopped. Our Female Veterans are SPECIAL! We need to do what

Willie Means Well

is necessary to make sure they don't wound up looking for safe places to stay. Everybody needs to be on look out and know of some place this population can be guided to for good care. I'm sure pride will be an issue with many but if approached correctly, these Ladies will be more than happy to take the help offered. They have earned it just as their male counterpart has. We show commercials about helpless animals surely, there are some higher-ups that can show compassion for our Veterans. GOD BLESSINGS!!!

Willie Means Well

Monday, April 19, 2010
(This would be Happy 47th Birthday to
'Hazelnut', my first Wife)
9:48AM

Politics!

Hello. I find an adversary or myself wondering if you are smart like that. I once had a teacher in U.S. Government and Foreign Policy tells me I was a 'HAWK' when it came to the rights of the Unites States. I in term told him that every person living in America should be feeling just like I do about our Country or they needed to get the 'H--L' OUT! I want people to know this, I don't agree with many things the President is doing but he is the President. The job did not change, just the person and the Party. I wish America would get off its' A-- and put me in the White House. I would show my love for this Country and put it back NUMBER ONE where it belongs. You see, first off, I'm a Christian, and I really believe what THE BIBLE says when it says "I WILL BLESS THOSE WHO BLESS MY PEOPLE

Willie Means Well

ISRAEL!" The GOD I believe in and serve is not dead! He's the same GOD he was yesterday, today and will be tomorrow. All these other gods let them speak up for followers. I feel the person who is president doesn't need to be playing politics but be taking care of the People of this Country. The number one job in this Country should not be regulated by whose Party shouts the loudest but by an honest to goodness all out effort to take care of each citizen in this Country. Give it to someone with the promise of letting them out of the position after two years if the Country is up and running smoothly and America, with the help of **ISRAEL** of course, is back number one and not depending on those countries that have their hands so deep in our economy and everything else.

Willie Means Well

Tuesday, April 27, 2010
9:34AM

A CHAT!

Hello Mr. President. This is former Army Sergeant Willie Means. Don't forget to get a copy of my book "Willie Means Well (But It Don't Work Out Sometimes). Pointed out something I didn't like what you did. Anyway, I was once told by someone in Military Intelligence (MI), there are as many levels under CIA Headquarter as there are above it. A nice place to consider for tea party people and Sarah Palin if she doesn't stop her treasonous activities. Do you know that we had people on the way to take care of the situation in Iran but former President Carter had them recalled and so our Country got into that embarrassing hostage situation with the "MOUSE THAT ROARED?" I once had a level of clearance that allowed me to see anything the Army had. It was due to the type job I had. For so many years, I had convinced myself that it was all a hoax until the Chinese guy tried to slip out the Country

Willie Means Well

with information on a particular weapon system we have for countries like China. Then, of course, with that 'Ivy League' education, I'm sure you were aware of the man named Nixon who was selling our most luscious areas in California to the Orientals. Mr. President, do you know our Military is so great that we did not have to endanger our ground forces during 'Desert Storm'? You can easily check this information. It was all over the NEWS. We wanted the world to see how generous we were and we would stop killing those people hiding out in their so-called safe, underground bunkers. War is HELL and you don't fight it being a gentleman when the other side is caught dragging our military dead through the streets and burning the remains. We have the 'MOABs'. What I'm pointing out to you is I don't see any glory in our people dying in any of those places when we have the capability to go in and end it all in a week. The French got their butts kicked in Vietnam and then we went over there and allowed Russia to dictate to us how we would fight that war for we got our butts kicked. (By the way, I

Willie Means Well

guess you have those who would like to see these Veterans coming home wound up in jails and prisons like the Vietnam Vets did rather than get them the help they need. Ask your military advisors what's the acronym 'REMFs'! That's their mentality to the ones who actually to the fighting.) The Russians got their butts out of Afghanistan and now we are over there doing the same thing. YOU don't have to make these mistakes Mr. President. Turn our Intelligence and Military loose and allow them to end that mess and bring that money back HOME and let's get the ECONOMY back in the right direction. NOW! Once again I ask that you appoint a CZAR over the VA and get this ENTITY back on its' feet. Today is 27 April and I have an appointment in Tuskegee Thursday (29th) at six in the evening, would you believe. I am going to add the results from that appointment to this letter and hopefully get it in the mail by Saturday. I was told the last time I had an appointment the workers are unionized. I have nothing against Unions, once belonged to one of the biggest when I worked for UPS, but that's probably why Veterans

Willie Means Well

don't get the best of care in many of these places. Just like having armed security in the VA places. I guess a Veteran survive "HOT ZONES" only to come home and possibly lose their life in a VA Clinic or Hospital. I will forward copies of this to the American Legions (which has an excellent article on how our government has made the Intelligent Community so weak in their last magazine), and various VA Regional Offices.

Willie Means Well

Monday, June 7, 2010
1:30PM

Where Is The Glory?

I was in the Subway on Victory Drive when four Soldiers came in. To many those Soldiers would not even get a second glance. However, being a Veteran, and with Memorial Day and "D-Day June 6th" just passing, I thought about our people fighting overseas. It was the Soldiers' patches on their right shoulders that caught my attention. One wore The Big Red One (first Division), one The 101st Division (Screaming Eagle), one the 2nd Infantry Division, and I couldn't recall the fourth. This was representation from four Divisions that have had troops in one of those hot zones. Recently, two Rangers gave the ultimate sacrifice fighting overseas also. One, the news said was on his third tour and the other was on his fourth. Been there, came home, been there, came home, etc then death. There is no glory in our people being killed over there when we

Willie Means Well

could ramp it up and end both those wars in less than a month. Many, if not all, Military people know this. BRING OUR PEOPLE HOME!!!

Willie Means Well

Saturday, June 19, 2010
9:22PM

So Sorry!

Back in 83 while in Public Affairs on fort Benning, I saw a stat that put the ratio 2.5 females to males in the "Tri-City". I saw that stat again several years ago at 22.5:1. They were referring to "QUALITY MALES". I can't but feel sorry for this generation of females coming out in this era. I also wonder how this ratio stands across the Nation. After 26 years, I find myself checking out dating sites and it grieves me to see so many ladies from their upper teens even into their late 60s looking for mates (psychology teaches there is nothing wrong with being 100 and having a sex life if you're healthy). Pretty soon all that female power is going to rise up and make itself felt in the world of politics and everywhere else. Guess this generation of males better get smart, get some education, and hopefully stay off the streets so they don't wound up in the justice system. Is there an answer out their somewhere?

Willie Means Well

Saturday, August 14, 2010
4:58PM

Georgia's Children!

I can't help but wonder why Georgia is at the very top when it comes to not taking care of the adolescent population. I worked at West Central Georgia Regional Hospital for three years with Adolescents and they closed the Unit. I worked on Bridge way Child and Adolescent Stabilization Unit at West Central and they closed that unit. This morning while with two of my adult consumers, there was this kid probably in his upper teens showing signs that said he really needed to be in a controlled setting. Unfortunately, today, if there is no insurance for the Bradley Center, it means jail, or worst, death on the street. I watched the kid and when one of my consumers came out the store, the consumer called the kid and gave him some change. The kid looked at him and said thanks. I must admit that I was frightened for my consumer. I guess that means at 55 taking a beating and LORD knows I got that at West Central. Perhaps that's what wrong. We've grown afraid of our children and adolescents and decided to let them fend for themselves. VERY SCARY PEOPLE because I guess they will go hungry only for so long before they began to do whatever it takes to get food and live.

Willie Means Well

Saturday, October 23, 2010
9:40AM

REGULAR AMERICANS???

"…when I PUT FORTH THAT Obama had created a gulf between him and some 'REGULAR AMERICANS,' Bill O'Reilly, Ledger-Enquirer, October 23, 2010, p. A16. I am credited with 13 years in the United States Army and would have gladly fought for this Country if required while I was serving; am I not a Regular American! In the paper earlier this week, someone said they could not believe four retired General Officers were supporting a Democratic Candidate. A while back at a Republican Convention, a speaker made the statement "We got friends in Hollywood too so let's get busy and get this Country back into the right people hands!" When I pointed this out to my wife, she looked at me in surprise and made the statement "I can't believe you don't know who that is." Well, I didn't but she informed me that it was Angelina

Willie Means Well

Jolie's father. I was speechless. After all this time, it is really coming out where people mentality really lies. It seem all the hidden racism is coming out and making itself known on a large scale and not nearly enough people are speaking up about it. I can see now that you have those that will go to any extreme to keep Blacks surprised. It is not the other Minorities... it is the Blacks. We are the only Race forced to come to America and still all these years' later people still want to keep the Black Race down. By the way, I could swear during my time in the military there were numerous other Blacks serving this Country too. So let's have our Elderly go back to eating cat and dog food as long as the Black Race doesn't get an even break.

Willie Means Well

Sunday, July 18, 2010
7PM

Poor America!

Our Country is in a very sad fix. All these new 'George Wallace's' openly campaigning to turn the time back to when Blacks was nothing but other people property. One person running for office just out and said, "let's get rid of the Obama…etc." You know people can at least buy a little food right now and a little gas. All these republicans have had their pocket change slowed down because they can't just give out contracts wherever they want. If the last thing the President do before leaving office, he should bring the draft, back so some of these rich people can see their children headed to all hot spots this Country is getting into. I wonder how long will any of this "MESS" last. Everything over there has been under false pretense. Get our people out and drop a few of those 'MOABs' and our people will stop being killed while these people back here are

Willie Means Well

looking for more ways to keep them fighting over there. The Country is SICK! James Dobson had to resign as head of 'Focus on the Family' because he was pushing the republicans cause. Now every time you turn on the television some preacher out of Texas is yelling and praying for God to end this administration. I'm a Veteran and I'm a Christian. I justified my time in the military because KING DAVID HAD HIS MIGHTY MEN AND ISRAEL SURVIVED. OUR COUNTRY NEED TO GET BACK ON 'ONE ACCORD' AND EVERYBODY GIVE A HAND AT HELPING EVERYONE AND NOT JUST THE RICH GETTING RICHER AND BEING UPSET BECAUSE THE POOR PEOPLE ARE HANGING IN THERE AND SOME ARE HAVING STEAK AND CAN AFFORD A NEW CAR EVERY NOW AND THEN.

Willie Means Well

August 24, 2011
(Time to get on with it!)

September 6, 2011

Well, since it is now two weeks from *'Time To Get On With It!'* I know you realize that I did not get on with it then. But! Here I am again. I truthfully believe I am trying to catch a cold. August hit us with some really hot days and now we finally got *Tropical Storm Lee* in the Gulf and a cold front is coming in behind it. By the time the remnants of *Lee* got to us here in Cataula, Georgia, it was moving so fast that I had to do some hard PRAYING. There were tornado warnings as the system moved and the trees around my house was swaying back and forward like dancers moving to an up-tempo, mellow beat. My son Ike was off with his new Lady Friend Alex. Which, by the way, means I guess I will not have my, who I thought would be my daughter-in-law someday, Brittney, edit the book for me. Well, I wish Ike the best of luck with Alex. She is a very nice young lady of 19 that is recovering from a bad relationship with a FOOL! With the ratio over 25 to one, and females to males, I will never understand why these guys get themselves in trouble trying to make a girl stay with them. I am sure there are enough bad girls out there who want guys who hit on ladies. I watched my mother raise six of us by herself and she told us to treat ladies with respect. She would say, *"I don't care if that woman wants to work digging ditches, don't you put your hands on her. There are enough good girls out there that want a man to be gentle and treat her right!"* I have had an occasional run in with my wife Denise and other females over the years, but when it came to physical altercations, I was strong enough to walk away. I was even in the process of calling the Police on myself one time to get me out of the house after Denise made me hit her. When I realized what I had done, I was calling the Police but she hung up the telephone. When 911 called back, she told them she had dialed the number by accident.

    Well, my other son, Bobby, was home with Denise and I and I asked them to join with me in

PRAYER. When the wind, rain, and thunder arrived, I was walking and PRAYING and Bobby stated, with excitement, *"Dad! Look! I see light through the trees!"* In addition, it was. GOD is a good GOD and he comes to the aide of his creations when we petition HIM for protection.

When I took those guys with me from the Army, I told them I wanted to show them something in a place down the road. Like good Soldier Boys, they were bold, challenging, and ready to tackle hell with a bucket of water. Well, I guess that man's face was just too much for my friends. I remember *'KD'* made the statement, *"Buster, we got to go. Why you had to show us something like that?"* Normally, it was PARTY! PARTY! PARTY! With my *'Inner Circle'* Buddies. However, that night, we all just sat in with my father and watched some television.

WEEKENDS SHOULD LAST FOREVER

Ed Eason was my friend
We suffered through it all, thick and thin
Ed, Des, and Willie Tee
We were just like brothers, people could see
Monday through Friday, we all did school
We all had to learn the 'Golden Rule'
Friday evening began our weekend
The grown-ups got together all the rules we could bend
Pullman's Steel Mill, the mines, or where they worked
The neighborhood got together, no one got hurt
The men got together, and they drank and clowned
The Ladies looked so lovely in dresses like gowns
The children ran errands, and they went to the store
A quarter bought a lot in 1964
Ice cream, cake, and candy
Man, those weekends sure were dandy
The time arrived, and we all split up
Something better for everyone, life c can be tough

Willie Means Well

That little neighborhood at the corner of Eighth Avenue and 28th Street set in a small hollow just off the railroad tracks. We all had outdoor toilets buy it was not so bad if you got to the toilet before it got dark. Sometimes Ms. Rosie McNeil and some of the other ladies and men would play dominoes while listening to the ballgame. As long as someone was still outside, it was not too bad going to the toilet. Of course, at night, we would burn newspaper to give us light while we did our business in the toilet. If it were too late, you would use the *'slop jar'* then take it to the toilet and empty it in the morning. When it was raining, you would pour the contents of the *'slop jar'* in the ditch that was behind the toilets and the rushing water would carry the waste on away. However, sometimes you did not want to go in the toilets for fear of those big spiders getting on you. These were times when I would toss the waste in the ditch anyway. This of course got me a bad whipping when Ms. Lucille caught me and rose a stank all over the neighborhood. At least after, I got the whipping my brother and some of the older boys when in the toilets and burned all the spider webs down.

Willie Means Well

FROM OUTDOOR TOILETS TO INDOOR PLUMBING

It is after midnight, I need to use the stool
The toilet is outside, it's dark, and I am no fool
The thing in the coal yard will make its presence known
The pounding on the oil drum makes you so alarmed
The spiders in the web are big and shinning black
The smell in those toilets makes you want to get back
Some weathered wooden sheds sitting to them
Covering a hole in the ground and of course, you know what else
Your greatest fear is to fall in
People wondering where you are, not knowing your end
Nine-twenty Fourth Avenue was our new address
Momma was closer to her job and she needed the rest
A new neighborhood and neighbors too
We had indoor plumbing, and this was all so new
Our wood heater was gone, but we had a fireplace

Willie Means Well

A toilet in the middle room, this put a smile on our face
The final room was the kitchen and another wood stove
Happy we were, but a story needs to be told
While out to play one day, my sister gave a shout
Did you see the little girl and boy? We had a problem no doubt

Willie Means Well

WHAT IS REAL?

(Here's To Reality)

These days I tell anyone who will listen, *"These people who do those paranormal pictures on television and the movies, don't realize what they mess with sometimes. Read the sixth chapter of Genesis and you will began to learn and understand that evil is very real. You will see how demons have strong desires to enter into the lives of mankind."*

Roxanne came to the back door and asked me what the little boy did and girl goes. My new friend, Philip, and I looked at each other and I told my sister we did not see anyone come out of the house. I continued to play, but this stayed in my mind. Roxanne was my oldest sister, and like the rest of us, she saw spirits. Momma said we all had been born with this stuff on our faces the 'Old People' called veils. From my understanding, this meant you were spiritual sensitive. Whether it is seeing, hearing, or feeling, you knew a spirit was around. Some like to say ghost. However, I was taught and learned there is a difference. You had a spirit; a ghost; and worst, a haunt (pronounced "haint" by many from the South)! At an early age, we had our "baptism of fire", so to speak, when Daddy put us out after Momma tried to kill him. Yes, my Momma tried to kill my Daddy. She found out, like many Black men back in the Fifties, he had more than one wife. Momma had put us all in the backroom in the house at 2731 Eighth Avenue North when it was almost time for Dad to get off work. If I have not mentioned it yet, I was always hiding under the beds or in the closet to see and hear what I could. Many times, I did not know what I was hearing or seeing, but it sure sounded and looked good. Probably the reason I got spanked a lot when Momma's friends would talk about how cute I was, grab me, and squeeze me to their chest. My hands, at a very tender age, had learned that the flesh on the inside of a woman's thighs was very soft and appealing. Anyway, as I was saying, I was peeking through the crack of the door and I saw Momma hiding behind the door when

Daddy got ready to come through the door. I do not know what made my Daddy jump back, but when he did; my Momma buried the cutting edge of a hatchet in the door frame. Years later, when I had found my Daddy again, I asked him about that day. As usual, he was surprised that I remembered such a thing. He told me to that day, he does not know what made him jump back, but he was glad he did. I always told myself that the LORD JESUS knew we needed our Momma and that is why she was unsuccessful at killing Daddy.

 Well, when Daddy put us out, Momma got this man to let us move into when we dubbed "The Little Round House." I never knew the address of the house, but it was across from the front of Mitchell and Thomas Coal Yard. Would you believe even in the daytime, I could not stand to look across the street at that place? There was always a man sitting outside the door smoking a pipe. I tried to show him to my sisters and brother, but they said they did not see anyone. I had figured out it had to be the security guard that had been killed over there and would beat *on those oil drums at night. One day, Joyce and I were playing in the house, I looked over, and I called Joyce and told her where to look. SHE SAW HIM! This, of course, scared me even more. That night, Joyce woke us all up screaming. On top of her screaming, she also had blood running down her face. Momma told us a rat had bit Joyce, but I never saw a mark. It was less than a week later Roxanne woke us all up yelling for Momma. Buy the way, Joyce, Dot, and myself, (Buster), we all were small enough that we slept in a baby bed together. When Roxanne woke us up that night, she told Momma she needed to use the pot (slop-jar called by many). She saw this lady standing by the pole in the middle of the room and she thought it was Momma. When she called Momma two times and Momma did not answer, she knew it was not Momma. She ducked her head under the covers and when she peeked towards the pole, the lady was gone. Roxanne said she thought she had imagined the whole thing and she threw the covers back from her head. When she did this, Roxanne said the lady was standing by the bed* looking down at her. That is when Roxanne woke us all up screaming for Momma. When Momma got Roxanne calmed down, Roxanne told Momma that as she screamed for her, the lady was floating back to the pole and repeatedly telling her to "call madea, call madea." Roxanne said when the lady got to the pole, she vanished. (A lot of our fifty-cent pieces, quarters, nickels, and dimes vanished into that same damn pole. Joyce, Dot, and I said it was our piggybank and we used to put the coins in a slot in the pole. When we moved and they tore the house down to build the Tabs' home, I will bet somebody got happy to discover our bank). The next day when J.D. (I remember this is what Momma called the guy) came, Momma explained to him what happened and called Roxanne, and J.D. asked Roxanne to describe the lady. I was looking through the door when Roxanne got through describing the lady. You could actually see J.D. turn shades lighter as he told my Momma that was his mother Roxanne described. He told Momma his mother said she did not want anyone living in her house, but he did not believe in *any of that stuff.*

    Well, Daddy contacted Momma and told her he was moving to Reform, Alabama, and the rent was paid on the house for several months and Momma could move back into the house. We did. So you see, when Roxanne asked me about the little boy and girl, it stayed on my mind.

    School had started in September 1965, and I was home sick one day. I was ten years old but from a very early age, we had been cleaning the house and cooking. I had the house to myself and I was feeling better, so I got up, cleaned the house, and was washing dishes when I looked in the middle room and I too saw a little boy and girl standing and watching me. My first thoughts were it was Donald ray and his sister Gwen from next door. When I looked closer, I realized it was not them. I asked, *"How did you get in here?"* The kids turned and walked to the front room, I followed and came in the front room just as the kids went into the fireplace. I opened the door and ran to the front porch. One of the neighbors saw me and asked was I feeling better and I told him yes. He told me I had to stay in the house so the truant officer would not see me and try to take me to school. I wanted to tell him what I had seen and that I was afraid to stay in the house. Instead, I went back through the house and opened the back door and let my dog, Rusty, in and finished washing dishes. When my sisters and brother got home, I had dinner ready, but I did not say anything to them about what I had seen. When Momma got off work, had eaten, and was reading her Bible, I began to tell her what had happened. Roxanne heard me and she told Momma she had seen them before too but did not want to bother her with it. Momma gave us both a scare when she said she had been seeing them almost every night but did not want to alarm us because we needed a place to stay. Momma said almost nightly the two children would sit in front of the fireplace and play jacks. She said normally when she made a noise; they would look up at her and vanish. Momma told us not to tell our sisters and older brother because she did not want them frightened.

Willie Means Well

I had not seen the children for a while, but we all heard noises in the hose, and had learned to live with it. One day, I believe it was in November of the same year, I was home, and in the kitchen cooking when I looked up and there, they were in the middle room looking at me. Once again, I followed them into the front room and they went into the fireplace. I remember I said, *"I am going to find out what is in this fireplace!"* I was bold enough to bend down and try to look up into the fireplace, but it was dark. I then reached up in there with the poker, a brick fell out, and then a 'hook-bill' knife fell out too. I jumped up and just stared at the knife. The knife was covered with reddish, black stuff and I had no idea at the time what it was. I took the knife, wrapped it in a cloth, and put it under Momma's mattress to show her when she came home.

Willie Means Well

MURDER AT NINE TWENTY-FOURTH AVENUE

When we first moved into this house, the children in the neighborhood told us a story about a lady and her husband who used to live in the house. The story was that they fought almost daily until one evening, it was worse than the other times. The lady who lived next door at Nine Eighteen said she heard the fighting as usual, but she never thought to call the police. Back in those days, Black people did not want the police in their neighborhood because many of the police were in the Ku Klux Klan. The lady next door said all of a sudden, it got quiet. Then there was a knock on her front door. She said the lady was standing at their door and said she needed to use the telephone because her husband had tried to kill her. The lady next door said she noticed the lady had her hand up to her throat, but she did not see any blood. She told the lady to come on in and she reached to get the telephone for her. She said when the lady sat down and her hand dropped into her lap, she then

Willie Means Well

saw that lady's throat had been cut from ear-to-ear. The lady next door said she told the lady, "Honey, he ain't tried to kill you, he done killed you!" The lady next door said the lady attempted to look up at her and this is when her head fell back and the blood came gushing out. The man was arrested and charged with murder, but no weapon had been found. Well, guess what? There it was, now waiting under my Momma's mattress.

When Momma got home from the funeral home, where she worked, I got the knife and showed it to her. I remember she said, *"Lord have mercy"* and took the knife and went next door to the lady's house. I saw them both go to the trash barrel, start a very hot fire, and put the knife in it. As I explained, Blacks did not want policemen in their neighborhood and it was more than thirty years later before I learned the significant of what they did by burning the knife. It was during my taxi driving days in Columbus, Georgia when a young lady name Netra, a regular rider of mine, introduced me to her mother and I was telling her mother about some unusual

Willie Means Well

happenings in my life. When I told her how Momma and the lady burned the knife, she explained the man was already in torment and by them burning the knife with that dried blood on it, it pushed his spirit further into torture and pain.

    Life is so funny and precious! Life is in the blood and people go to great extreme to keep the blood in the body. Then, you have some 'two legged predators' that are so sick and take joy in taking that life from people. A dispatcher of mine, Ralph, told me of getting his throat cut while taxi driving in Atlanta. Ralph said he picked the fare up at the airport, and was headed downtown. Ralph said the guy did not talk but when he stopped at a traffic light, he saw the guy leaning forward out the corner of his eye. Ralph said when he turned to see what the guy was doing; it actually helped the guy to get his arm around his neck. Ralph said that guy cut his throat so fast he did not realize he had been cut until he felt a stinging on his neck. Ralph said he reached up with his hand and it came away bloody. Ralph said his first instinct was to grab the mike and call for help but he was afraid to talk. Ralph said he then recalled the guy did not try to rob him he just got out the taxi and walked away. Ralph said he kept his chin tucked down and kept trying to send a 'sos' with the mike button. Ralph said he drove himself to the hospital and all the while, the dispatcher kept talking about she wish whoever was playing with the mike would *"cut it out!"* Ralph said they later told him by him not talking saved his life. Had he started talking, it would have started the blood pumping from the wound and he would have bleed to death...

Something that happened to one of my female drivers one night is still a mystery to me today. Betty J. almost was killed but according to her, the guy got frustrated because she fought back. When I went to the hospital to see her, she explained, *"Willie, he could had killed me at anytime but he wanted to cut my throat from ear-to-ear. He had his 'behind' on my steering wheel and was trying to wrap one of his hands in my hair to force my head back. I kept moving my head and trying to stop him from sticking me with the knife and would you believe he stopped,* *looked at me, and asked, '**WOULD YOU PLEASE BE STILL SO I CAN GET THIS RIGHT?**' I told him he was a crazy son-of-a-bitch and I grabbed the knife, pulled it from his hand, and threw it out the window. Then I pushed him against the steering wheel and the horn started blowing. That's what probably saved my life. People started coming out their apartments and yelling what was wrong. He jumped out of the car and ran. One of our regular riders called the police. But I'm telling you, it really gave me cold chills when he asked me to stop so he could get it right."*

That guy did cut Betty's throat but it was not deep. She also had cuts on her hands where she had been fighting with him, grabbed the knife, and pulled it from his hand. Betty and Ralph both got lucky. However, it was a different outcome with one taxi driver who the dispatchers claimed was working off his radio and had not checked in. To this day, I will dispute this with them because I could have sworn I heard them talk to the guy as I was on my way home. Jim Sharpe was managing then and he called my house the next morning and asked me to come to the cab station. I asked what was wrong and he told me we had a driver killed. This kid we had been riding from Fort Benning apparently had been kicked out and the driver had been riding him as a *'Regular Rider'*. We found out later the kid was looking for drugs and he killed the driver to get money to buy the drugs. The driver was stabbed over twenty times. They said look like he tried to fight the kid off but he was overpowered. Normally we want a single passenger to sit up front but it backfired on the driver that night.

September 16, 2011
(I May Have Found Netra-'Lil Lover')

I was going to continue where I left off but I am in a state of joy this evening because I may have found my Lil Lover, Netra Brooks. So very funny! A young lady who has worked with us on second shift for almost four month came to relieve me today and as we were walking, I asked her age and what school she had attended. The young lady told me she was 23 and she had graduated Kendrick High School. Anyone I run into that has attended Kendrick I always ask did they ever know a Netra Brooks. To my surprise, she said she knew a Netra and as a matter of fact, the Netra she knew was her cousin. I stopped and stared at her and she of course asked me where I knew her. I explained to her during my taxi driving years I had met Netra and she became my regular rider. Netra's mom and dad were separated but she came from a good home but liked the *'Bad Boys'*. The young lady told me it might not be the same Netra because the Netra she knew was around

31 years of age. I calculated her age and kept coming up with the mid-twenties until I realized I was calculating the age for someone else. I told the young lady of some of the crazy things Netra had done and she said, *"Yep! That's my Cousin alright."* The young lady started playing with her cell phone and I thought she was perhaps looking for her sister's phone number. She said Netra, her sister was close, and she thought she had the number somewhere. What the young lady had turned out to be better than a hundred phone numbers! She had a picture of Netra and as I looked at her face in the picture, I could see I might as well have been looking at Mary, Netra's mother. Perhaps this is all I will see of her but it did me good and has brought me joy. She is alive. Looking at the picture, the young lady said she believe it was taken in March of 2011, Netra looks really well but I can see traces of sadness in her face. I hope I get to meet my Lil Lover so I can tell her that I did her poem for her and I am going to print it again her for YOU! Thanks!

Willie Means Well

YOU TOOK MY LOVE FROM ME
(A Thought for Janice, Pay)

Oh, Bessemer, You have been so cruel to me
You took away my love before we could be free
She was my breath of spring that carried me through the year
I can now only hope she knew, to me, she was so dear
It was a time in the South when one's color was a burden
Yet she was a Girl Scout and forced to be with the others
A family affair it almost came to be
Our sisters and brothers were paired just as we
We were forced apart as my family moved North
It broke my heart; hopefully, she knew this, of course
We left for the bus, the family walking down the street
I could not believe my eyes, and she was approaching me
She was so cute in her Girl Scout suit

Willie Means Well

As I looked in her eyes, I saw that she knew
"Y'all go to Chicago?" My love she asked of me
Yes was my reply as I drank of her beauty
Too young to be in love, I was told it was not true
But time, it yet rolls on and still I am so blue
She was taken from this world, a great disease, I was told
I never tasted of her goodness
However, my love will never grow old

Willie Means Well

JANICE (*PAY*)

I met Janice when I entered fifth grade at Carver School located in Jonesboro, Alabama. To us, all it really was a different side of Bessemer. We moved into the house at Nine-Twenty Fourth Avenue over the summer in 1965. Our little neighborhood located in the cul-de-sac at the corner of Eighth Avenue and Twenty-Eight Street had begun to clear out with the families that had children. Ed, Des, and Willie Tee Family had moved across Ninth Avenue. I cannot remember if the Woods Family had moved yet but they had begun to talk of leaving. All of us children had begun to grow-up and look like as one, our parents had decided we needed indoor plumbing. When school started in September, Grandmother had moved in with us while waiting to relocate to Florida. I do not remember how Momma and the six of us along with Grandmamma, Trisha-Baby, and Carolyn all lived in that three-room house but we did. We had an abundance of food. The lights and water were on and we had a television. I do not know if perhaps Grand momma's reputation had got to the neighborhood before we did but we had no problems becoming part of the neighborhood. I am sure a lot of you out there have heard *'Old Battle-Ax'!* That is what my Grandmother was. People did not mess with her. I always heard the greeting of the day and people would move on with respect. Do not know if I shared it with you or not, One Saturday morning when I was in third grade back at Dunbar on the North side of Bessemer, I got out early on my bicycle before I could be tasked with any chores. Man, I believe the whole neighborhood was looking for me. I believe my Grandmother saw me when I was approaching her house and she walked into the yard and called me. I decided I was going to ride by as if I did not hear her but she said it just loud enough for me to hear her as I was going by: *"You go ahead and ride by like you don't see me and hear me. If I don't stomp you, Mary ain't my name."* I rode my bike into her yard and just sat looking up at her. She sent one of my uncles to get Momma and I will always remember, Momma was eating a peeled cucumber as she whipped me with an extension card. Grandmamma finally told her *"RoeLee, that's enough. Now you take him on home and don't let him get on that bicycle for a week."*

I guess you might say leaving the North side of Bessemer and moving to Jonesboro was the end to our time in Bessemer. I do not know what mystic doors came open or what began to work on our behalf, but less than eighteen months after we left our Lille safe haven on the North side, Big Bud had us all in Chicago.

I was in Mrs. Hill class in fifth grade at Carver. This lady was supposed to be mean but one of the better teachers and that suited Momma just fine. We were like the sister in Stevie Wonder's song *'Living for the City'*. Our clothes may have been old but never were they dirty. On top of this, we were smart. I believe that is how my brother Bobby wound up with Emma Glover. She, like her sisters and brothers were smart also.

Have you ever been in a class where regardless to how mean the teacher is suppose to be, you got somebody who has to act up and constantly gets the entire class in trouble? Well, my *'Bane'* was Frederick Lockett. On top of everything else, he was a bully. Frederick and I had our difficulties with each other because he immediately started at me and was not happy until we had it out during recess the first week of school. Mrs. Hill would leave the room but tell everybody to put their head down on the desk until she returned. When she would leave, Frederick would make the other boys do things and they would because he threatens to get them during recess. One of these kids became my best friend at school because he was a small guy and Frederick would pick on him. One day at recess, I do not know what made me do it, but I tackled Frederick and held him down until he promised not to mess with William Bell again. When I let Frederick up he started talking crazy but began to throw some of the other guys down because they would not help him when I had him down. Later when we were lining up to get out of school, Janice came to me and told me *"thanks Willie Means. William is such a little guy and*

Willie Means Well

Frederick doesn't need to be messing with him anyway." I am Black but I am sure I must have turned darker from embarrassment when Janice spoke to me.

Then there was the time when Mrs. Hill left the room when I, Frederick and his little gang of followers left the room and got on to the roof of the school. It did not dawn on us that kids in the other classrooms would see us and of course, they did. You had kids lined up at the windows looking at us on the roof and word must have gotten to Mrs. Hill that some of her students were on the roof. There was this light-skinned kid named Edward who spotted Mrs. Hill when she turned the corner and was coming up the hall. He yelled to us, took off, and went through the window in a dive as if he was in the circus or something. To this day, I do not know how Mrs. Hill did not see me but she called out every boy name that had been on the roof and sent them to the principle. I looked around and every girl in the class was looking at me. I was waiting for one of them to tell on me when Janice said, *"Mrs. Hill, they tried to get Willie Means and William Bell to go but they kept their heads down and were quiet."* She saved my butt a whipping because the other guys got their butts paddled by the principle and had to stay late for school. I was feeling good and William started teasing me that Janice Glover liked me. As pretty as she was, that was fine with me. When I got home from school, Joyce told me she had seen me on the roof. I argued with her and told her she did not see me. When Momma got home from work, it was not Joyce that told on me but 'Bobby. Apparently, he and some of the high schoolers were outside and they spotted us on the roof. Simply? I got away with it at school but Momma gave me a real good whipping when she got home from work.

    I was ten years old in 1965 and today I look back and see that I, along with Philip Adams, Leonard Studimyre and his cousin Little Junior, had our life spared many times by GOD. From sneaking to go swimming under a small bridge in the White people neighborhood and getting chased off by a White man with a rifle, to walking through the woods and coming up on a Ku Klux Klan rally and out running them in their white sheets, we challenged life and we got away with it. Little Junior's Mother had just bought him a pair of sneakers with *Batman* emblems on them and he ran out of his shoes. We tried to explain to the grownups what had happened but none of them would believe us. Little Junior even got a whipping and had to stay away from us a couple of days. We could never figure out why his Mother made him stay away from us when that night after the klans chased us they drove through our neighborhood early that next morning with crosses burning on their cars and calling us all kinds of niggers.

    Fifth grade went fast and it was right before school was going to be out in May 1966, my brother Bobby got a job throwing the *Bessemer Sun Newspaper.* The route we took had us delivering to Janice home on Sixth Avenue. By now, Bobby and Emma Glover were spending time with each other and so were Roxanne and Alexander Glover. One of the Glover Boys came around and cut our grass and he would always have another brother with him. They would always talk to Joyce and Dot: "....*A family affair it almost came to be, our sisters and brothers were paired just as we...!*" One evening we were delivering papers and when we got to Janice house it seem like the entire family was sitting on the porch. Emma came down the stairs to get the newspaper and she and Bobby stood talking. Of a sudden, she yells at the house, *"Janice! Willie Means is out here."* Everybody had their eyes on me and started laughing because I took off down the street slinging papers on porches as I went. When I looked back, they were still laughing and Janice was standing with her feet on the bottom of the gate, holding it with her arms and hands, and leaning over watching me. Man, she was so beautiful but I only saw this from a glance because I took off again tossing my papers as I went. I do not know how a person could be so lucky. To have two beautiful young ladies take an interest in your well-being. Here it is Janice was showing an interest in me, and I did not think I would ever find another girl as pretty as the one I had left at Dunbar... *Debra Nunn.*

I do not remember if it was Second or Third Grade when I met Debra Nunn. What I do recall from those days absolutely hates school because I did not have any nice clothes to wear like the other children. We may start the school year in clothes made by Momma or if she had the money, she would go to the *Top Dollar Store-"Every day is dollar day, at your Top Dollar Store!"* Probably got rich off just the Black Folks alone. However, looking back, I am sure my Mother and lots of others appreciate those stores allowing them to shop in them. Sometimes the salespersons were mean but you tolerated them because the Ku Klux Klan always seems to know where you lived and they would come to your neighborhood.

Debra Nunn was not dark skinned. Neither was she light skinned. The complexion of her skin reminded me of the female Indians you saw on television back during the old black and white days. During recess, she would get out there and rip and run like the rest of us boys. She seem to prefer playing with us boys rather than sitting around with the girls talking and giggling. It had to be Second grade when I met her. I remember the teacher was Mrs. Cole. I had been sick but it was coming up to Thanksgiving and I believe one of the requirements to get a *'helping hand box'* the children had to be doing well in school and not trouble makers. I probably have this wrong but even now, I recall it was the good kids that got the boxes. I had been out several days, Momma sent me back to school on a cold day, and I had on Bobby's coat and some socks on my hands to keep them warm. The classes were taking turn in the gym because it was too cold outside for recess. Mrs. Cole had the gym set up for the class to dance and I remember the one song played over-and-over was *"Twister Loop"*. Mrs. Cole was teaching the class a sort of square dance and the boys, girls were alternated in a circle, and you had to change partner throughout the song. I was so shy and I had been keeping up with the music but I had my head down because I figured the girls did not want to touch my hands. It was almost the end of the class when it was time to change partners and I was looking down and I could see my new partner was Debra Nunn. First, she reached and grabbed my hand. Then she told me, *"Willie Means hold your head up. I've been watching you all class and I've been wanting to dance with you."* I looked her in the face and I could swear looked as if she was ready to cry. She was so beautiful with her hair in three, thick ponytails with pink ribbons. She had on a gray dress and the crinoline *(we called them 'Cane, Cane Slips')* slip made the dress sway and move with her body. We only had a couple of minutes together but when the music was over, she squeezed my hands and then we all clapped and lined up to return to our class. I think we did third grade together also. Mrs. Rolle was the teacher and that was the year they assassinated President John F. Kennedy. I remember Mrs. Rolle sitting on the floor by her desk and crying.

  Debra Nunn lived in Dunbar Court. So many days I would find a reason to walk over there in hopes of seeing her but I never did. My friend

American Best People lived in Dunbar Court also and he told me she did not come outside much. It was *Easter* 1963 and we all headed to *Saint Peters Primitive Baptist Church* located near Dunbar. Joyce had gone to the bathroom and she came back and told me, *"Buster. Debra Nunn is sitting over there and she asked was you here."* With all the leaning and peeping I did, I still could not see her. Finally, I asked Momma could I go to the bathroom and when I walked behind the Pulpit, I saw her sitting with some folks in the corner. She looked at wave, and me, smiled. We were only eight years old but man, I am telling you the look that lady sitting with her gave me told me I had better stay away. Lucky for me, after Church was over, my Grandmother called Momma over and introduced her to Debra Nunn's Grandmother. Her Grandmother spoke up right away, *"Oh! So this is your grandchild that he and my granddaughter were making eyes at each other."* All these years later, I recall she was dressed in a beautiful blue dress with blue ribbons in her head. I did not see much of her anymore. I finished Fourth grade at Dunbar then we moved to Jonesboro. I had started Sixth grade at Carver when *The Abram Blue Devils* came to play *The Carver Bulldogs* at the stadium in front of our house on Fourth Avenue. Once again, it was Joyce who brought me the message that Debra Nunn was with the Blue Devils' Band. I went down to the area right behind where their band was sitting and I saw her. She was a Majorette and WOW! For her to be only eleven like myself she sure did look older and she was so BEAUTIFUL! I remember she spotted me and came to the fence and told me hello. I never saw her again to this day. What I did find out Monday in school was that Janice was at the game and she asked me who was that beautiful girl I was talking to that went to Arbam.

    Sometimes I wonder. Life is full of crooks and turns. You figure you want to go left but you wound up going right. I have looked back so many times and wonder where would I be today had I learned to do my athletics and Church together. Alternatively, had we remained in Bessemer and I played football.

Even at eleven years old, I was very fast and the older boys always wanted me on their side when we played football on Saturday afternoons. When I ran track and field, I was only five feet six inches and weighed one hundred forty-two pounds. When I played football for the brief time that I did, I played at one hundred sixty-two pounds. I was good in both sports but it never crossed my mind during those times that I probably could have gone on to play at the professional level.

Rest in Peace Dearest Janice '*Pay* 'Glover! Perhaps someday I will meet your daughter and see if she favors you and tell her how you befriended someone from the poor side of town.

Ms. Debra Nunn. I do not know whatever happened with you but I hope the world was nice to you and brought you a beautiful life with love and happiness.

WILLIE MEANS
(My Grief)

As the bus rolled out, of Bessemer, Alabama
Only eleven, my life was in a shamble
To the North, Chicago, my family was bound
To new hope, a former lover, my mother had found
Marzett was a baby, only three years old
For my Mom, my sisters and brother, I tried to be bold
That lovely, soft-eyes girl, her face was before me
I reached to touch her, probably never more to see
Chicago, Chicago, such hope, and such joy
Sometimes Destiny plays with you just like a toy
As the bus rolled on into the night
They were not aware of my feeling of fright
To see my love, nevermore, I wondered
This dreadful feeling strikes me with thunder
Janice, Dear Janice, I wanted to tell you
My love for you I will forever hold true
I fell asleep, and a lonely tear did escape
My sister to the rescue, she wiped it from my face

Willie Means Well

Cupid, though a baby, a cruel mistress is she
You Took Away My Love Before We Could Be Free

Willie Means Well

INTERTWINED

It seems the hurt would heal with time
However, that doesn't happen when two families are intertwined
Opposite ends of life, one family struggled with toil and strife
Bobby/Emma, Alexander/Roxanne, The Boy who cut grass/Sister Joyce
Lovely, soft-eyed Janice, she was Buster's heart
My dear sister, Dot, and another of the boys
"Oh, Bessemer! You were so cruel to me
You took away my love before we could be free"
When one family moved North in '66
Who could have thought it would come to this
So much violence for young eyes to see
Surely, it wouldn't be long before they saw grief
However, the grief didn't come, they adapted and survived
Another tale was told in the South by and by
One sister, two sisters stricken in their primes
Here comes the hurt when families are intertwined

Willie Means Well

Roxanne married, Alexander heartbroken
To an early grave, so much love unspoken
Bobby was a medic in that Southeast Asia Land
However, nothing struck him as hard as when he lost Emma's hand
Buster trying so hard to become a success
Missed out on telling Janice he loved her, perhaps for the best

Willie Means Well

CHICAGO
1703 West Walnut Street

We arrived in Chicago the week of Christmas 1966. On such a very short notice, but Momma and Big Bud made sure we had something for Christmas. A few toys for a great Christmas meal, and us the temperature was frigid outside but we were safe, snuggly, and warm. We had a daddy again. Even though we tried to hide it, we all missed Bessemer, Alabama. Momma had turned us on to music when dad put us out back in Bessemer. We became a Gospel Singing Group called *The Heavenly Gospel Singers.* Momma taught us to sing by listening to WENN radio out of Birmingham. I remember we went from *"Shelly the Playboy Show" and "Tall Paul"* on WENN to WVON in Chicago with *Richard McGee, Purvis Spann the Blues Man, Jay Johnson-Jay Johnson,* and of course, *Herb Kent, the Cool Gent!* There was so much music. I did not find out until later on, that there was a lot of recording studios downtown on Michigan Avenue. You had the Motown Crew out of Detroit, but a singer could sell a ton of records just by getting WVON to play their records. My sisters and brother looked forward to Saturday because WVON would play "Old Gold" all day and we could sit and talk about Bessemer and our friends.

Big Bud worked with the Postal Service, he got Momma, and Bobby jobs at the Greyhound Bus Terminal downtown Chicago. Everything was great. The first week of January, Joyce, Dot, and I were enrolled in Birney Elementary School. I remember walking in the snow and it was so pretty and white. Some kids made fun of the way we talked. We enjoyed our time at Birney and Joyce and I have to go off to Cam Hasting for a week. We were both in Sixth Grade, she was twelve years old, and I was eleven years old. We had never experienced anything such as camp but it was a joyful event that I will remember the rest of my life. On the morning we were to leave, Joyce and I were the only two who showed up with shopping bags to carry our belongings. The children laughed of course but we got over it.

    Some kids, I guess, are just naturally smarter than others are, but Joyce, I showed RESPECT to the grown-ups, and this amazed the other children. They laughed at the way we talked and seems everything we did was the exact opposite of what they did. My Sixth grade teacher was Ms. Cash. I do not remember what contest she had us boys do in the woods but I won. She presented me with a pack of Wrigley's Doublement Chewing Gum. First, the damn boys tried to get me to share it with them, and then they dared me to throw it out on a pond of ice..., which like a fool I did. They immediately went running to Ms. Cash and told her what I had done with the gum. I remember she asked me why and then just looked at me. I so wish I could have just melted into the snow. As we walked back to our barracks, I walked in the rear with my head down until she came to me before we went inside and told me if I was going to allow others to influence the things that I did, I would have a hard and unhappy life in front of me. There, right off Jump Street, I began to develop my feelings about the other Races. I could tell I had done something that had hurt her in some way but she did not get angry with me but took the time to give me a little advice. Now the boys began to spread the word that I was the teacher's pet.

Our time at Camp Hasting really was an *'A Winter Wonderland'!* There were signs in the lunchrooms that stated, *"Take all you want! Eat all you take!"* Wow! In addition, I sure enjoyed myself. The evening before we were to head back to Chicago, we had a talent show. The guy that was in charge of our barracks played guitar and he taught us a song titled *"Tell Ole Bill".* I shall list it for you. I do believe we took second or third and we were feeling good about the *'Bliss'* we had brought to the crowd. We received a nice round of applause and walked off the stage. However, our joy was short lived as these guys from another barrack did *"The Duke of Earl" by Gene Chandler.* We had gotten a good round of applause from the adults and the students, however, the DAMN females went crazy during the song and after it was over. Damn females standing, clapping, yelling, and trying to get on the stage to touch the people. *SHIT!!* As I said, *"do I have to say they took first place?"*

We were all in a good mood that Friday morning after breakfast. When it was time to load the buses, the guy who played the guitar, and had introduced us all to this crazy song to finish off the talent show, began to play the guitar and we all immediately knew what he was about to sing: *"THE CAT CAME BACK!"* All these years later there are times I find myself humming that song and it still brings me moments of joy and pleasure as I look back and remember that time at Camp Hasting. Wish I could teach it to the World. Laughter is the best medicine and today, I feel we could all use a ton of laughter. As I look back, I recall only one other time I recall a song that was almost as crazy. There was this Variety Show, I believe, called *"The Smothers Brothers Show"*. This guy with a guitar was singing a song about working in a club owned by the *"Mob'*. The only lyrics I recall is at the end of each stanza he would sing about a red rose being placed in the label of these guys suit. At the end of the song, he sang *"...Now there's a red rose, in the lapel, of my black suit..."* something like that. But we need all the laughter we can have.

TELL OLE BILL
(Leave Them Downtown Gals Alone)

"Tell ole Bill when he comes home he better leave them downtown gals alone; this -morning, this- evening, so soooon!

Sal was home she was baking bread this- morning!

Sal was home she was baking bread this evening!

Sal was home she was baking bread when she heard the news that Bill was dead... this- morning, this- evening so soooon!

Sal said no this couldn't be so - this- morning!

Sal said no this can't be so - this- evening!

Sal said no this can't be so, Bill was here just an hour ago, this- morning, this- evening so soooon!

The hearse come rolling it was brining Bill home, this- morning!

The hearse come rolling it was brining Bill home, this- evening!

The hearse come rolling it was brining Bill home; Bill was all dressed in rags, this- morning, this- evening so soooon!

Tell Ole Bill when he comes home, this- morning!

Willie Means Well

Tell Ole Bill when he comes home, this- evening!
Tell Ole Bill when he comes home, he had better leave them downtown Gals alone, this- morning, this- evening so soooon!

Anyway, what I wanted to share is that when Momma, Bobby, and Roxanne picked us up the first day, we returned home a different. I later heard Momma telling Big Bud that a man had gotten his throat cut right in front of them on the way home that morning and the snow was covered with blood.
WELCOME TO CHICAGO!

Willie Means Well

SNOW

For those of you who do not know
Chicago always gets some snow

1967

It was early 1967 when the city of Chicago was brought to a halt by the downpour of twenty-six inches of snow that fell in less than twenty-four hours. To people who live in warm climates, this may seem unreal, but believe me, it happened. I remember Big Bud coming home from work at the Post Office and rushing my mother to get ready to go to the A&P. I had learned to look forward to going to the grocery store because Big Bud had this little sort of push/pull cart that I enjoyed playing with, that is right! I was twelve years old now and simple things like this brought me happiness. In the South, this we unheard of for a black family. If you were not lucky, enough to get a ride, then you and your sisters and brother had to carry it all by hand. I think there was one or two taxi cable in Bessemer, but when your Momma is making only thirty-two dollars a week,

Willie Means Well

you seldom had lour utilities on, let alone have money for a taxicab. The snow was falling very heavy during our trip to and from the grocery store. I went to sleep that night looking out the window. The next morning, WVON was broadcasting no school. I was dressed and called myself going to sneak out and play in the snow. It was a great idea and I would probably be whipped for it when I returned, but I could not pass up this chance to make a snowman. The only other time I had ever seen even a fraction of this much snow was around 1963 while still on the North side of Bessemer. I managed to get the door locks off (all three of them) and get down the stairs. I was surprised, and I thought to be able to get the lock off the downstairs door. However, you would have to be with me or in my shoes to get an idea of how I truly felt once I opened the door. I found myself looking up at a wall of snow that completely covered the door entrance. I cannot remember all the thoughts rushing through my head, but I know fear finally made me slam the door and run back upstairs, into the bedroom, and into the bed. I remember my sister, Roxanne, coming in and asking me what was wrong with me. After I told her, she told me, *"Serve you right. You know you're not to go out by yourself."* Well, she saw I was scared and that probably stopped her from telling Momma because she knew I would get a whipping. I think we got to stay out of school for an entire week, and it was fun until being shut in together like that we learned my sister, Roxanne's secret.

Willie Means Well

ROXANNE

She was my big sister and I loved her
She watched over us like an Angel from above
She was quiet, pretty, and very friendly
All the boys wanted her, but she didn't want any
Alexander came along in his mohair sweaters
He even had a Corsair, none could be better
All the girls wanted him
He paid them no mind
His eyes were on Roxanne, to her, was so kind
They began to step out, Momma did approve
They each had the other, together, so cool
When she left for Chicago, they both had to know
She was carrying his child, tragedy for sure
The child came along in July '67
To an early grave, I am sure this helped HIM!

Willie Means Well

ON THE MOVE

Roxanne was pregnant with her first child when the family moved to Chicago. For some reason, everything fell apart once this was discovered. Something happened at the bus station where Momma and Bobby were working, and she put my brother outdoors. When big Bud returned home and found what she had done, he made the statement, *"if bobby can't live her too, then none of you can live here."* Momma, always a proud woman, left the house and later that day, we moved out of Big Bud's place.

  It was an arrangement that none of us wanted because we had to split up. I didn't find out until later that the lady Joyce and Dot stayed with was related to Big Bud somehow. This lady then found Momma, Roxanne, Marzett, and I a place with a lady named Mrs. Franklin. I guess the Lord Jesus was with our family because he protected us. He definitely took care of my brother, Bobby, because I learned he had moved into the YMCA. I have to see my sisters daily because they were brought to Mrs. Franklin daily so Momma could go search for work. Once together again, we knew it would be a matter of time before something caught our attention.

THE MAN AT THE TOP OF THE STAIRS

    I believe it was my baby sister, Dot, who first began talking about the man at the top of the stairs. Mrs. Franklin had a church in her basement and we were required to keep the church clean. The church was in really bad shape, and I guess Mrs. Franklin figure she had some cheap labor. Roxanne was showing Joyce and me what to do when we noticed Dot was gone. We rushed out the basement and we could hear Dot talking in the stairwell. When we opened the door, Dot jumped and we jumped, but there was no one else in the stairwell. Dot was ten and she began to act silly and started talking about where did her friend go. We went on upstairs, where Mrs. Franklin had let Momma have this little room for us, but there was no one there.

    We all sat outside until Mrs. Franklin returned and began to tell her about the man Dot said she met in the stairwell. Mrs. Franklin laughed, but we noticed she was very careful when she pushed the door open. When Momma came and Joyce and Dot were carried back to the lady's place, Roxanne explained to Momma what had happened. Momma told us to just pray about it because she had felt a spirit in that stairwell and in our little living area.

Our sleeping arrangement was Roxanne, Marzett slept with Momma, and I had a small couch to sleep on. I remember I had not been sleep long that night when I heard a loud "SLAP!"

Roxanne was groaning and Mommas asked her what had happened. Roxanne was holding her stomach, but I was pointing at the wall behind Roxanne and telling Momma to look, there was a forearm and a hand being pulled back into the wall. Momma turned the light on and said, *"Now Lord, what is this?"* I remember Momma getting on her knees and Praying and then had me get in the bed with them. When she told Mrs. Franklin what had happened the next morning, I remembered Mrs. Franklin laughed, but told Momma she would be glad when she found somewhere to live because nothing had ever happened in her house like that before. A week later, we moved into an apartment in the 2600 block of Jackson Boulevard.

JOURNEYING

Our **stay** on Jackson was a really short time, but we met some friends and Momma met Mr. Cliff and Ms, Doris. As I told you, we were in a gospel-singing group named *The Heavenly Gospel Singers*. Mr. Cliff had children that sang also. I guess it was a gene thing, but three of his children were blind. The two oldest girls were twins and were blind and their little brother named '*Peanut*' was blind. If you ever wanted to hear how Angels must sound when they sing, all you had to do was listen to those twin sisters sing. All these years later, I can still hear and see them standing together, holding hands, and singing '*Just the two of Us*'. I heard years later, both twins, Peanut, and Ms. Doris all perished in a fire. I think Mr. Cliff had a heart attack.

Between Mr. Cliff's five and Momma's six, we used to go to a place called *'Riverview Amusement Park'* out on the North side of Chicago. We had a number of beautiful weekends at *Riverview*. Back in Bessemer, Alabama on the North side, there was a yearly carnival before the Civil Rights troubles and that turbulent year of 1963. In Bessemer, there was a large field across from the house and the carnival was set up there. Can you imagine how thrilling it is to a child to see such wonderful sights and hear all the gaiety of people having such a good time? *Riverview* never moved. It had one ride that swung out over a river. I do not know why *Riverview* finally closed, but I believe someone got hurt on one of the rides and *Riverview* closed down.

    Momma spent a lot of time with Mr. Cliff and his family. We got jealous, of course, but Roxanne was there for WVON and us on the radio. So many beautiful songs like *'Make me yours' by Bettey Swan; 'Made a Believer Out of Me' by "Ruby "Andrews,* and the song that was blasting everywhere the summer of 1967, *'Sweet Soul Music by Arthur Conley.* I cannot remember if Bobby was back home permanent, but I recall him being in and out a lot. Every time I hear *'Jimmy Mack',* it takes me back to the place on Jackson. It was early in the fall after school had started that one evening we moved to 1307 South Saint Louis.

Willie Means Well

1307 SOUTH SAINT LOUIS

I had never really been exposed to gang activity. However, I got my first taste of it before we left Jackson Boulevard. On my wan to the store one night, out of nowhere, I was suddenly surrounded by a group of guys chanting, *"Seven Crowns all around. Seven Crowns up-and-down. Seven Crowns on the ground."* The guys then tried to throw me on the ground and take Momma's hard-earned money. I was getting ready to fight when two brothers I had met, Stanley and Andrew, showed up with baseball bats and chased the guys away. I am not sure but I think one, if not both brothers wound up playing professional baseball.

When we moved to South Saint Louis, gang activity was multiplied. For the first two days going to the store, I was jumped on and had my money taken. There was a kid named Larry that we called *'Fat Larry'* and the Johnson family lived across the alley from us. I met Johnny Johnson and he had a brother named Larry, too. We were headed into a lot together and I figured we would be friends for life. In 1974, Larry turned on me when his sister and I wanted to get married. She married the guy from their hometown of Monroe, Louisiana. Anyway, the four of us, Johnny, Larry, Fat Larry, and me were having the same problem going to the store. One day we just started talking and we formed our own little group called *'The Ring Gang'*. We really were no gang, but we started watching out for each other's going to the store and playing in the neighborhood. The Johnson family and our family soon became like the Means and The Glovers were back in Bessemer. Bobby and Mary Lucille, Roxanne had met William through Bobby, Joyce met Johnny, and I wanted JoAnn (and we eventually had a daughter together named Katina, but I call her Josey); and Dot liked Larry and they had a son together.

From my stay on Saint Louis, I wrote my own version of *The West Side Story* when I was a sophomore at John Marshall High School on the West Side of Chicago. It started out as a short story for Ms. Helen *'Lundragon'* Lundergan's English class, but some guy in the English Department suggested I make it a Play. Looking back, I do not know if he was being jealous or just having fun with me because I never knew what happened to the story. I do know that it helped me earn an *'A'* from Ms. Lundergan that year and she told me, when I found her again many years later, that she still tells people about me and I was one of a very few she ever gave an *'A'* to.

Johnny, Larry, Fat Larry, and I eventually wound up with an area on the West Side where we could walk with no problems. We did a lot of fighting, bit it ended when the Johnson family had to return to Monroe to bury their grandfather and we moved to the 2800 block of Lexington. Sometimes, it is like a dream. We fought so much and then we would make the boys move that caused the problems. I never knew how this all worked, but it did. The neighborhood became quiet and people actually came outside to play.

One day Larry, Bernard Davis *(Also-Known-As-AKA- Man)*, Johnny, and myself were walking on Roosevelt Road near Douglas Park. Two guys on a bicycle came up behind us and told us to keep walking down this pass in the park. One of them stated, *"If they try to run, shoot them!"* Johnny and I looked at each other and knew they probably only had a *'zip-gun'*, a gun made at home and only fires one bullet at a time. We both had schooled each other and the guys when something like this happened, everybody run in a different direction and then we would double-back. Johnny and I knew Larry and Man were too scared to run so we marched along whistling as if the guys told us. We got to these bushes and they actually came alive with guys. From two on a bike, we now had about twenty to deal with. The guys wanted money and we had a few dollars, so we gave it to them. All of a sudden, one hit Larry in the stomach and another did the same to Man and told them to get out of here. When Johnny and I saw, crying had worked for Larry and Man; we decided to try it also. One of the guys who had been on the bicycle told us not to even try it. They knew who we were and we were going to have to fight our way out.

Willie Means Well

Johnny and I were getting ready to fight these two big guys when a guy jumped in front of me and must have hit me at least six or seven times. I hit the ground, rolled over and came up running. I remember hearing shouts of *'CATCH HIM, Y'ALL! CATCH HIM!"* I looked back and I saw these twins running after me. Johnny told me he could not tell me for sure if two guys were running after one or me because a lot of them had on the same thing. In addition, when he saw me come up off the ground, one of the guys knocked him down and they began to kick him. He said he did recall thinking, *"they're not going to catch Buster."* I found a Police Unit and told them my friend was being jumped on. The Officers both looked at me and told me to get in and show them where. We came across Johnny walking out the park, they told him to get in, and they would take us home. We started to tell them where we lived and they told us they knew where we lived and they knew who we were. It did not go well with us being brought home in a police car. Would you believe we both got whippings?

Willie Means Well

Therefore, as you can see, we might have been co-leaders of our little gang, but our Mommas still had the upper hands. After Johnny left for Monroe and we moved to Lexington, one day, about a week later, Man showed up at my house and told me the guys told him to bring me and Johnny a message. Neither of us was to return to that neighborhood. I remembered I thanked Man and told him I would get with Johnny when I could. He told me the guys were serious. Man said he had gotten up three mornings in a row and followed blood trails to somebody badly hurt or to a body. Where as we did it with chains, rings, bottles, and our fists, these guys had graduated to guns and knives.

Willie Means Well

LEXINGTON
(2800 Block)
When I die, have no pity
Bury me deep in Vice Lord City

    I was introduced to an entirely new world when we moved to 2818 West Lexington in the summer of 1968. The gangs had already rioted with the slaying of Doctor Martin Luther King Jr. in April of 1968. Then it started over again with the assassination of Robert Kennedy. There were two gang powers in that area on the West Side of Chicago at the time: **THE CHICAGO VICE-LORDS, and THE ROMAN SAINTS.** There were others, but these ruled the streets. After the rioting over Robert Kennedy's death, The Roman Saints were no more.

VICE LORDS DON'T DIE
THEY MULTIPLY!

Willie Means Well

LEXINGTON 1968 - SUMMER 1970

If ever there were an area I considered a Utopia during our moving around, it would be our first stay in the twenty-eight hundred block of Lexington on the West Side of Chicago. There was so much fun and games from day one that we moved in the neighborhood. Had you visited Lexington in 1968, you would have seen fenced-in yards with nice green lawns. The sidewalks and the street were clean. Even the alley that separated Lexington from Flournoy was spotless clean. The very first day while walking down the street, this dog chased me. Her name was *'Queeny'*. She was a meany and her owner, Charles, was just as mean. I later found out all the guys in their teen years belonged to the Vice Lords. All my friends were made to join, and the only reason they left me out was because my Mother was a Minister and they knew we went to Church.

From playing a softball game in the street called *'Piggy'*, or sitting on the roof and eating Hostess Twinkies and drinking Papaya Juice, we were always into something. Can you imagine what it is like to see so many pretty girls? You could not talk to these girls unless you wanted to be jumped on. It was one thing if you could fight the one person who wanted to fight you, but as I said, almost all the guys were in the Vice Lords, and you would answer to another-and-another if you got the better of any one of those Vice Lords.

However, once the neighborhood accepted you, then the neighborhood took care of you. I never found out what happened with the guy, who took care of our building, but he somehow got on the wrong side of the Vice Lords and they made him move. I do not know why our landlord did not know this right away, but his apartment became a playhouse for us that lived on the first part of the block.

These are the people I remember from such a wonderful time. Benjamin *'Ben Grim'* Taylor, and his cousin, Evelyn, who came to me one Saturday morning. After this guy called out to her to come across the street where he was with some other guys, and told me *"that motherfucker think he is going to get some pussy from me, but my stuff belong to someone special, don't it Buster?"* I was fourteen, she was fifteen, and even today I wonder was I suppose to be that someone special. Timmy, *AKA, Theo*. His sisters, Pat and Juanita were *Vice Ladies* and whipped many of men's asses. Zeke and Joe Stanford with their pretty sister Martha, Brother Bud, and their Mother with eyes that still haunt me today. The Banks, with cousins Princilla, Marva Jean, and Shirley Jean. Marva Jean's mother, Jill, was a very good friend of my Mother... both in person and Spiritual association. So much to the tune, that Jill came to my Mother and told her she had been killed in a bus accident somewhere in Mississippi. When my Mother came to my door and woke me up early one morning, I believe it was 1974; it scared the dickens out of me. We were living at 2842 West Lexington several years later, and there was a Church in the basement where we lived. The preacher's dead wife haunted the apartment we lived in over the Church. With my trusty companion, 'Old

Man, AKA King, my dog, I was bold enough to sleep in the back bedroom when no one else could. That early morning when Momma showed up at my door and made the statement, *"Willie Earl, Jill is dead!"* I jumped up and told Momma she had to be dreaming and had a nightmare. She once again repeated, *"No, Jill is dead. She just came to me and told me her neck has been broken. The bus she was on has been in an accident."*

    I walked Momma back to her bedroom and told her to try to get some sleep. From my bedroom, I could hear her saying a Prayer to the tune for the Lord not to have let her friend suffered if it was true that she had been killed. Next morning I was getting ready to go to school at Wright College, *"You Can't Go Wrong At Wright"*, where I participated in track and field. It was roughly 6:30 when the phone rang. The person on the telephone was Marva Jean. She asked me how I was doing and she apologized for calling so early. She wanted to know was Momma up yet and I told her she had a bad night and was still sleeping. At that moment, Momma called from her bedroom and said she was awake if someone wanted to talk to her. I told Marva Jean to hold on she was coming and then I asked her what was wrong. She confirmed that her Momma had been killed in an accident early that morning. She had been on a bus and the bus was struck by a train right where Jill had been sitting. Then she gave me the chills by saying, *"they say Momma's neck was broken,"* I was stunned and could not speak. She called my name a couple of times, but I just stood there, looking at the telephone in my hand until Momma came and took it away. I heard her crying in her bedroom as I returned to my room and dropped down on my knees to Pray and ask the Lord to please help me to understand what I had gotten myself into. While still in high school, I had started playing a game with Arnold "Victor Wethersby, Glenn Brown, and Monroe Eugene Bidding about *'ESP' or 'Extra-Sensory-Perception.* A friend on the track team hooked me up with his girlfriend and her mother became my personal tutor in ESP and believe you me, even today, my hair is gray and things happen because I touched something that I thought was a game; a Ouija board.

Willie Means Well

OUIJA

I thought it was a game, but the spirit knew my name
This had to be a joke, and somehow it must be broke
An encrypted board and a triangular piece of plastic
This thing knew all my secrets, my thoughts put in a basket
I met a Satanist priest; she paid a price to become free
I knew a Wicca warlock, what he learned left his mind blocked
There was a kid who practiced magic, and Ouija let him have it
Milton Bradley claimed it was a game, but many are left insane
To dabble with black arts, your soul and you will part
I have good mind frame, but sometimes I don't know my name

I will tell you more about Mr. Ouija and my messing with *ESP* later. Especially when we moved

Willie Means Well

into the Cabrini Green Housing Projects.

 There was Paul Luther Fairly, *AKA 'Country Cool',* my closest and best friend who became part of the Vice Lords and I was told became very ruthless when it came to dealing with guys in different gangs. Paul should have played professional basketball for somebody, but like many of the guys, once you become a gang-banger, you cannot go to school at times because someone is always looking for you. My friend Ben was another guy this happened to. We entered Ninth grade together, but Ben had to drop out when it was time for us to transfer to Marshall on the other side of the expressway. Manley Branch of Marshall was around the corner from us, and a new gang called *'The Black Souls'* had to cross the expressway to come to Manley. A lot of them paid for crossing that expressway. I got away with it because my Mother, bless her heart, once again moved us into an area that had a neutral zone and I was able to walk to Marshall.

 My friend Wilfred Smith lived under us at 2818 on Lexington. Very pretty boy, if I must say so myself. All the girls were crazy about Wilfred's curly hair and light-skin complexion. Poor Wilfred, I remember him getting three pair of new boots taken off his feet by guys in the gang. His Mother brought him a fourth pair and told him he would go bare-feet if he let someone take those. I remember seeing Wilfred with a black eye but he kept his boots.

    Jesse Burrell lived on the first floor in our building, and poor Jesse stayed in the bad boy's home more than at home. He was a great guy, however, even when I took his paper route from him one morning and sold all his newspapers, then went to school. I was no bully, but as I said, all my friends were in the Vice Lords and they accepted me because we lived in the same neighborhood. There were times I had to hold my own with my fists, and then there were a couple of times that I totally got the stuffing's bead out of me. I remember one time looking between this guy's legs as he was pounding on me and seeing my girlfriend, Margaret, and another girl, Bell, standing at the fence. I know I heard one of them say, *"Oooh! That man is beating up Buster."* That is exactly what he was doing. I think I was maybe fifteen and this guy was over twenty-one. Margaret and Bell at least went and got Ben, the guys, my sister Joyce had run upstairs and got my brother Bobby, and my brother-in-law William. By the time, any of them could get there, one of the other guys who knew this guy pulled him off me and told him my brothers were coming. Once the Vice Lords found out what had happened, they said it was over. We could not get the guy back because he was somewhat mentally retarded. He sure did whip my butt. I remember Margaret came out and talked to me after we finished out meeting with some of the Vice Lords and told me how she would be too embarrassed to come out if her face was messed up like mine. I actually looked at it as my *"Red Badge of Courage!"*

    Ben's sweetheart was Constance Marie Smith. I wanted her, but Ben was more mature than I was. You talk about a fine, healthy, and good-looking girl, then Constance was it. All the boys wanted to talk to her, but were afraid. I got her to talking by inviting her to my fifteenth birthday party, but Ben wound up being the one to explore her goldmine.

You had Janice *'Pap'* Smith and her sisters and brothers, Margaret Delores Dugger, whom I was utterly crazy about, and her family. To be thirteen and fourteen, Margaret really had me broken up when word got around that I had been talking to another girl. She and Pap had me and this other guy on a *'Kiss Schedule'*... funny right! The schedule went by the moon. As the moon changed quarters, we went from three on the first quarter to a whole bunch on a full moon. I was content to be getting such goodness from Margaret. However, Pap's sneaky sister and her friend Lois actually picked the schedule out of my pocket as we were standing up talking and damn if they did not tell everyone. As I said, we were only fourteen and thirteen, but when the guys and girls found out that Margaret and I were not having sex, they began to tease us relentlessly. I remember I started seeing this girl who all the guys said was *'Easy'* since I could not get Margaret to give in to my begging. I recall walking by her and

Pap coming from the store and Margaret began to sing this song done by Diana Ross and the Supremes with the Temptations *'I'm Going To Make You Love Me'*. Only thing, she would sing, *'I'm going to make you hate me!'* Would you believe the damn guys started laughing about it but the girls told me I had better be glad Margaret told them not to beat-up that girl I had started seeing? Guess What! I never got anything from that girl but a lot of teasing. I found out she only gave it up when you gave her something in exchange. Guess you can say she was a young whore. We moved from Lexington without Margaret and me ever making up. She came to Marshall as a sophomore but I was so into track and field by my junior year I spoke when I saw her but I never tried to get back with her. I heard my pretty, little baby was strung out on drugs and died. I did not find this out until more than thirty years later and do you know I found myself crying for her. I will always remember her Mother calling me to go to the store for her because Margaret was sick. When I got upstairs, her sister Cynthia answered the door but Margaret came to the door and told her to go finish her homework. When Cynthia left, Margaret looked up the hall to make sure her Mother was not coming, then opened her housecoat and just stared at me. My baby had on a whole slip and at thirteen she definitely had not began to develop but I do not know, for some reason at that time it sure made me feel like it was she and I alone in the world. When she heard he Mother coming, she gave me a quick kiss on the lip and just stood staring at me.

Bell and El *(Beverly and Evelyn)* twin girls and their family all lived at 2820 Lexington, in a building owned by Pap's Father. You had fine, super-fine Florida and her yellow cousin, Tony, and some kids that never came outside. The Triplets and the family who lived above them that the Vice Lords made move away after the man hurt Wilfred. See what I mean about the neighborhood taking care of its own?

As I have said, Lexington was a whirlwind romance for all of us. Sometimes I wish I could return to that era and never leave. We all learned of life and death on Lexington.

Willie Means Well

Linda was a beautiful, quiet young lady. Ben and I had included her brother in our little group hoping this would get us in the door with Linda. She was queenly and had a nice thick head of hair. Now that I look back, I recall she would always talk to us from the door, but would never come outside to us. Even when Linda would be out talking to girls in the neighborhood, she would immediately leave when we guys came up.

Ben and I were young and we did not understand we somehow made things happen. First, there was the incident with Wilfred while we were swimming at The Social Center at Manley. Ben and I both had lifeguard training, but Ben could swim and skate circles around me. That night, I had just swum down to the shallow end of the pool when Ben jumped in beside me and asked had I seen Wilfred. I made the statement, *"You know Wilfred. He is probably on the bottom of the pool holding his breath and trying to fool us."* Ben replied, with his hands in motion, "Yeah! On the bottom of the pool screaming for help." We both laughed, but our laughter was cut short. Right at that moment, Mr. Brown, lifeguard and assistant principal, looked into the deep end and dove in. He came back up with Wilfred and began yelling for someone to call the fire department. Ben and I looked at Mr. Brown perform life-saving steps on Wilfred, and I remember foam and blood came out of Wilfred's mouth. Mr. Brown continued to work on Wilfred until the fire department got there and took Wilfred away. Social center was over for that night, but fortunately, Wilfred did live.

We found out that a guy from the street gang called the *'MTs'* had pulled Wilfred under the water and stood on him. What Ben and I tried not to laugh at was Wilfred told us he actually did cry out for help when he realized he could not get up for air. This situation also set off fighting between the Vice Lords and the *Mrs.*

The Vice Lords would go to the *MTs* hangout and shoot into the place. One night, I was told of one such raid when a couple of Vice Lords' cousin was killed. The guy was up visiting from Mississippi and did not know his way around. I was told he was very excited that the cousins were going to allow him to see what they did at night. After shooting up the hangout, the cars pulled off and left several of the guys. While running down the streets, trying to get back on friendly turf, the cousin from Mississippi fell and could not keep up. I was told the guy ran into a gangway and several of the *MTs* ran in behind him. The guy who told me what happened said you could hear the gunshots as they continued to run. When they went to claim the kid's body, he had been shot over twenty times.

"AIN'T NO LOVE IN THE HEART OF THE CITY
AIN'T NO LOVE IN THE HEART OF TOWN
AIN'T NO LOVE AND AIN'T IT A PITY
AIN'T ANY LOVE WHEN YOU AIN'T AROUND!!!

Those are the lyrics to a popular Blues tune that was out around that time. Poor kid. Anyway, as I was explaining, Linda stayed away from boys. However, I always liked to think that she liked me some. It was winter early 1970 when Ben and I were at my house and talking about people hurting themselves to get away from bad situations. I remember Ben and I could be heartless at times and we fought with each other, too. We were discussing how Linda would not talk to any boys and how she might as well blow her brains out for being so STUCK-UP! Barely had we finished laughing about it when we heard a gunshot followed by another shot. Ben remarked, *"Damn Mean-mo! Maybe she heard us."* Less than five minutes later, we heard the sirens and went to the window to look out because the sirens sounded close. We saw the police and the fire department in front of Linda's house, and Ben and I ran down to see what was wrong. Her brother was crying his eyes out and we kept asking him what was wrong. He looked at us and said, *"My sister just shot herself!"* At that time, the firemen brought Linda out on a gurney. Her face was not covered and she looked so peaceful. We figured she was alright. We later learned that she was already dead, but the police and firemen did not want to possibly have a situation develop. Lindah had literally blown her heart out of her body. Her brother then told us how their father would chain her in the kitchen until dinner was over or how he would chain her to her bed at night so she could not get out. This information was passed to the leader of the Vice Lords, and that night, they marched. When one of the guys knocked on the door, the only thing that saved Linds's father life was he slammed the door and fell to the floor. The guy from the Vice Lords shot the door and the windows up pretty good. They then marched away. The next morning, the entire family was gone and we never heard what happened to them.

MARSHALL HIGH SCHOOL
(Track and Field)

The summer before my sophomore year, we moved to the thirty-nine hundred block of Jackson Boulevard and dead in the middle of *'Four Corner Hustlers'* territory. Here, it was my sisters who saved me from the gang; they became *'Hustlerettes'*. This was a very sad time for me, but a happy one, too. When school began, I tried out and made the track team, *'The Marshall Mercurians'*. After trials and beating everybody out the starting blocks ten consecutive starts, the guys, both varsity and junior varsity made me feel welcomed and special. Mr. Jody Poole was coach and Mr. Randolph Sweeney was assistant coach. I will always remember Mr. Sweeney had a Volkswagen Van and we sometimes got twenty of us in it on the way to track meets. Tor three years I lettered in track and field but never got my letter until my senior year. Then I got some little silver track foot pin to pin on my jacket. I DID NOT WANT IT! I wanted my large *'M'* so I could sport it on my jacket like everybody else. Those people always made me out to be something more than what I was and I simply did not know how to handle the attention. I was very gentle and did not know anything about socializing except being myself. Had you told a joke in a room with one hundred people in the room, I would probably be the one hundred and first to get the joke. I was truly that *'naïve'*.

I was always fast and it was a guy, *Albert Milton*, from my old neighborhood on Lexington who told the track coach about me. Albert went on to run the hurdles for the United States in the *'76 Olympic Games'* held in Oakland, California. I should have, and will always wonder why I was not, on that same Olympic Squad. I always tell myself it was my coach from Wright College who used the *'76 Games'* to get back at me for causing him misery my two seasons I ran for him. I say this again, *"I WAS NOT A BAD KID! PEOPLE JUST MADE ME OUT FOR MORE THAN WHAT I WAS AND I WAS NOT ABLE TO HANDLE ALL THE ATTENTION!"* If I could do it all again, I wonder, would I. I am sure any athlete places himself or herself in competition with superstar athletes they see compete in their field of sports. For me, it was seeing *Carl Lewis* win the *200 meter* in the Olympics. He finished the race in nineteen seconds and some tenths. I remember my second season of running for the coach at *Wright* when this *Italian Guy name Mike,* a track-mate of mine, and me, both broke twenty-one seconds. Mike worked hard and had the guys pushing him and the coach helping him, to surpass me and become *the number one sprinter.* Me, I had gotten more into JoAnn and preferred to spend time with her. It got to the point where the coach would ask me was I going to practice instead of kicking my ass and making me practice with everybody else. Instead, once I realized how much they wanted me to run for them, I dropped all my *'Core Classes for Engineering'* and just kept those pertaining to sports. This kept my getting a check in order but the coach would call me on the telephone and ask me to come to meets and run certain events. I did, however, practice enough to remain on the *440 yards relay.* I had been out with a hurt ankle from playing basketball for about a month when the coach called me and asked me to come in to practice with the relay team because *Outdoor Regional* was coming up. I drove to the stadium where they told me to come and I found out they had put together a second relay team that they wanted me to *lead off* and run against the primary relay team. I was going to run against Mike on the first leg. I could not believe they had video camera set up and guys had cameras to take pictures. Before the race started, I heard guys laughing and saying things like *"kick his ass Mike!' He won't come to practice, he deserve to lose his spot on the relay team.* I heard Mike mumbling but he did wish me luck and I remember my friend Henry Milton, who son plays with the *Chicago Bears,* now, told me *"just run your race Mean-mo. Don't hurt yourself."* Now, knowing Mike, he probably wanted to tell them to shut-up. Mike probably was remembering the *220 yards dash* we competed in a couple of months earlier against these four-year schools at *The University of Chicago Track and Field Invitations.* Mike and I was in the third *'heat'* to run and he was in lane two and I was in lane three. This guy walked up to the sprinter in lane four and made the statement, *"you got this easy man! Anybody that is somebody was in the first two heats!"* When we got down into the starting blocks, I had made up my mind to try not to get embarrassed. When the man brought us to *'Set'* and the gun sounded, I remember I went by the guy in lane four so fast, he was just coming out of the blocks. I heard him say very loudly **"SHIT!"** I could not help it. I was running, but I was laughing so hard I almost stopped. I heard breathing on my left side and Mike came by me and told me, **"STOP BULLSHITTING MEAN-MO AND BRING YOUR ASS ON!"** I recovered enough to run the race and finished second behind Mike, he did 20.6, and I did 20.7. Coach and his brother came up to us as Mike, I was walking back up the track, and coach had this frown on his face. His brother was clicking a stopwatch. *"Willie! Did I see you laughing,"* the coach wanted to know. Before I could respond, Mike spoke up. *"Yeah this 'Moth-fuc' was laughing. I had to tell him to come on."* Coach brother-in-law, who was also the assistant coach, looked at the watch and made the statement, *"damn it Willie! You and Mike just did 20.6 and 20.7. Think of what it could have been if you were running all the way!"*

So you see, that day when we were getting ready to run against each other, Mike realized that the guys probably had just motivated me and he was right. When the gun sounded, I did run my race and did not think anything about it until I heard Mike swearing. *"God damn moth-fuc won't even come to training then come out here and beat everybody!"* Our team won and coach and his assistant came walking over, and his assistant was clicking the stop watch. *"Damn it Willie! You did it again. We are never going to know your true potential because you won't practice regularly."* Coach started to say something but instead asked his brother-in-law, John was his name, to check the video and see what it looked like. Mike was still mumbling and some of the guys were around him trying to get him to settle down.

When coach and John checked the video, I

heard them say, *"Where's Willie?"* Now, everybody was gathering around the camera trying to see what coach was talking about. Suddenly, you heard this *"DAMN!"* Coach turned and looked at me and told me to come and watch this. Everybody was looking at me and John made the statement, *"Willie, you've got to put your heart into this. Man, I'm telling you, there's no telling what you can do if you decide to focus on running."* What the camera caught was Mike running first leg and passing off to the second leg on his team. The guy on my team was not even in the picture but when Mike and his second leg exchanged the *'baton',* the camera caught me walking back round the track. Coach had John slow the video down and *pan* it in reverse back to the starting blocks. Once again, there was Mike coming out the blocks but I was nowhere to be seen. One of the guys asked John to go forward slowly because he thought he saw something dark on the screen. When John *panned* forward slowly and came to the dark blur, he froze the camera and focused the len. There I was already almost a good 15 to 20 yards down the track. I had come out the blocks so fast that the camera only caught a blur. Coached later told me that he and John decided it could only be backed-up energy I had been storing up from not practicing for a while. I knew what it was. Ever since *Indoor Nationals* held in Joplin, Missouri in spring of that year (1975), I had finally gotten my start down pat and not too many was beating me out the block the reminder of that year. That reminds me why I got upset and decided not run from coach anymore. I made the finals in the *60 yards dash and should have placed second or third. Mike was crying once again because I had beaten him and coach went to Mike instead of checking to see why they did not give me my place in the finish. When I asked him about it, he told me those were just the breaks.* I decided then I did not want to run for him anymore.

As I have said, I was not a bad kid. People just made me out for more than what I was. The first year of track and field at John Marshall High School, we set the record for the *880 Relay* for Junior Varsity at the '*Oak Park Relays*' early in 1971. This was done even with me up on Bobby Polk's back trying to pass him the baton. Kevin *'Rockchild'* Cherry held the starting blocks for me and later told me no one was within thirty yards of me and it seemed I was trying to go faster. Well, to tell it like it was, I was trying to go faster because I heard someone breathing behind me and I was trying not to let them pass me. Coach Poole later told me I heard myself breathing. That was the beginning of a wonderful time in my life. I really enjoyed track and field, but I have always felt with better coaching, I could have been one of the *Superstars* in track and field.

    While running for Wright College, there was a track meet at the University of Chicago, where everyone was talking about a sprinter named Mike McFarland. There was a television crew there to film him and nobody really expressed to me about where beating this guy could lead to. I was working on developing a new style, and when the gun went off, I ran my normal race but McFarland beat me about five yards and I beat the rest of the pack about five yards. I remember coach coming up to me, shaking his head, and telling me, *"Willie, you could have beaten him."* Coach turned and walked away ant the guys on the team were also angry with me.

I never understood the significance of that race until 1980. I was in military journalism school at Fort Benjamin Harrison, Indiana. One of our study guides was the *AP Associate Style Book.* While looking under sports to see the proper way to dateline a sports article, I wanted to cry and it put me on a downer for a while. Mike McFarland's name had been used as an example for track and field. I tried to tell my friends how I had the chance to beat the guy, but I did not understand what it could have done for me. I have always wanted to write a book and tell young athletes not to make the same mistakes I did. I guess I was destined to **'DIE UNBORN!"**

On the other side of the coin of life and living in the neighborhood I was now in, was always the threat of being killed. I was going to the store with my dog, King, one afternoon and I saw these female Hustlerettes crowed in this gangway. I walked up to see what was happening and one of the girls turned and said, *"Get out of here Buster! You don't want to see this."* I got away as fast as I could. I heard the sirens coming back and when I turned the corner and got near the gangway, I could see they had a body under a sheet, but I could not make out head or tails the way the body was positioned. As I approached the building I lived in, some Hustletetts were sitting on the steps next door. The girl who had told me to get out of there looked at me and winked. I later found out that the Hustlers had the girls block off the entrance to the gangway while they killed a kid who they thought was a member of the *'Black Souls'*. I was told they kicked the kid's face in. It was done as retaliation for the killing of a Hustler who had been killed the day before at a hotdog stand on Pulaski Road. They said the Hustler had walked out the hotdog stand and some Black Souls had shot him six or seven times. This really saddened me to think that some mother was waiting for her son to come home and he was being stomped to death in some gangway. I was very glad when we moved.

Willie Means Well

OUT OF THE FRYING PAN AND INTO THE FIRE

Summer 1971 through spring 1974
(THE CABRINI GREEN HOUSING PROJECT)
-Death Walks the Streets-

When Momma told us we were moving into the housing project, I got very worried. You could not have pets in the projects and my dog, King, had been with us since late 1968. King was lake a member of the family. That dog and I had fought the fights together. There were times when I would put him on one guy while I might be fighting with one or two others. Then, there were times when I would stick my hands in the middle of him fighting and pull him away when I knew he was overwhelmed. Actually have a couple of scars still on my left hand from where I reached in to pull a dog off King and the dog put two rips in my hand. When I yelled, it must have scared the dog because he tried to run. That was enough for King to grab the dog across the belly and he would have ripped the dogs' stomach out had we

Willie Means Well

not separated them. Theo told me he was sorry and some of the older guys wanted to take me to the nurse at the park and let her wrap my hand. **I was not** interested in getting my hand wrapped, I just wanted to get King home and try to give him a bath before Momma go home. She had told me, *"You bring King home with one more scratch on him, and that's gone be your behind!"* As soon as I walked in the door, Joyce, who normally kept me from getting whipping, looked at King and yelled, *"Momma! Buster done had King fighting!"* I replied back that I had not had King fighting but Timmy's -*AKA- Theo,* dog jumped on King and I tried to stop it. Momma came from the back with a stick in her hand and was reaching to grab me when Dot yelled, *"Buster! Why is your hand bleeding like that?"* I did not say a word I was looking at Momma and thinking about pulling that stick from her hand. I guess I had just been fed up with getting a whipping at my great age of fourteen. Probably would not have, but would have taken the beating. Anyway, with Dot yelling, Momma stopped and grabbed my hand. I told her the dog had bit me when I was trying to get King. Mother told me I had better be glad because she was ready to beat my behind.

KING

The guys on Lexington had come up with a new way to get some spending money... Sale dogs! This was a good idea, but where were the dogs going to come from? Theo and Grim had the answer. Every other morning or so, a trip would be taken to the suburbs and we would take dogs we thought would make good watchdogs. How were we going to get the suburbs? On the train, of course. I saw failure in this straight out the blocks.

Steal somebody's dog and return to the city on the train. Unbelievably, this worked well for two weeks and netted us ten dogs; including my future dog, King. I was too much of a coward to sneak on the train, let alone go steal somebody's dog. So guess what? We organized. I and several of the guys would prepare the garage where we were going to keep and train the dogs. The others would be the pick-up team.

We had a good week one before I was to meet *Mr. King* for the first time. A man had come to us for a watchdog because one of his had died. I remember

Theo talking about a dog they had seen and he believed the dog would make a good watchdog. The man was going to give us fifty dollars if he liked the dog. I remember that morning we were walking to school and Grim told me Theo and a couple of the guys had come back with a pretty German shepherd. Grim said the dog had bit Theo but he would not let the dog go. Hearing this, I decided to make sure I carried a stick or something with me when I went to the garage when I got out of school.

  When I got to the garage, King was the only dog there. The guys had gone off to sale two other dogs. King was lying down with his ears back. I started talking to him and he got up wagging his tail. He allowed me to rub his head and scratch his ears. Had you looked in h is face, you would had swore he was crying. I fell in love with him at that moment, got a chain on him, and took him home. I was trying to figure out how to tell the guys I wanted this dog when two of them came to my house and told me the man only wanted to give us twenty-five dollars. The guys said no and they would find someone else to buy the dog.

    I let King sleep on our patio that night. I got up early the next morning and went out to give him some water and food. The dog was lying in the corner and I said, *"Good morning boy, how you doing today?"* That dog got up just as casually and came to me. He jumped up on me and I thought he was going to lick me. At the last moment before his head reached the side of my face, I heard the growl in his throat. I snatched my head to the side and that damn dog bit me on the shoulder. Had I not moved my head, he would have grabbed my throat.

    I threw him off me, ran back in the door, and just slammed it before he bumped into it. I took a couple of deep breaths, went, and got a stick. When I opened the door back, would you believe that dog looked at the stick in my hand and came over to me peeing on the floor? He lay at my feet, whimpering, and that is when I realized that dog was smart. I put the stick down and then he jumped up and licked me.

    On the way to school, I told Grim what had happened and that I was going to keep the dog. Grim told me the guys were not going to like it, but he would back me up. That is how I began an eleven-year journey with my best friend. He truly was my best friend in more ways than even I did not understand until years later. Once again, I must ask you, *"What is real?"* Here is to Reality!

JOANN AND I
(Our Grief)

Joann and I met when our families lived on Saint Louis. She was a skinny little thing, but she believed in wearing dresses, and that made her very appealing to me. Her brothers were Johnny, Larry, and William, who married Roxanne. It was only *'Puppy Love'* between the two of us until she returned to Chicago from Monroe, Louisiana in the *fall* of 1972 with her first child.

I was with Helen Jean Blossom at the time but when I saw JoAnn, all the times I had teased at her, and kissed at her, I now wanted this to actually take place. I remember the lyrics from a song that went, *"Wish I h ad a girl like you, baby. You make an old man stand up straight and drive a young man crazy!"* That was JoAnn. She later told me the guy knocked her out and stole her love the first time she made love. That guy created a very hungry lady when it came to sex.

Anyway, JoAnn and I became *real lovers* in the

Willie Means Well

spring of 1974 and we wanted to get married. Her family said no! They wanted her to marry the guy from their hometown of Monroe. We were going to try to go it alone but I guess it was not to be. My sister Joyce told me JoAnn's Brother Johnny came to their job and talked about JoAnn like a dog until she agreed to marry the other guy. She did, and I got very sick.

To many, I guess you would just have shrugged this off and go on with your life. Me? My Momma told me I lay in the bed for three days and did not move. The only thing I remember from those three days is every time I would turn my head; King would rise up by my bed and look at me.

I should have known then that something had changed about my friend. You see, by this time, I had become a student of Extra-Sensory-Perception, *better known as ESP*. I might have said it earlier, *"I touched something, and it touched me back and did not let go."* Out of my dabbling, to include an Ouija Board, I had crossed into something that is very real. Now, I believe King had what is calling a *'familiar spirit'*. The dog was *TOO* smart. If you had gotten around Johnny before he died, and some of that other crowd that knew me back in Chicago and started talking about animals, they would tell you people could say what they want about how smart animals are, but they had never run across a dog smart like King.

An ex-Satanist priest I picked up one night during my taxi driving days in Columbus, Georgia explained to me what I had done.

I had recently had a hair-crawling experience with a ghost in the neighborhood of Tenth Street and Britt Avenue. I had gone on a call early in the morning and I could not get to the dispatcher. While waiting for the dispatcher, I saw this beautiful lady in my rearview mirror looking in at me. When I turned my head to look back, she was gone. Logic was trying to tell me she could not had gotten away that fast but when the dispatcher gave me my call, I backed the car looking for the lady and I saw her standing on the porch of this house at Tenth street and Britt avenue. The house had four column poles and she was standing by one of the columns. As I backed the car so my headlights would shine on the porch, it seems she was playing a game with me. As I got lighter on in the area she was standing, she seem to move around the pole from the light. When I got to point that I could shine my lights directly on the porch, I hit the bright-lights switch but there was no one on the porch. I felt a chill go over me but I figured I had been pushing it too long and it was time to go in and get some sleep. I told myself to call it a night after this fare.

 I did not get anyone where I was blowing my car horn, so I decided to ride up Tenth Street to see if maybe I was seeing things and the lady had walked up the street. As I got to the rear of the building, some guys were playing cards and began to yell that they had called the taxi. When my fare got in, I asked him did they see a lady come up this street. He yelled my question to the other guys and they informed me that had a lady came that way, they would be talking to her.

 When I got ready to pull off, the guy asked me

Willie Means Well

why I asked that anyway. When I explained what happened, he stated, *"Man! I wish you had said that. The lady who lived there was killed about a year ago and we have called the police thinking someone was being raped over there because sometimes you can hear a woman crying and sort of screaming. We have called the 911 and had the fire department come out thinking the place was on fire because you can see yellow like light through the windows. Nobody ever find anything wrong. We all stay away from there because we know she is still over there."*

    I had several more people confirm that I had actually seen that lady. That night I picked up the priest, she was in a wheelchair and in the same condition that the fall from the horse left Christopher Reeve. Her companion had been the leader of a *'Wicca'* group. The more I think of this and put it down, the more I am finding myself looking in dark corners.

    That priest told me I had opened a *portal* in my bedroom where I played with that Ouija Board. She also said she bet no one was able to stay in that apartment too long since I did not close the *portal*. That was at 1159 North Cleveland, apartment 906 in the Cabrini Green Housing Project. you are a movie person, they did *'Cooley High', 'Sandman',* and a couple of more movies in those Projects I believe. They did not realize just how close to evil they really were.

DEATH WALKS THE CABRINI

It Was a Tuesday night, the summer of '72
I was coming from the store, a little scared too
I rounded the corner of the building where I lived
A shotgun blast delivered, somebody was killed
As I took off running, I took a quick glance
Somebody should had run, instead of taking a stance
I heard the buckshot hit the wall around me
I wasn't hit, and God's Love is astounding
The shooter killed his man, and the he became a victim
Shot in the head himself, death quickly came to take him
As I ran, up the stars and hit the Ninth floor
My family stood in waiting so did the neighbors next door
Now it is like a battlefield; you run and do not walk
Take your time and fool around, your life it will be lost
From building to building, the killers, they came
It all seem unreal, but this was not a game

Willie Means Well

By the time the killing was over, it was a Sunday afternoon
Fifteen guys and a baby, lives forfeited all too soon

The Vietnam Conflict was going on when we lived in those projects. With the way those guys killed, I used to wonder why didn't the military just wait until around 2 a.m. and come and make a massive sweep and take them all to Vietnam. They killed like professionals, so why not let them go and serve their Country and this would get them off the streets.

Willie Means Well

A WHIRLWIND ROMANCE

(Reform, Alabama)

Christ**mas** 1975, my dad came to Chicago to visit us. I was very happy to see him. We had not seen each other since fall 1966 before we left Bessemer. Dad only spent a short time with us and then he was going to fly back to Alabama. I told Dad I would be glad to drive him home. He thought I was playing around. Truth be told, I was looking for any reason to get away from Chicago for a while.

Around Christmas 1975, I had a 1964 Buick Electra. My brother-in-law William had worked a deal with the company he worked with and I believe I got that car for fewer than one thousand dollars. We have all heard about the great bargains at car places where the salesperson tells you, *this baby was owned by a little old lady who only drove this car to church on Sundays after her husband died!"* Ring a bell?

Well, unbelievably, I really did luck up on such a deal. That car had a four-fifty-four under the hood and it was heavy like all American cars were until

Willie Means Well

everybody began cutting corners to save material. That car had been customized so the dashboard lights or turn signal would not work until the engine had warmed up properly. Many nights that winter, I left work with no dash lights because I needed to hurry and get home to my three hours sleep before being back at Playbill Enterprises at seven in the morning.

When I got ready to take Dad home, Johnny, Jimmy Ray, and Jean all decided to go with me. I appreciated it. If you get lost, you don't get so scared when you have people with you.

That car held the road like a Cadillac. The ride was so smooth that if you were not driving, you were sleeping. Dad later told me he always preferred Buicks or Fords. I truly understood about the Fords when I returned to Reform to live with him. Dad had three Ford sedans and five Ford pick-up trucks.

We stopped off in Bessemer so Dad could show me off to old friends and family. I was very glad to spend some time with Ed, Des, and Willie Tee. I had seen them a little over a year earlier when we returned to Bessemer to bury my cousin Arthur.

Arthur had popped up in Chicago in August of 1974. He and I had not seen each other since we left Bessemer in December 1966. He was more mature than I was but I did not begrudge him that. I had heard that life was rough for him since his Momma had moved them to Florida. He fit right in with the guys I knew on Lexington. In 1974, we had moved back to Lexington, but we were farther down the block and most of the people we knew in 1968 were gone.

    My brother Bobby, who was still in the Army during this time, had came home and left me with a knee-length leather and suede coat. Arthur asked me could he wear it and I told him sure just be careful. Unbelievably, someone tried to take the coat from him but the story I got was one of the guys recognized the coat and told the other guy they thought it was my coat. When Arthur told them he was my cousin form Miami, they left him alone.

    I was thrilled to spend time with my cousin again. Like I said, he was rough and took some getting used to but I had begun to bond with him. He

Willie Means Well

teased at JoAnn and she loved it. She did tell me that he told her he did it to see how much I loved her.

I remember everything was going great. I had found him a job through one of the employment agency. I had turned him on the grilled polish sausage and hot tamales. He had talked to me of a plan to get Momma, *Aunt Rose* to him, in a house. I remember he said, *"Hey Buster. Why is Aunt Rose not in a house? All her sisters are in their own homes; don't you think she would like this?"*

Everything was great! Then I went to pick him up from work and he told me he had to go back to Miami to get his brother, *'Red Button',* out of jail.

I took my cousin to the Greyhound that Wednesday and saw him off. I cried once he left.

Our telephone was off and Roxanne and William had been over that Friday checking on Momma. Momma was forty-three years old and she was pregnant again. Almost an eleven-year difference since Marzett had been born. Roxanne and William had been gone less than an hour when the doorbell rang and it was they. I asked why they were back and Roxanne asked me was Momma lying down. I told her yes and asked her what was wrong again. She looked at me, put her finger up to her lips to silence me, and said, *"Arthur is dead,"* I looked at her and told her to stop playing. She then said it again and William shook his head yes.

I turned and walked away. I had been sewing something on my track bag. My knees must have given out on me because I heard myself cry out, *"NO!"* and then someone was helping me up off the floor. I heard Momma call my name and ask what was wrong with Willie Earl. I could see her sitting on the side of the bed as Roxanne, William, Joyce, and Dot tried to calm her down. Then I saw her breakdown and they were trying to get her off the floor.

The way we heard it, Arthur had gone to see his baby and somebody shot him the stomach. They said he might have lived, but the girl gave him ice water when he asked for it. The water chilled the blood and he died from internal bleeding. He was a week away for his twentieth birthday.

Willie Means Well

I want to share something else with you here. Earlier in the year, my grandmother had become seriously ill. Ill to the tune of the doctors had told her daughters in Florida, if anybody wanted to see her before grandmother died, they had better get there. They were not giving her twenty-four hours to live.

I remember everybody immediately went into some hard Praying and begging GOD to spare grandmother. There is power, real power, in GROUP PRAYER! Momma was waiting for Roxanne and William to come and take her to O'Hare Airport. When Roxanne and William got to the house, Roxanne was telling Momma she was not going to believe it, but the doctors could not find anything wrong with grandmother that morning. Momma left to call Miami. It was then several months later that Arthur called and wanted to come and see me.

I would like to give a word of warning to anybody who will listen. ***"WHEN DEATH COMES TO YOUR FAMILY, DEATH IS GOING TO GET SOMEONE!"*** It was years later when someone else got sick and everybody was asked to Pray and I informed my mother that I would Pray but it would be in the fashion, *"LORD, LET THY WILL BE DONE!"*

I have no doubt that our Prayers were answered for grandmother's life. However, death was there and it had to take someone. Arthur was nineteen years old. I had just got to Germany in July 1977 when Red Cross called with the information that grandmother
Was dead. My brother, Bobby, went home to the funeral, but I did not. I had told Momma before joined the Army, I would not come home to any funerals. Death took Arthur at nineteen and still came back and got grandmamma three years later.

Well, it all must end so I will end for now and give you a few of my poems. I did return to Reform, Alabama in June 1976 but returned to Chicago and joined the Army in March 1977. Perhaps I will get to tell you about those Army days next.

Willie Means Well

I ONCE WAS A SOLDIER
BUT THAT WAS LONG AGO
WHEN I WAS IN ARTILLERY
AND MY MORALE WAS NOT SO LOW

Willie Means Well

Hazelnut

You were eighteen, and I was twenty-six
In Barstow, California is where we met
A young Catholic Girl just out of high school
You walked with a smile, your eyes so cool
The music of Pat Benatar, you loved so dearly
I wanted to walk on the WILDSIDE with you
It showed so clearly
In Beacon Bowl, we rolled and rolled
Trouble came to us, so strong, so bold
They tried so hard to keep us apart
Nothing else matters when love touches your heart
In a dark hole, they threatened to put me
Everyone around use were put in jeopardy
My friend abandoned me and asked me to move
We only got tighter, in our own lovely groove
You gave me your love, so sweet, so completely
I didn't know I was your first, my love you needed
You cried out in pain, in pleasure, too
You said goodbye, and you thought we were through
I wanted to assure you that my love was seal

Willie Means Well

In Vegas, we brought closure to the deal

I really cannot remember **which** bowling league I was in when I turned from getting a strike and she was standing there watching me. *'Seven Year Itch'* by Rose Ann Cash is currently playing on the radio. This song, like others, *"Waiting for a Girl like You,"* and *"Can I see You tonight,"* and *"Sea of Love,"* and when trouble came so boldly to us, *"Trouble"* by Lindsey Buckingham. It wrapped Jennifer and I in their lyrics, music, and supported us through the very turbulent time of *Fall League 1981 in Beacon Bowl,* formerly in Barstow. Hazelnut and I mail each other sometimes and she tells me her sister Peggy gave up the bowling alley a long time ago.

That first night I saw her, I walked back and spoke and she told me, *"I've been watching you and you're good."* Made me feel good and I told her thank you. That probably was the league George and Billy, my roommates, we all bowled in together on the same team. They were White and I, being Black, wanted to talk to Jennifer but they each showed an interest so I stayed in the background while they both had dates with her. Jennifer was beautiful, but like I said, she was only eighteen and just out of a Catholic Girl School. Jennifer was, as a former female soldier of mine, *Tracy Spiva, Kohler*, funny story about her becoming a Kohler. Tracy Spiva married Tracy Kohler and they became Kohler and Kohler. Broke poor *Richard's* heart, another soldier of mine. Perhaps I will get to these soldiers when I do *'once a Soldier'*. Tracy said their hair was what you called *'Dishwater Blond!'* Jennifer had hazel eyes, so my special name, *Hazelnut*. She uses to laugh when I called her Hazelnut but I could tell she loved it. I in my own way really loved her. Since I have found her again and explained to her that I used to expect someone to try to hurt me over her, she said it surprised her that I felt that way. I told her of the *Military Police Investigator (MPI)* who use to ride with us home from post who told me how he use to ride with a biker gang who would definitely had hurt me for messing with her. I cannot remember his name now but I remember I heard distain in his voice as he told me. I knew he was telling the truth and with Barstow being an old hangout for numerous biker gangs, I started watching all around me when I would give him a ride. Jennifer was mine and at that time, I really expected someone to take me away from her. I use to stop off in the desert on the way home and have Jennifer fire off a clip of ammo so she would get use to the weapon we had. I taught her exactly what to do if I left that apartment and did not return when I told her I would. I remember one particular evening when the assistant Public Affairs Director, Marsha Polk, who also lived in the same complex, called me over to go over a project. I left Jennifer cooking dinner and told her what time I would be back. I do not know if Marsha just wanted some company because we went over the project but she kept going over the same thing from different angles. There was a knock on the door and when Marsha opened the door, it was Jennifer. Marsha started shouting at Jennifer how she knew I was her husband and she was not going to eat me, and she just did not appreciate her coming to get me as if I couldn't go anywhere. All the time Jennifer kept telling Marsha how sorry she was but she did not want my dinner to get cold. Finally, Marsha told her *"Just take him! My goodness, act like I'm gone eat the man up!"* I did not say anything but followed Jennifer home. When we got in the apartment, I followed her into the bedroom, and she took the weapon out her pocket, dropped the clip, ejected the round out the chamber, returned the round to the clip, replaced the clip, then placed the weapon back on the nightstand and put a towel over it. She turned, look at me, I told her *"Very good Jen,"* and we had our dinner.

    Billy dated Jennifer first and told us she was a nice lady but he wanted this soldier named Laura, which he got while she was drunk and tried to get Billy in trouble. George took Jennifer out and was back at the house the three of us shared in less than an hour. George asked Billy did he know Jennifer was a virgin and told Billy she was not going to be being stuck on him. I told them both they were being ridiculous and Jennifer was a nice lady. They both told me then I could have her. I was bowling four

Willie Means Well

leagues during this time and I must say California was the peak of my bowling days. I would have loved to get Jennifer to come to Columbus; we would have won all kinds of tournaments. She could have showed the ladies what bowling was about. I really expected to see her on the *Ladies Professional Bowling Tour (LPBT)* someday. I use to keep up with the tournaments and browse the bowling sites looking for her name. She told me she had moved back to Barstow in 1986 after our divorce but bowling was never fun for her anymore.

    When Jennifer and I started seeing each other, we did not realize it brought trouble to Peggy at the bowling alley. My Company Commander called me in the office and yelled at me, *"God damn it means! What is wrong with you and Marzec? I just got him out of trouble messing with that Spanish woman in Barstow and now I got people calling my house at night and telling me they're going to put you down one of those mines in the desert if you don't leave some White girl alone. What is this? Do I have to have you guys move back on post?"* The Captain was serious and this would probably have ended the relationship because Fort Irwin is thirty-eight miles in the desert from Barstow. By now things had heated up and Jennifer and I had ran off to Las Vegas and gotten married and did not tell anyone. A week prior to us running off to Vegas, we had finally had sex and she told me *"I know I probably won't see you again now that you've gotten what you want from me."* I looked at her and realize she was for real. I asked her did she think her car could make it to Vegas and she looked at me and told me yes. I told her that Friday when we got off work we were going to go to Vegas and get married. She said ok but I could see she still did not believe me. We did the Vegas thing at the *Circus, Circus Hotel at the Chapel of the Fountain* December 11. We returned to Barstow, she dropped me off at the house with George, and Billy and she returned to her Sister Peggy. That Saturday morning she came and got me and we stayed the entire day together. At eight that evening, my friend Elizabeth with her friend Laura, who Billy wanted, came to the house. George's lady friend had come down from Fort Ord and Jennifer and I got up and went into the bedroom. Liz and I had spent some serious time together since we both had been stationed there in September 1980. As a matter of fact, I think she was number 95 and I was number 96 to be stationed there. From the beginning, we did everything together except have sex. If you looked up in the evening time and saw one of us, you probably saw us both. I will tell you about Liz and me in the next chapter.

Liz, Billy, and Laura were drinking *'Salty Dogs'*. I heard Liz when she asked Billy, *"What's Willie doing with that girl over here?"* I could not hear Billy's reply but after about five minutes, I heard Billy yell out, *"Liz! What you doing with that gun?"* I heard the front door open, and then *"POW! POW!"* The casings from the rounds hit the window to the bedroom Jennifer and I were in and Jennifer grabbed me and stated, *"My goodness, Bilbo! She's shooting at me?"* I told Jennifer to remain in the bedroom and George and I both came out the bedrooms at the same time. Poor Billy, who had been shot before when one of his friends back in Indiana accidently shot him in the leg, was standing by the kitchen door, as he was ready to run. George took the gun from Liz and I just looked at her and went back into the bedroom. I could hear Liz crying and Laura telling the guys that she was sorry and would drive Liz back to post. Because Liz and I use to hang out, everybody thought we were dating. However, Liz could not take the talk and pressure when they started calling us *"Salt and Pepper."* She started seeing this White guy and this of course broke my heart. Jennifer and I still did not tell them we were married and we also spent Sunday together. Monday morning, everything came to a head.

    Peggy called me while I was sitting at my desk laughing with the editor, Eugenia *'Goldie'* Dawkins, Sergeant Norm Bothun, Specialist Kohler, and Private First Class *(Pfc)* Richard Milhouse Saunders. We were doing our version of *'Quill and Stroll'* before getting ready to layout *'The Combined Arms Monitor'* our first newspaper after reopening Fort Irwin. Peggy was always soft spoken and she always used my bowling name, *'Bilbo'*.

"Bilbo, you, and Jen have got to break this thing off. Bilbo, I'm not prejudiced and I would love to have you as my brother-in-law but Dale has shown me a side of him I didn't know. Dale talks to the guys in the bar at the bowling alley and Bilbo he said they're talking about hurting you. Bilbo, I don't think this thing is worth you getting hurt over."

My reply was, *"Peggy, we're married."*

"Bilbo, if you tell Jen--what did you just say."

"Peggy, we're married."

I heard a very soft audible *"Oh!"* and then Dale got on the phone.

"Now Bilbo, that's just totally irresponsible of you. Why would you go and do something like that?"

"Dale, we are not asking any of you for anything. Just leave us alone. I'm sure my command will help me get what I need so I can take care of Jennifer."

Peggy got back on the phone. "Oh Bilbo! How am I going to tell my Mom and Dad? Jennifer came down here and I am responsible for her. Well let me *call Jen and your first stop is here when you two get off work today."*

Monday was really busy. I went by to see this Captain at *'AER' (Army Emergency Relief)* and he told me I couldn't get any special treatment I would have to fill out some forms and wait my turn to get help. I told him thank you but decided to see just how much the *'Higher-up'* I had helped would take a step to help me. I started with Lieutenant Colonel *(LTC)* Filbert, Director of Personnel, and Community Activities *(DPCA)*. After I called Forces Command *(FORSCOM)* that night and talked to Colonel David, *Chief Public Affairs Forces Command,* they had LTC. Filbert in charge of me until they could get a Public Affairs Officer in place for Fort Irwin. Everybody was already jumping around trying not to upset me because Colonel David had talked to Brigadere General *(BG)* Bramlett, the Post Commander, and General Bramlett had told them to give me what I needed to do my job and get Fort Irwin up in the local news. With LTC Filbert to run *interference* for me, I stayed at the radio and television stations in Barstow. I enjoyed working for LTC Filbert and then one day he asked me to write a story and told me how the story should go. His desk stayed covered with paperwork because after Colonel Zimmerman, it was LTC Filbert's people that kept that Post operating. That day, I took all the information he gave me and returned to my office. I went over that information numerous times and I could not write the lie I had been told to write. I finally went back to LTC Filbert and told him I would not write the story. He simply looked up at me, by the way, they all had combat time in Vietnam, leaned back in his chair and stared at me. I looked down and mumbled to him that it was not the truth. He let out a sigh of frustration and told me, *"It's ok Sergeant Means, I understand. Just return the information to me and I'll write the story myself."* I stood looking at him and told him I was sorry. He repeated again that he was sorry. Then he said, *"Sergeant Means, I know you be busy. These other folks don't really understand Public Affairs. I know you have a million things to be done, but I have five million to be done. However, you're ok. Bring it to me."*

I returned to my office and less than an hour later, I returned with the story done. I handed the story to him and returned to my office. He called me on the phone later and told me the Chief-of-Staff to him to tell me it was a good story and to keep up the good work. When word got around that Sergeant Means had run off to Las Vegas and got married, I found out later that LTC Filbert had cleared it with the Chief-of-Staff to provide me with whatever help I needed to be settled down with my wife. I was allowed to live in emergency quarters, which was at the Holiday Inn, until we were able to get our own place out near Barstow Community College. Jennifer and I had settled down in our room at the Holiday Inn but Peggy allowed us to stay in her house over Christmas. The family returned home for the holiday but Jennifer was asked not to come because the family had to go over the fact the she had married a Black man. I will tell you that I was not called *'Mean Sergeant Means'* for nothing. I knew my job as a Sergeant E-5 but what so many did not understand, I might have only been an E-5, but I held a position that was on the Commander's Special Staff. That made the General's door open to me at any time. I must admit that I used my position to get back at some NCOs that out ranked me. I even got back at a few field-grade level officers who antagonized me until I called Colonel David. However, I caught Jennifer crying when she realized she could not go home for Christmas. You must remember, she was only 18 and her father absolutely loved her and she loved him. When I seen how much it meant to her not to be with her family, I made myself available to her every disposal. I remember hearing it from so many females that they wish their husbands would take a page out of my notebook. I was far from being a wimp but I loved Jennifer and I wanted her to see I was there for her. That song by Bertie Higgins, *'Key Largo'*, really explained that first winter, comes to think of it, our only winter together. We married December 11, 1981 and I was sent to Korea in September 1982. She refused to join me in my assignment that had been changed from Fort Myers, Virginia to Fort Benning, Georgia. Her sister told her she had word from a friend that they were not supposed to send mixed couples to the South. Her sister's friend was a Marine and I believe The Marines really try to accommodate Marines who get into such situation. Our divorce was granted June 29, 1985. So you see, out of four years of knowing each other, and being married for three of those four years, we only spent a little more than a year together.

When Peggy and her family returned from Oregon the day after Christmas, she made the statement, *"Bilbo, I don't know how you're going to get the time off but you and Jenny need to be at Mom and Dad for New Year's Eve."* I looked at Peggy, and said, *"I'll see what I can do." What's going on?*

"Mom and Dad want you guys there so you can meet the family and Jenny can stand in front of them and tell them that she loves you."

My boss, Major Mike Williams, was a total jerk when he came aboard as Public Affairs Officer. As he explained to me, I knew how to be an NCO but I did not know how to be a Public Affairs Supervisor. The Major gave me a *'69'* on my first *'Enlistment Evaluation Report (EER),* when as a Sergeant E-5 I was not supposed to get under *'121'*. He picked up a lot of dissension from the Senior Officers and NCOs that knew me. I was advised not to sign it but go back to my old *MOS (Military Occupational Specialty)* with one of the *Line Units*. I gave that all of two seconds thoughts. I did those three years in Artillery and that was enough field duty to last me a lifetime. I decided to stick it out and since he was getting so much dissension, he raised the score to a *'74'* and acted as if he was doing me a great favor. I believe he had something to do with the information getting out about Mein Li and he told me a general told him he would not make another grade. If I recall correctly, he turned down another assignment and did retire a major. When Sergeant Norm Bothun came aboard and I explained what the Major had done, Norm's mouth dropped open and he told me I was lying.

"Willie, you lying to me! You mean to tell me

that low-life son-of-a-bitch didn't max you out on your 'EER'?

"Norm, the major said I had a lot of people happy with what I was doing before he got here, but they don't know anything about Public Affairs."

Norm jumped up, grabbed his hat, and walked out the door. Tracy was looking at me and told me she was glad the son-of-a-bitch didn't do her evaluation.

I could hear Norm when he walked in the major's office and told him he needed to talk to him about '*Willie*'. I heard him very clearly, when he told the major, *"We're all under a hardship stationed out here in this desert, and everywhere I go everybody tells me Willie did an excellent job with the Public Affairs when he was by himself. Now Willie tells me you gave him a low EER.*

I could hear them mumbling back and forth through the wall then the major called me around.

The short of it was Norm pointed out to him what a great job I was doing as *'sports' editor'* and other stuff beyond my job with the newspaper. The major put in a special *'EER'* on me and raised it to *'121'*. The *'Chief-of-Staff'* called me over and told me he had heard what the major did but they were going to try to find another *'PAO'*.

Major Mike William really was a burned out individual. He repeatedly made comments about things I had done, which showed he was on top of what went on in the *Public Affairs*. What he did not know, however, was my influence on events that took place with the staff. Richard Saunders received a *'Fourth Estate Award'* for a photo he shot of a tanker truck and a helicopter that looked like it was some type of new machine. I pointed the shot out to Richard, told him how to shoot it, and told him he would get an award for it because *FORSCOM* was looking for things to put Fort Irwin in the eyes of the rest of the military. Eugenia *'Goldie'* Dawkins would change words in my copy and the Major never failed to jump on me and tell me I was *editorializing* in my writing. I would look at *Goldie* and she would look away. Norm would later ask me had she done it again and I would tell him yes. However, the Major did step up and told me to go ahead to Oregon and he would fix it for me. I even recall the major laughing and joking at the little get-to-gather they gave me and Tracy presented Jennifer and me with a *Crock Pot*. I remember the major looking at me and saying *"Now Willie. You really don't expect to find a Crock Pot in that box, do you?"* It was moments like that when I could see he probably was a good officer before that shit in Vietnam messed up his career. That crap at *Mien Li* probably messed up many people.

Jennifer and I were at her parents in Hillsboro, Oregon for New Years Eve. Dad was a Veteran of World War II and I really enjoyed getting to know him. Dad had a heart attack while I was in Korea but he recovered enough to live again. I came home on emergency leave to be with Jennifer while he was in the hospital. I even went through the procedure and had been given a *Compassionate Reassignment* so I could be close to give support to Jennifer and the family. This was after I had already done seven months of a thirteen months assignment. I was going to be assigned to Fort Lewis, Washington which was about three hours driving time from Hillsboro. I was happy until the sergeant told me when I came down on *levy* I would be headed back to Korea. Korea was not bad once I got use to it, but at that time, I told Jennifer I would rather go back and complete the assignment rather than be separated all over again.

I look back at those times with fond memories. I do not believe many would have tolerated those times. I actually enjoyed the short time I had with Jennifer's Mom and Dad, although I was afraid of Mom, for a couple of weeks in January and again in late August and early September before heading to Korea. While there in January, I met the oldest female of the family clan and I swear it was like being in an old movie. I am so sorry I cannot remember her name now but when I was introduced to her, she sat in a chair in all black attire, to include a veil over her face, and she pointed to a small stool for me to set on in front of her. I remember Mom and Dad giving me this pleading look and Jennifer being so nervous. I probably could have told them not to worry because my Mother had taught me to be respectful to my elders regardless to their race. Would you believe I lost track of time I was enjoying the conversation we were having so much. Finally, she held out her, black, laced covered right hand for me to kiss, and I could see she was smiling under the veil, and she made the statement, *"There's room for you in this family bill."* To this day, I wonder if they had some kind of room monitor where we were sitting and downstairs. As soon as we finished talking, everyone came upstairs and began to shake my hands and present Jennifer and me with gifts. That is when I was told the family had made money in the lumber business in Washington State. If I have not told you before now, I was given a book on beginning flying because I had to learn how to fly. I was given a book on boating, because I had to learn how to drive a boat. In addition, from my understanding, they had a yacht that was not very small.

    Jennifer and I were snowed in but I really enjoyed the time with her. I have to meet two of her partners in crime, who also was a couple, *Kirsten and Don.* I later told Jennifer I felt a little uncomfortable because they seemed younger than being eighteen. Kirsten had been in the Catholic Girl School with Jennifer and Don had attended the male counterpart Catholic Boys School.

    I think we had been their almost two weeks when the weather broke. We told Mom and Dad we were going to make the break back to Barstow. Coming up, we came through the *Shasta's and the Siskiqous Mountains.* I Prayed to God that if he let me get back across those Mountains, I would never be caught in those Mountains during wintertime again. Jen and I traveled that same route in late August of '82 on my way to Korea. You talk about two areas and scenery different as night and day, and that was travel *Interstate five* going from Northern California into Southern Oregon. I am sure, given the opportunity to acclimate to the area, you would never want to live anywhere else. The area is beautiful.

    Jennifer was an obedient child and I am sure at

times, she probably called me a devil. Dad had given her some money for us to dine on and get sleeping accommodations for the night while we were on our return trip. As the day grew into evening and I kept driving, she began to squirm and wanted to know where we were going to spend the night. When I told her I intended to keep going until we got home to Barstow, she became a little irate and began to tell me Dad had given her the money for us to relax and enjoy our evening together off the road. When she told me about the money that only reinforced my desire to keep going. Whatever money she had, could be used for any emergency that might be waiting for us when we got home.

    Jen and I made it back to Barstow and we both slept the day in when we returned. The atmosphere was so much better with the family now. Peggy and the girls came by and invited us to dinner that evening and I will always remember Dale shaking my hand and apologizing for the 'WHOLE MESS' people had put us through. I appreciated his change of heart and since he was a teacher at the college, he was able to get Jen and I back in school. Jen and I had an English class together and on a couple of occasion while doing homework, I caught her crying over stories that ended sadly. That is why I wanted to reach out, take her in my arms, and protect her from everything. She was my *'Child-Bride'* and still so innocent about life. She shared a piece with me she had done on abortion as a senior at the Catholic School. She read it to me as a song titled *"Music Box Dancer"* played on the radio. Over the years when I have heard this song, I can see Jen and I sitting in our living room and she reading to me.

    I do not know if Jen ever talked about it with any of her family members. However, I took her with me when the Army returned me to Fort Benjamin Harrison, Indiana for photography school before sending me to Korea. Since I did not have orders allowing Jen to accompany me to school, I had to find a place for us to stay when I got there. I called my Mother in Chicago and Mother said she would be glad to have Jen stay with her while I got things settled in Indiana. What I want to share with you, is,

Mother told me the first day she had Jen go to the store with her, which was right across the street from where Mother lived, two guys got to fighting and one of the guys killed the other guy in front of the store while they were all looking through the door at the store. Momma said another guy approached Jen and tried to talk to her at that same store but Momma said she told the guy Jen was her daughter-in-law. Momma said the guy made a comment about Jen being White but then said *"Yes Ma, am! And she is a pretty little lady."*

    I will bet it never crossed Momma's mind about any of those guys turning on her. Momma's *'Faith'* in the LORD JESUS saw us through many dangerous situations.

    Jen really enjoyed her time at Fort Benjamin Harrison. It really was not so bad for me either. I learned to do some really neat things with the *Canon F-5 Camera.* Over the years I have said many times *"the camera does not lie!"* On top of learning to be a real photographer, the journalists learned to do everything from load the camera, take the photo, process the film, print and develop the picture. Learned some neat stuff to do while the lens of the camera was open. I spent a lot of time with Jen because I felt she missed her sister Peggi and her nieces Dina and Sara. Jen and I had only a short time together of the nearly four years we were married but I really learned to love Peggi and her girls. Jen, Dina and I were playing tennis at the college one afternoon and because of my track and field days; I took them both on in a game of doubles. Dina was only thirteen but she knew more of the game than Jen and Dina kept hitting shots that should had set up winners for them. After running down shot-after-shot, Dina finally tossed her racket in the air and yelled, *"HOW IS HE GETTING TO ALL THOSE SHOTS!"* I could not help but laugh. At that time I would had been twenty-six. I was so deep into track and field that my body remembered the discipline from training and I always put my best into everything. I really thought Jen and I would be together for years but being separated got me one of those *"Dear John Letters"* when I only had twenty days left in Korea in August of 1983. I have always felt had I housing on the base I was stationed at and gotten the opportunity to get Jen familiar with the Army, we would had made it. I might have said it earlier, but the break eventually sent me to the hospital with a nervous breakdown. When I found Jen again in 2010 and told her of some of the things that I went through, I could hear the sincerity in her voice when she said no one had the right to keep information from her about what had happened to me. It really made me feel good to know that she cared.

ELIZABETH
My dear...

Elizabeth, my dear! My dear friend
I shall walk the Earth and search to the end
Elizabeth, my lover
There shall never be another
Elizabeth, my Woman
So much the child, we held hands
Elizabeth, we had our world
There was no room for another girl
Elizabeth, in the desert we met
You looked upon me and knew I was a wreck
Elizabeth, from Germany you came
Your love you left behind, I asked you his name
Elizabeth, you asked me of my life
You said you knew I had a wife
Elizabeth, you told me I was lying
You had saw me and I was crying
Elizabeth, we came together
You and I became one
Elizabeth! When we walk this Earth no more

Willie Means Well

I shall turn down Heaven, and meet you in Limbo

I was sitting outside the front door to the barracks when Liz got out of her car and walked up with her arms wrapped around a box of personals that she was moving into the barracks. Wanting to be a gentleman, when she got close enough, I asked if she needed some help.

"Good afternoon. Need any help with your stuff?" I asked as she walked up.

"No, I think I got this, but you should can have been a help yesterday," she responded.

Not wanting to impose, I sat back down and began to think of a way to get into town to get to the bowling alley. My assignment to Fort Irwin, California was nothing new to millions of other military personnel and their family members. However, unfortunately for me, this assignment had me 38 miles out in the *Mojave Desert* away from the city of Barstow. I do not know how true it was, but word was, measurement only listed Fort Irwin as being 35 miles away because the Army had the *Military Police (MP) Gate* set three miles out from the Cantonment area and that put Fort Irwin within the City Limits of Barstow. By doing this, Fort Irwin would not be considered a *'Hardship Tour of Duty'* thereby eliminating the need to pay us hardship pay. (*Now that would be dirty, wouldn't it?*)

Fort Irwin was my second permanent duty assignment after coming into the Army. It was my first in the Public Affairs Field. My first assignment I was a *"Fire Direction Specialist"* in Artillery. I was stationed in Friedberg, West Germany and hopefully I will someday do a book about my experience over there. Anyway, since coming into the Army in March 1977, the first thing I would do when I went on pass or had some free time, I would find the bowling alley. I knew Barstow had to have one because during the '70s, Bowling was the number one family recreation activity. In addition, I had looked in the phone book and saw the name of the bowling alley was *"Beacon Bowl"-(had no idea at the time that I would meet my first wife there).* After sitting and watching Liz carry several loads from her car into the barracks, she surprised me on her last load when she stopped and began to talk to me.

"Hey, when I get done with this, I'm going to go over and hit some racquetball. You want to come along?"

"Sure, I don't know too much about the game but I would be glad to cheer you on."

"That's interesting! Well, let me change and I'll be right back."- (so interesting; I have been using "That's Interesting" since I became a student of Psychology in '94. I have looked for Ms. Elizabeth 'Ann' Vereen since finally getting myself back together after leaving the Army in March 1985. Using that phrase all these years, I now realize she has been with me all these years. Liz was a 'Behavior Science Specialist', which is the Army's field of Psychology Studies).

Liz came back in some shorts and we hopped in her car and went to the courts, which were inside. She got two rackets out the trunk of the car and was handing me one when I told her, *"hey, I said I would watch and cheer you on. I really can't play because I have a bad right knee."*

"Oh, well I'm sorry. I'm just going to hit a few then ride into town to get something to eat. You want to come.

That was the beginning of a really wonderful year. As a matter of fact, many thought Liz and I were going to do what many of the soldiers were doing out there; running off to Victorville and getting married. Liz and I actually did get closer-than-close but so much talk sprung up around us that I believe she could not stand the pressure.

California is WIDE OPEN! California might as well be another country instead of another state. Elizabeth was the 95th person to be assigned to Fort Irwin when they reopened the Post to make it *"The National Training Center-NTC"*. I was the 96th person to be assigned to the Post. However, I really was in the first fifty to be assigned there but I tried to get out of the assignment. When school was almost over at Fort Benjamin Harrison, everybody was getting their assignments. When I opened my assignment, I spoke aloud, *"this is not Fort Ord. This is some place called Fort Irwin."* Two Army

E-7s (Sergeant First Class) heard both and I asked at the same time, *"Where did you say, Young Buck Sergeant?"*

"Some place called Fort Irwin."

"Whoa, Sarge; you don't want to go out there. Let's go over to the 'MOS' Library and we will show you where you're going on a map."

We got to the MOS Library and pulled a map of California out. Right there, close to Nevada, and ten miles from *"Death Valley"*, was Fort Irwin. The place was in the *Mojave Desert*.

"See what we mean Young Buck?"

"My goodness, it's out in the desert."

"You're pretty damn observant Sarge. They us to use that post as a jump off place for soldiers headed to Vietnam. General Patton also trained his Armour Units out there during World War II."

I should have been in California by the first week in July. Between hurting my right knee again and other stuff, I did not leave for California until the second week into September. I remember Sergeant First Class Haddock in Branch at the *Pentagon*,

Willie Means Well

called me at school and begged me to take the assignment.

"I Will Be Back!"

Willie Means Well

SUNDAY

November 20, 2011

Wanted to take a moment and share something about my son Bobby. I have shared information on him before. He is my youngest child. Therefore, even though he is 21, he is still my Baby Boy. I look back on Bobby's school years and he being ADHD. *I recall things happening to him and the dumb look on teachers and others faces as if they haven't a clue what happened to him. I guess I can chalk it up to my Army discipline training that I am sitting here writing this book instead of being in prison for getting back at the ones who have hurt my son over the years. Bobby has always tried to be friend to everybody and so many times, I have seen children laughing behind his back. I guess once again I am the blame because I raised both boys to be gentlemen and not take part in the trend of wearing their pants hanging off their butts or walking around swearing in public and doing other indecent stuff to get attention. Bobby confided in me that he would like to* have his own place. *I told him that was great and he needs to show me how serious he was by showing me he could get his drivers' license. I don't know what I was doing but when I came back in the house, Bobby was in the process of cooking him some hamburgers. It made me feel so good to see him cooking and he was cooking with confidence. I asked a few questions and he gave me the right answers. I told him to try not and get smoke in the house because the fan is out on the jen-air. He fixed him two double hamburgers, got him some chips and returned upstairs to watch football. I don't know what the future holds for me but I have to get a family business going to secure my son the rest of his life. The way things are going currently; don't look like we'll be able to get him in Columbus Technical College in January. Bobby is really smart when it comes to computers and electronic games. My goal is to get him certified in some field that deals with 'software'. He is also good in mimicking broadcasting sporting events. I love my children and grandchildren but for some reason people always want to say nasty things to me about*

Bobby. *Every time I turn around, somebody is trying to tell me that I should let him get out there and be with the other young adults. I would love to see such a thing happen but as I have said, He tries to befriend everyone and they only seem to want to take advantage of him. If all goes well, I will have a program titled "Just a Chance" that will cater to children and adolescent everywhere that gives them a chance to grow up and learn of life and society at a pace that will allow them to fit in when the proper time comes.*

Willie Means Well

ELIZABETH

Ms. Elizabeth Ann Vereen and I, Ann to everyone, but I called her Liz. In addition, I believe it was my calling her Liz that rather opened the door for us to spend so much time with each other. I would call her *'Lizzy Ann'* and she would tell me her Mother called her that. Liz and got together and went to a local disco called *"Rossetas'"*, named after the wife of the guy who owned the place. Rossetas was a disco and eatery. The main course was Spanish Food Stuff. Our **first outing** there was pretty low key. We had dinner then decided to check out the disco and see what kind of place it was. The two dominant races in Barstow were Whites and Hispanics. There was Blacks but they were greatly outnumbered. As a matter of fact, do not know if I mentioned it with *'Hazelnut'*, but I actually had the klu Klux Klan gets involved with my dating Jen. It got so even the families we bowled with intervened into their daughters seeing my roommates and me. I remember one very pretty, petite blond name *Kim Sick* who was absolutely gorgeous. I missed the last bus back to Fort Irwin one bowling night and everybody I called had an excuse why they could not come and get me. I had forty some dollars in my pocket but there was no such thing as a taxi service that was reliable out there. It was after eleven when I struck out to walking and I figured between walking and jogging, I could get to post by '*PT*' time. I told myself it was only 38 miles and I was in great shape. I had made it maybe three miles from the bowling alley and was just getting ready to go across the bridge over the dry riverbed that led into Barstow when a car passed and I thought it was Kim. She blew the horn and then I saw her brakes lights come on and she backed up, rolled the window down, and asked me where I was headed. I explained to her about missing the last bus and could not get anybody to come and get me so I had no choice but to walk. Kim looked at me and told me I had to be joking. I told her there were too many '*Higher Ups*' who would love me to miss Morning Formation and would try to take my rank away. She looked at me and told me had she the gas, she would give me a ride. I told her I had the forty dollars and she told me we would put it in the tank and she would take me to post. I just looked at her.

"What's wrong Bilbo? I don't want you to get in trouble, this is my car, and Mike, her husband who was in and out of their marriage, wouldn't mind me giving you a ride. Besides, we could use the gas."

I got in, she turned around, and we went and got gas. That was during early *'81* and everybody in *Beacon Bowl* really was like family. I think I was bowling three or four leagues and had bowling the next night. When I walked in, I could not believe the number of people telling me they were so glad I had got back to post all right and had not gotten into trouble. When Kim and Mike came in, before he got his bowling shoes, he came up to me and told me thanks for the gas. I'm looking at him to see if he was serious when here comes Susan and Gordon Beal, two more bowlers, and telling me next time don't do anything stupid like that call them and they would give me a ride. As I was standing with my mouth open, Susan told me to shut it or was I trying to get a kiss. That is when I realized those people took their bowling serious and once they have to know you, they would do anything for you if they could. I do not exaggerate when I say Kim reminded me of the girl the group *'Hot Chocolate'* sing about in their song *"Emmaline"* that was out in *'74 or 75'*. Later that year when I met Jen and this fat, ass Staff Sergeant named Chuck Stewart, was spreading racism and poison about Blacks and Whites dating, the bowling crowd kept their daughters away from my two roommates because they did not want them possibly getting involved in the situation we were all going through. After Stewart used his influence with Haddock in *Branch* to get me sent to Korea, my sister-in-law, Peggy told Jen and I how he had sat in the bar at the bowling alley and bragged on what he had done. Peggy said Stewart made the statement that maybe her sister would get her mind back while I was gone. We later found out that Stewart was a practicing member in the klu Klux Klan. I heard he suffered later after being put out the Army but I sure would have liked to have had him one-on-one for a while.

Willie Means Well

THANKSGIVINGS
(2011)

However, I am getting ahead of *November 22!* The date is a *'Black'* date in our History because it is the day our government killed our own President. I have always believed that this Country would never had gotten into that squabble with Vietnam had President Kennedy remained alive. President Kennedy was a military man, a religious/righteous man, and a President this Country believed in. It is so sad that just because he decided to do something about the way Minorities, especially Blacks, were being treated in the Country, they got rid of him. The rich, rich will always panic when someone comes along and try to give the Poor a taste of real meat and potatoes. That is what is going on now with this current administration. I know there is a better way for healthcare in this Country but still the President is trying. I still say it is time for people to start taking up residency in those nice quarters under *CIA Headquarters!*

Willie Means Well

Elizabeth and I began to hang out together all the time. Every Friday and Saturday night, we were at Rosettas'. During the weekday evenings, she and a young lady name Carmen had begin to come and get me to jog with them in the evening time and they took great pleasure in running me until we had done at least five miles. Looking back, it is amazing how those miles seem to float under your feet when you are having fun. In addition, have fun we did. Being trained to run and sing cadence really prepares you to run and have a conversation. Those two had some glorious conversations and every so often they would throw in some *'girl talk'* to see how I would respond to it. They both worked in *'Army Community Services' (ACS)* Captain Johnson with a couple of *LTC's* wives who volunteered. Lieutenant Colonel Filbert wife being one of them.

    Liz being White and my being Black did not sit well with many but because of our positions and who we worked for, it was very seldom that anyone would outwardly show their feelings about the two of us spending time together. I did not really care at that time because I had just enough of the streets of Chicago in me to get in anybody's face. I knew my rank and that I was on the *'Commander's Special Staff'*, but those *'SF' Types* who had trained me Germany, had me believing that I could seriously take a person down in three blows. Could probably do it today but old age would make it nasty and not a clean thing.

Liz had to go *TDY* to Fort Rod and she would be gone 30 days. I had been on field assignment for Brigadier General Bramlett, the post commandeer, when every office I went to, I got the word, *"Specialist Vereen is trying to get in touch with you!"* I went over to *ACS* and Carmen pulled me into her office.

"Ann told me if I see you to tell you that she is lonely. I know you guys go dancing together because she can't wait to tell me when she gets back. But I thought maybe we could keep running and maybe have a few drinks together while she was gone."

*"You know what Carmen? Everybody thinks Liz and I are girlfriend and boyfriend but we are just

Willie Means Well

friends. The guy in the Chow Hall asked us if we thought we were salt and pepper. Liz told him to mind his own damn business. He started to get smart but I told him we could take it up with his NCO. I admit I miss her but she knows how to call the Public Affairs Office."

"Well she gave me the number and told me to give it to you and she really wants to hear your voice."

I returned to the *PAO, locked up,* and found the newsroom empty. I called Liz and had to leave word for her that Sergeant Means from Fort Irwin had called. Time passed while I was sort out my information to do a news story on my field interviews. I looked up, it was almost six o'clock, and I realized I was about to Miss Chow. I was in the process of turning the lights out when the telephone on my desk rang.

"Public Affairs, this line is unsecured, Sergeant Means speaking."

"Willie?"

"Hello Liz. How are you?"

"Willie, I'm lonely."

That is the way the conversation began and it was almost seven o'clock when we hung up. That was on a Wednesday and Liz and I made plans for me to come up and see her that weekend. I was broke but Liz told me she would pay for a round trip ticket I just had to get to the bus station and get on the bus. I explained to this guy named Terry what I was going to do and he told me he would give me a ride to the bus station. I got word that Stewart and Terry decided I did not need to be bothering Liz while she was *TDY*. Would you believe the son-of-bitch left me? I do not remember how I got into Barstow to get the bus but I did. I always tell people California might as well be another country instead of a state. The ride on the bus was 12 hours and then I had to call this number posted for rides on Fort Ord. I got me a room at the guest quarters then got me something to eat at a snack bar. I was tired and was trying to stay awake incase Liz showed up. I wonder had I made a mistake by coming. I dozed off then I heard a light knocking on my door and she called my

Willie Means Well

name. I opened the door but she would not come in. We hugged and she told me to come on we were going to barn fire down on the beach. We got to the beach then I realized Liz had made other plans because there were several girls and guys there and this one guy kept focusing on Liz. I finally told her I was going to find my way back to post and would catch the bus out the next morning. Some blond came over and asked Liz to introduce me. Damn lady was a captain. Then I found out all of them were officers except Liz and me. When I realized that, I told them I was tired from the bus ride, was going back, and get some sleep. Liz told me I was not taking a taxi and that she would give me a ride back to post. Looking back on that event, I should have known then that Liz was selfish. We rode back to my quarters in silence and she did not even come in. She did tell me she would be to get me for breakfast in the morning. I really did not care. I had planned to be out at first light and at the bus station to return to Fort Irwin. Even today, I tell people at times that Chicago side comes up in me and I do not give too much about anything then except what I want to do and feel is right. When Jen and I moved into our apartment in Barstow and those people started giving me trouble about Jennifer, when I was fed up with it, I told the *Military Police Investigators* they did not have to do anything. I was going to stop on the way home and get my gun out the shop and was going to knock anybody who came bullshitting around my door over the balcony. While still living with George and Billy when Jen and I were dating, Billy came in one evening and caught me on the phone with some friends from Chicago offering to pay for them to come out and help me clean up the situation I was having for dating a White girl. Billy went to screaming at me on the phone not to do that and to hang the phone up. It was all over post the next day but it made people leave me along for a while.

    I really felt like a fool for going all the way up there and then telling myself that I really did not know Liz as if I should anyway. Every damn body and their brothers and sisters thought we were sleeping together because we were together all the time. What they did not, was Liz had left a lover name *'Mills'* back in Germany and I had left *Mary* back at Fort Benjamin Harrison and Liz and I pulled together to comfort each other but I guess it got deeper than what we wanted it to be. Liz outsmarted me the next morning and got there when I was checking out. I told her she could go back to her friends but she was very much the Liz I had come to visit and keep company this morning and after she cried all over me and begged me not to leave yet, we got in her car and she drove us to *'Fisherman's Wharf'*.

MONDAY
November 28, 2011

Good morning, raining out this morning. We even have a promise of some snow by Tuesday morning. Really did not intend to write this morning but must take advantage of the feeling when it hits me. (I swear, lately, this computer is talking to me more and more. Probably wants me to get back to the unexplainable.)

Fisherman's' Wharf was cold and very damp the morning Liz and I went there. She could tell from my silence I still was dwelling on the night before. I recalled minding some of my friends from Germany telling me of the cold mornings at Fort Ord. They swore that sometimes in Jun they would have to wear *field jackets* to Formation because it would be so cold. The fog was still on the shore when we arrived at *Fisherman's' Wharf.* Liz and I were the only customers and the guy really brought us a nice breakfast. However, as *B.B. King sings in his song,* "*The Thrill Is Gone!*" Liz could tell my heart was

Willie Means Well

not there anymore.

"You know Liz, I really care for you, but there are times when you can do some really crazy things. You know that hanging out with officers is fraternization but I know you being here you got to take friends wherever they come from."

"Well we do work together but she invited me to hang out with them since I am here training. I am sorry we did not get to spend time together last night but I had already accepted her invitation to hang out. Willie, I am sorry."

SATURDAY
December 17, 2011

Wow! Off today, and, slept the night away. I have so few of these since my second surgery on my left shoulder November 2010. Sitting here listening to *'Youngblood'* on *'Hot 104.1 FM Atlanta,* this song *"Breezing",* is playing and I just want to take this moment and remember the Guys in *Bravo Battery, Second Battalion, Twenty-Seventh Field Artillery (B-Btry 2/27) in Friedberg, West Germany 1977.* My little Buddy, *Andrew Steve Lee Boris Moore - "Lil Bit",* and myself was assigned to *B-Btry* in July when we got to Germany. The Battery was training in *Graffenwhor* so Moore and I have to really walk around and learn the *Kasergn*. The *Tank Battalion Elvis Presley* was in when he was in Germany was on this *Kasergn*. One thing I have to say about *Tankers, they have the worst foodstuff in their dining facilities.* I guess it is because those guys have to be able to get inside those *"Rolling, Cumbersome, Behemoths,* they must remain small. If you have

Willie Means Well

never looked inside a tank, check it out. A tank crew normally consists of three to five men and believes you me; those guys know how to put steel on the target. Everything in Europe was *mechanized* then and the Unit Lil Bit and I were in had One hundred and fifty-five millimeters Howitzer *(155mm)*. Lil Bit was part of a gun crew and I was in the *Fire Direction Center (FDC)*. A tank is a *direct-fire* weapon and our guys are suppose to take out at least five of the other guy tanks before getting *'killed'* themselves. The weapon system Lil Bit and I worked with was an *indirect-fire* weapon system and would normally be miles away from it's' *'killed-target'*. Once had a Drill Sergeant tell me when he got to Vietnam, he use to go out with the *Forward Observers, the eyes of the Artillery,* and watch enemies get pounded by artillery fire. Staff Sergeant Reynolds said he use to get all kinds of mixed-emotions watching those guys are blown apart by the incoming artillery rounds. I use to hear guys in the *Battery* make the statement, *"In Vietnam the Infantry found the enemy and fixed them. But the*

Artillery killed them." If I get around to doing my book *'Once a Soldier'*, I will tell you of Lil Bit, Ralph Edward Hunter, and the other Guys I met while serving in Germany from 1977 through 1980.

Willie Means Well

DEATH IN THE FAMILY
December 19, 2011

My wife has lost another aunt. She was the oldest female and now only the baby of the girls is left. I really never have to know Dee's family like she really never have gotten to know mines. After almost 27 years together, there is still strife between her family and me and my family and her. I so wish it was not but I guess that is what happens when one is raised with sisters and brothers versus being an only child. So many times, I have wanted to walk out and try to find the happiness that I know is out there for me. However, Dee and I get to talking of things from our past and we both began to wonder if we really were destined to meet each other. Dee tells me of having an offer from *Northwestern University* in Chicago when she graduated from Carver in Columbus, Georgia in 1971. I had an offer on the table from them when I was to graduate in 1973. Northwestern wanted both of us for *'Academics'*. From what I have learned of Dee, she has been smart with book learning from beginning school in 1958. Myself, I started my sophomore year at John Marshall on the West Side of Chicago with one *'C'* and the rest *'Ds'*. My first year of high school I experienced being cut in the head by a window falling out in the Science Class; I got hit by a car; and then my hand was almost cut on a band saw in *'Shop Class'*. I was told had not the blade hit my fingernail, it would have taken off several of my fingers and possibly had cut into my hand. However, by first semester of my senior year, I was on the *'An Honor Roll'*. I do not recall what I did on the *'SAT'*, but years later I was told I did a *'14' out of 17'* on the *ACT'*. I will tell you of what I attribute that to later.

DENICE--'Dee'
(Denise Elaine Hale Hardaway Means)

*Two years after brining her first son into the world, she was in a head-on collision with a drunk, old White Man on Forest Road. She told me how it was explained to her that this young White Fireman saved her life. Apparently the Police, being in the South, had determined that the drunk White man was way more important than some young "Nigger Gal"; which is how they saw Blacks back then, even though it was 1975. Dee said she was told the Fireman walked up and the Police were all focusing on the White man so he told them, "**If you get your asses out the way, I will save this child's life!**" She was told they just looked at him while he performed life saving steps and got her to the hospital. Through the 27 years we have been together, I will tell you of what I recall from memory.*

She was the Son her Mom and Dad did not have.

Willie Means Well

SWEET MELISSA

(My contact with my, hopefully, publishing company)

She is bubbly and sweet. Sounds so very neat. Have to get me a *"Skype"* to see her when she says, "this man sounds so sweet, maybe he too, is neat!"

NAW!
Fuck It!

I do recall, however, a '70s group singing a song about "Sweet Melissa". In addition, she probably is. Therefore, I will leave her alone without the radical influence of yours truly, Willie Earl Means. This will make somebody happy.

WHO AM I?

Dammed If I Know!

Think I am going to leave you hanging. Been waiting to get in a writing mood for months now. I was really pushing it and making myself write when I thought the election year was November 2011. When I found out it is November 2012, it seems everything about the book stopped. I have been searching my mind and trying to figure out what happened and cannot come up with an answer. I do know this much, however, I accidentally ran across the *'Ed Show' on* **MSNBC** *(I think)* found this man giving the republican party a run for its' money when it comes to slandering the President. This made me happy because any **'DUMMY'** can tell they are not giving Mr. Obama the **RESPECT** the Office of The President demands. I guess it is people like me that you pray will never get into a position of authority because I would fill all those rooms under CIA Headquarters.

Willie Means Well

WHAT IS REAL

Here's to Reality

Mary, Pic, Pete

She **came to me in my hour of need.**
Mary, Pic, and Pete, came the three.
From a plane above, they came with love.
Come to help me out, without a doubt.
Failing in my subjects, 'D's I got.
Then I got 'A's I don't know how.
Seven centers unlocked.
My mind unblocked.
The teacher thought I cheated.
The competition got heated.
Straight 'A' student, on the honor roll.
A triangular piece of plastic, some letters on a board.
That's how it all started, my innocence and I parted.
It is a dreary, foggy morning today, in December 2008. I gave my wife a ride to our Son in Columbus. These days so many things are pressing in on me that, I just want to walk away and not look back. I know, however, this would probably be the

Willie Means Well

end of my two sons at home because I know they love me dearly. On my way, back up the highway I was repeatedly given mental nudges to stay on the road. It was not until I realize I was about to drive by my exit off the highway that I realized once again **"SHE"** was with me.

MARY

When I began to learn *'ESP'*, I was told that I would need to gather a *'Spiritual Band'*. The Band could be one and not more than eleven. I was also warned to beware because there were those out there who were very strong and would try to move in and control my life. Needless to say, this was all so exciting to me and scary at the same time. My friend had told me some things and I could not wait to try them on my own. When her mother began to teach me, she told me if I ever get lost while meditating, always look for the light and it would bring me back to my body. This probably sounds funny and crazy to you but I want you to know that evil is very real.

There are seven psychic centers in the body that I was introduced. You may not know this, but you have them too. There are three lower centers, and three upper centers. There is a middle center to regulate the flow of energy from the lower centers to the upper centers when you are meditating. If you get a copy of Doctor Howard G. Manning's book

'Helping Your Self with ESP', pay close attention to what it says about falling asleep before completing all the centers. The results can be very difficult on someone with sexual hang-ups.

You hear people use the term *'Guardian Angel'*, I was told from my earliest days in Church that we all have guardian angels. If you are not a Church person, I guess you must have a guardian demon. I pity you if that is the case. Demons are very real and their leader is *Lucifer,* the former Morning Star. Lucifer let his beauty and pride get the best of him. The *BIBLE* states he was cast to the earth along with his followers and the *BIBLE* warned mankind to beware.

As wild as it sounded when my teacher told me of this, I had to get some help from somewhere because I was barely passing my classes. I was smart once I got the hang of something, but between working at Sears in the morning, running track, and field after school, and for the first time in my life, getting into a real relationship. I think I told you of Helen Jean Blossom earlier. If not, I will tell you a little and more later in *"Willie's Girls"*. I did not have much time for anything. You want to know how crazy high school was for me. In Ninth Grade, I was cut in the head when an entire windowpane fell out when I was trying to adjust the blinds to get the sun off my desk. Talk about Guardian Angels. I had yet to even think of *ESP* but I was raised a Christian. When that window fell out, I was looking up and squinting because the sun was in my eyes. I heard something make a snapping sound and right before that windowpane struck me above my right eye, I felt a hand push my head down from the back. Whatever it was that pushed my head saved me my right eye and possibly my life. Had I been still looking up when the glass hit me, it would have gone into my right eye. I remember hearing someone screaming and yelling to take him to the bathroom. I was holding my right hand up to my head but I did not recall placing it there. I remember asking who was screaming and I lowered my hand from my head. If you have ever heard anybody talk about how water gushes out of openings, you will get a picture of how the blood gushed from my head. I guess I was pretty giddy. I made the statement that someone was bleeding and the girl screaming yelled at, *"that's you bleeding Willie Means!"* I put my hand back to my head and I remembered everything going red. This guy who I later found out was one of the leaders of the *'MTs'* street gang yelled for one of his boys to get the gym teacher Mr. Ward and he got me by the sleeve and guided me to the bathroom. That incidence kept me out of school for at least a week to ten days.

    I had not been long returned to school when one afternoon the workshop teaches asked me to help him out with a project. I was to feed this wood to a table saw. The teacher reminded me of our safety class and told me not to push the wood. I was doing well until been ran in and told me the Vice Lords and the *'MT'* were about to fight. Now I was not in the Vice Lords but all my friends were Vice Lords. If they were going to fight, I was going to be standing with them. I tried to hurry with the piece of wood I had in my hand so I pushed it. When I pushed the wood, that saw kicked up the back part of that wood so fast I did not realize what had happened until Ben said, *"Mean-mo, you're bleeding!"* I looked at my right hand, and that wood had kicked my hand on to that saw blade so fast; I did not feel it. I was later told I was lucky the blade hit the fingernails or I would had lost two fingers. When I showed my hand to the teacher, he raised his goggles and simply said, *"You pushed it, didn't you?"* I had to have two of the fingers on my right hand, which was my writing hand, splinted up. I only missed two days from school but if I could not get someone to write for me, I had to try to use my left hand. Several of the teachers understood but my math teacher was really hard on me.

    The last thing that happened to me in Ninth Grade was one Saturday morning Jesse Burrell and I rode our bicycles into another gang's neighborhood. The guys were chasing us and I was looking back trying to make sure Jesse was ok. When I looked up, I was riding into the street in front of a car. I swear that car hit me hard enough that it knocked my bike up against the curve and the kickstand came down. I heard some girls screaming and Jesse ran to try to get me up. I was screaming because I could not breathe well and I was telling Jesse to take me home. Somebody must have had the sense to tell Jesse not to move me. I must have passed out because next thing I knew the police paddy wagon was there and they were putting me in the back on a stretcher. This frightens me more and I tried to get off the stretcher. The police officers told me it was all right and they were taking me to the hospital. I told Jesse to go and tell my momma. I remember that was April 14, 1970 and they had my leg in a cast through the middle of June. I guess I did not help the situation because I kept breaking the cast racing with guys in the streets.

  There is something else I recall that happened each time my mother would take me back to get the cast changed. I broke five of them. Every time I returned to the emergency room, somebody would die in the room next to me. The sixth time I returned to the emergency room, the doctor was baking the cast on before I could leave when the nurse ran in and told him this guy had got shot five times. When she and the doctor went through the door, the door did not close and I could see the guy on the table trying to breath. The nurse was showing the doctor where the guy had been shot, she pointed to four places from his stomach to his chest, and then she pointed to the right side of the guy's neck. When she pointed to the one in his neck, the doctor shook his head and at the same time, the guy hand just dropped off the table and hung down at the side of the bed. I snatched my leg out the oven it was in, jumped off the bed, and ran. I met my pastor, Reverend George Clark, coming in the door and I told him, *"You better hurry and get momma. That guy just died in there!"* You see, violence is so real in Chicago and places like Chicago. I recall the Military sending medical personnel to the hospitals in Los Angeles because the wounds being inflicted on gang members out there were so similar to battlefield wounds. A medical officer told me the weapons the gangs were getting was so similar to the ones utilized by the Military that doctors could get a jump on what to expect when they had to deal with treating wounded during a war.

Anyway, what I am pointing out is that I was hurt so much my Ninth grade is that the highest grade I received was a *'C'* from my English teacher. I got a *'D'* in all my other classes. The teachers said I at least showed up.

My Tenth grade year I made the *'C'* Honor Roll and I decided I would try for the *'B'* Honor Roll my Junior Year. Here I got my introduction to *'ESP'* and began my personal Odyssey.

You probably have heard someone us the statement, *"I've been here before".* Hollywood even has people using the ritzy term, *'d`eja`vu'.* Three terms I want to tell you of that go along with **'ESP': *Clairvoyance, Clairaudience, or Clairsentience.*** To see, to hear, and to feel at an upper level above your normal senses. You also have **Premonition,** and **Out-of-the-Body-Experience (OBE).** Another name all these fall under is simply, **"The Sixth Sense".**

From my earliest childhood, as mentioned before, I have been able to see spirits and other things. If you read the Bible, you will find numerous times where the Children of Israel have been warned against spiritual activity.

PSYCHOLOGY

They've all gone and left me behind, seems to think I've lost my mind. My psychological studies, with my peers, have taught me a great deal and given me fears. I see something in passing and think it's gone, then my mind comes alive, and I'm off on a roam. Why did he do what he did, probably thought his actions were hid. I love Dr. Freud and his studies on kids. Many frowned, and disagreed, and they do not understand the id. Had me confused one night, with my peers I had a fight. ***"Ids taken on the second floor!"*** I knew that couldn't be right. Back and forth, I paced, trying to figure it out; a peer brought me about. "That's ids taken," it was explained to me. With a jolt of reality, I knew I had to flee. These psychological studies will never let me be. I took them to try to help others, now I will never be free.

Willie Means Well

THE STUDY OF THE HUMAN MIND!

Now there are a lot of you shaking your head and saying this person needs some serious help. However, the things I mentioned about seeing, hearing, and feeling when no one else around you is picking up what you are is real. Can you truthfully say without any doubt that you have never experienced the same thing? I will tell you this. To simply dream is such a great example of the spiritual abilities God created within us. *"And God made man in his own image."* Think about this simple passage from the Book of Genesis. This simple verse gives people so many problems. Look at the verse with a simple approach and you will realize that God imparted part of his spiritual being into us, and his creation. Since our spirit belongs to God, our spirit longs to be with the Creator. Therefore, our spirit roams. Thereby we all have dreams and sometimes those dreams burst into reality. Too bad, we do not know how to harness this great ability. Think of all the achievements we could claim. We all dream each

Willie Means Well

and every time we sleep. Fortunately, God is a merciful God and do not let us remember everywhere the spirit has roamed. I think in the very near future conventional psychology is going to be turned up side down. I formerly worked with a Child and Adolescent Unit and some of the clients we were being stayed from three days to two weeks. Many times Staff agreed that we would see the clients again after their discharge and it never fells that are what happened. I am going to focus on *'Reality Therapy'* by Doctor William Glasser. I feel **Reality Therapy** can handle anything that is getting ready to come down the pipe because it do not accuse and point fingers at people. It practically allows the individual to assist in their own therapeutic approach to getting their life back in some kind of order.

As I said, many of you will simply say, *"This man is crazy."* To you, I will allow you this because it is your right to think what you like. However, there are those of you out there who know and understand what I am telling you are very real.

Willie Means Well

A FIGHT WITH MY SISTERS

My sister Joyce and I have always been extremely close. As children, one always knew what the other was doing. Joyce was born February 1 1954 and I was born February 14, 1955. Even today, I do not understand how this connected us but it did. When Joyce started first grade, she could come home and tell what time I took a nap, what I had been given to eat, and even what I had watched on television. I, in term, would take her reader and attempt to read what she had read in school that day. I will always remember sounding out and announcing the word *'temperature'*. My mother snatched the book, looked at the word, and had my oldest sister pronounce the word. Momma then called Joyce and asked her to pronounce the word. When Joyce could not pronounce the word, momma shipped her. I remember I went to Joyce crying and she was mad at me but we hugged and comforted each other.

My baby sister is Dot. Before the age of two, Joyce, Dot, and I were playing with some brush

Willie Means Well

brooms in the house. All the ladies in the neighborhood preferred to have brush brooms. There were store bought brooms but most of the ladies would have the children go across the street to this field and bring them a bunch of straw and they would tie the straw together and make brooms. Joyce was four, I was three, and Dot would soon be two. We had a potbelly stove in the front room. There was only two rooms and we called the front room *'the front room'* and the other room was the kitchen and back bedroom. There was another coal and wood burning stove in the kitchen. You would not believe the meals prepared on that stove daily and at Thanksgiving and Christmas.

    Daddy was at work across the street at Mr. Carl's Service Station and momma was at her job in Birmingham. Bobby and Roxanne were in school. We had that potbelly stove *'red hot!'* We would stick the brush brooms to the stove and when they caught fire, we would swirl the brooms around fast and make sparks. Joyce had put her broom down, gone into the kitchen, and started washing dishes. Seems strange for a four year old to be washing dishes, right? At that age, she probably did not have to but I am so glad she was washing dishes. Dot kept asking me to let her do it. I put the broom down and Dot picked it up and stuck it the stove. Dot had on this print dress made of nylon and when she tried to swirl the broom the flame caught her dress and fire flared up. I screamed and ran towards the kitchen and Dot was behind me. Her running fanned the flame and I remember she was screaming. When we came through the door, Joyce turned and threw the dishpan of water at the same time. Even in this, at such young ages, I know we had guardian angels because the pan of dish water should had been way too heavy for Joyce, at 4 years old, to lift. Not only did Joyce lift the dishpan but also not a drop of water touched me but also it all went on Dot. The flames were doused and Joyce was holding Dot crying and I ran next door crying outside our 'Big Momma's' window. I was telling Big Momma Dot had been burned and all the way across the street and under a car, my daddy yelled, *"What did you say boy!"* Daddy came running, people came out on their porches yelling, and asking what was wrong. Everybody came running to the house. Daddy burst in the door and saw Dot and he grabbed a blanket and wrapped her in the blanket. I remember he kept repeating repeatedly, *"Oh my Lord! Oh my Lord!"* Dot was a bundle of charred clothing and burned flesh. Somebody called my mother and the people she worked for had her there in what seem like five minutes. I do know that daddy slapped me around a little while rocking Dot. People were gathered in the house and on the porch. The people who brought momma home took Dot to the hospital. Daddy did not go but took off his belt and began to whip me. Somebody finally told him to stop shipping me and use his head. By the time Roxanne and Bobby got home from school, daddy had gone to the hospital. People in the neighborhood brought food for us and we just sat around waiting for momma and daddy. Daddy came home that night but we did not see momma for nearly two days. When momma did come home, she told us she needed some sleep and she would return to the hospital the next morning. Momma had just climbed into the bed and we were sitting around the stove when a rocking chair Dot liked to sit in began to rock by itself. Look like we all saw it at the same time and Bobby cried out. Momma got out the bed and said, *"Now here!"* She reached out, stopped the chair from rocking, and stood looking at the chair. Just as momma, climbed back into bed the chair began to rock again. Momma told us to leave it alone it was just Dot sitting with the family. Momma then told us she did not want to tell us yet but the doctors said that Dot had swallowed that fire and she had also died but they brought her back. Momma said when they got to the hospital with Dot, the doctors and the nurses were just going to let Dot die. Momma said she cried, begged, and pleaded with the doctors to save her baby but they all acted as if they did not hear her. Momma said the man she worked for came in and told the doctor his family had an interest in the hospital and he would see that none of them worked there any longer. Momma said the doctors and the nurses began to work on Dot and the man she worked for stayed with her until the doctor came and told momma they had did everything they could but Dot had swallowed a blaze of fire and it had damaged one of her lungs. Dot had died but they were able to bring her back. Sometimes I wonder if this thing happened to Dot because we all loved Dot so much. Before Dot was burned, she had a beautiful thick head of hair and skin that people said was like the Hawaiians. Unbelievably, some had even asked momma for Dot. Back then, it was not uncommon for people to actually allow someone else to raise their children. Well she is still with us today with a family of her own. If you see her two daughters, you could see how Dot probably would have looked had she not been burned? Dot was burned over eighty percent of her body including her face. She has put up with a lot from people but she accepts it and continues to live her life.

  Anyway, we were living in the Cabrini Green Housing Projects on the north side of Chicago my senior year when I met a girl from Dot's school name

Helen. Helen was one of those girls that always kept a coat on and you did not know what was under that coat. Well one day Helen did not know I was home and I caught her with the coat off and let metal youth hat was and is one beautiful girl and lady. Beautiful light complexion, thick, dark, shiny hair, and a stare that pulled you into her deep, dark eyes. I had been sleep but I came full awake when I saw Helen. First, she just stared at me and told my sister she did not know her brother was home. She grabbed her coat and was headed for the door when I made the mistake of reaching out and grabbing her arm and tried to talk to her. Helen turned, and at the same time buried her left fist into my stomach. I must say that I was in fantastic physical condition from participating in track and field. That girl knocked the wind out of me and snatched her arm away. She was headed out the door when she realized I had backed up and plopped down in a chair. She then came to me and asked had she hurt me. I was shaking my head no but could not speak because I had no air in my lungs. My sister Dot came from the back and asked Helen

Willie Means Well

what she had done to her brother. I remember Helen had this quizzical look on her face and seemed astounded. *"Buster, did I really hurt you? I am sorry. Dot, I did not mean to hit him hard."* Helen left and Joyce and Dot told me, *"That's what you get for messing with our friend."*

Helen called later and I answered the telephone. She once again told me how sorry she was for hitting me and I told her I bet she ran all the boys off because she beat them up. She told me that was not funny because she did not have a boyfriend because boys did say she played too rough. Helen and I talked for more than thirty minutes before Dot asked who was on the telephone. When I told her Helen, Dot snatched the telephone and asked did she call to talk to her or her brother. I laughed and went to my room but Dot came and told me Helen wanted to speak back to me. We stayed on the telephone for an hour and Helen told me she was going to come back over. I did not say anything to Joyce and Dot but I went out on the balcony and waited for Helen.

It was December 1972 and Helen and I became

inseparable. I remember *'WVON'* had two songs playing, it seem like two or three times an hour, titled, *"Is that loving in your heart that you had for me finally gone away"* and *"If"*. There was a place off *Wells* and *Division* called *'Old Town.'* If you walked into *Old Town,* you would have thought you had walked into the Chicago of the *'Roaring Twenties'*. The streetlights cast a dull yellow glow and the atmosphere was so tranquil. For me, I found it hard to believe that such an area could exist right down the street from such violence that went on in the Cabrini Greens. Helen and I loved to go to *'Piper's Alley'*. The name should had explained itself but all Helen and I cared for was it was a place that allowed us to sit down and enjoy each other's company without anybody bothering us. I will tell l you more about my tryst with Helen perhaps later. Especially about we both being virgins and our first attempts at sex. I am sure most people get this part of a relationship done at first try. With Helen and me, it took us three attempts and then it scared the hell out of both of us. Like I said, more on this later.

Willie Means Well

Joyce and Dot turned on Helen as if she was *'Public Enemy Number One'* when they realized she was my girlfriend. I believe Helen could have stood her ground with either of them one-on-one.

However, Joyce and Dot wanted to jump on her together; that *Hustlerette* mentality; the gang they had been in. They also had this extremely, slim and gorgeous friend of theirs named Cheryl Ann, that lived next door, who also wanted to get her licks in on Helen. There was this wine named *'White Port'*, very cheap and extremely effective in getting you drunk, that Cheryl Ann liked to drink. She and Joyce were only eighteen but guys were always hanging around outside the package stores ready to purchase for under-age buyers. I recall one night Cheryl Ann came over to visit Joyce and they got into some *'White Port'*. Even today it amazes me how when a good guy wants to treat a girl right, the good guy wounds up on the losing end because he do not know how to give the girl what she wants. I remember being in my room and listening as Joyce and Cheryl Ann began to talk dirty to each other. When I heard them began to curse each other out and laugh about it, I decided to go and see what was happening. I do not recall what card game they were playing, but I noticed half of the fifth of *'White Port'* was gone. They both stopped talking and just stared at me. I acted as if I wanted something in the refrigerator and was lying around until Joyce told me to hurry and get what I was looking for and leave. I returned to my room but kept listening at those two laughing and cursing. They stopped cursing and began to play some music then I heard Cheryl Ann began to cry and start telling Joyce how low down this guy was she was seeing. It took another thirty minutes but both stopped talking and the record player played the same record repeatedly. I ventured back into the living room again and both were passed out. The bottle of *'White Port'* was empty and Cheryl Ann was lying back on the couch and Joyce had her feet up in the big chair with her. I stood there, stared at Cheryl Ann, and was wishing she were my girlfriend when she eased her eyes open and asked:

"Can I help you with something Buster?"

"I really don't know. You want to go to my room and talk about it?"

"What would you do if I did come to your room?"

"Well, first, I would kiss you like this," as I leaned down and covered her mouth with mine. I almost jumped back as she reached up and placed her arm around my neck and eased her tongue into my mouth. I kneeled down and was just easing my hand under her dress when Joyce woke up.

"Buster! What you think you're doing to my friend? You take your hands off her or I'll tell momma you were being "mannish!"

Before I could come back with a response to Joyce, Cheryl Ann spoke up.

"It's ok Joyce. I was just trying to see if he really knew what to do if he had the chance. Buster, you're still a virgin ain't you?"

My sister was staring at me and I was beginning to wonder where they really drunk or trying to set me up. I looked at Cheryl Ann and told her, "I've always wanted you but I didn't want my sisters to turn on *you like they did Helen."*

    I did not get any that night and I was still a couple of months away from February when Helen and I finally did it.

    I would always meet Helen at the elevator when she came to visit me. She always came and visited me because I could not go to her building and visit her. There was a gang in her building that killed like professionals. I am talking about incidents like starting a fire on top of the over-head you walked under to get into her building. When the firemen came to put the fire, those guys in the gang would drop glass gallon jars filled with water down on them for the fourth-tenth and fifth-tenth floors. This was disastrous when it would hit one of the firemen being dropped from that height. Another thing that gang would do, they would catch somebody who did something to them and close the elevator door on the person with half the person on the outside of the doors and the other half inside the elevator shaft. One of them would have stopped the elevator a floor above the person but when the elevator was started again, it would tear the person in half. Remember when I said they killed like professional and I did not understand why someone did not think of waiting until two or three in the morning and rounding them all up and sending them to Vietnam. One killing that chilled many others and I when we heard about it was the way that gang killed a ten year old boy.

Cooley High School was right down the street on Division. Apparently, this boy saw some of the gang rape this girl. The police came around asking questions and nobody told anything except this boy. You know how a kid is when he has an audience. I did not see what happened I, but heard some of the ladies in our building talking about it. Seems the kid told the police what he had seen and everybody stood around listening. A couple of days after the kid talked to the police, the lady came home from work and the elevators were stuck so she had to walk up the stairs. Not only was the elevators stuck, but the lights had been put out in the stairwell. The mother said she was afraid and tried to get the guard, yes, there were guards in the White High Rise, to walk up with her to her apartment. The guard could not leave his office and the lady walked up the stairs. The lady said when she got around the third floor in the stairwell she felt something sticky she was walking in. She said when she turned the corner to go up the stairs to the fourth floor; somebody grabbed her, and put their hand over her mouth. They did not physically hurt the lady but they made her watch as gang members cut her son up.

    The place was atrocious and it bred savage individuals. Everybody who stood around that day and let that little boy talk knew he was signing his death warrant. I am not sure but I think the mother eventually moved away from the projects. I do not recall anything ever being done about that death or many others that happened in those projects. I called the police numerous times I would see a crime about to be committed. They did not care. I saw this old White man following a Black lady into 1157, the other side of our building, one night. I was looking out the window on the ninth floor and I could see at least seven or eight guys standing in the stairwell waiting. That lady ran up between the guys and the guys began beating that White man relentlessly. They got his wallet and began to stomp the man. I called the police and told them what was taking place. The police wanted to know my name. I was young, but I was not stupid. I told them a concerned neighbor and hung up. It took about ten minutes then I heard two car doors slam. I looked down and saw two policemen strolling and talking as if they were taking a walk in the park. They walked up those stairs and looked like guys came out the concrete. They commenced to beating those policemen and at least this provided a distraction to the ones beating the old White man. One of the policemen broke away and ran for the car. I got back on the telephone and called the police and told them *"they got your policemen over there now and beating them too!"* The policeman who ran back to the car came back with the *'riot gun'*. Two of those guys had sneaked out and hid behind the bushes. When the policeman ran up, the two guys jumped him, took the gun from him, and began to beat him with it. All at once about ten cars of police and detective pulled up and all the guys ran. I guess the White man was not dead because the ambulance got him.

MARCH 1, 2012
(Talking About a Mess)

You know, I am fifty-seven, and I sure do want to cry to see the condition the America is in right now. Recently, I was surfing and came across some guy on *'NPR' (National Public Radio)* and he was stating his opinion that America is not a Christian Nation. He was saying that everyone has the right to do what they pleased and anybody who tried to take away those privileges is the ones who are the real criminals. The whole thing came from them discussing *'same-sex-marriages, gay rights'* and other things that need to stay private and behind closed doors. You got all these people with money to burn sitting back and laughing while the gas prices get closer and closer to five dollars. Some of the people in Washington act like the one they care when in actuality their pockets will be lined with green backs too as long as they do nothing. I really wish it were in my power to get a following that would put me in the *White House*. From health-care and every

Willie Means Well

other controversial thing that is causing the people in this Country to suffer, I would right those ships and put many of those people in Washington behind bars. There is so much wrong going on behind closed doors in this Country and other places in the World. I would right the wrongs in this Country first and then have the rest of the World *put-up or shut-up!*

    In each city across America, I will bet you can find large empty buildings that would make great accommodations to hold *'government funded'* healthcare facilities. In each city across America, I will bet you can find places to establish food places to provide hot meals and then give out foodstuff to last people weeks at a time. It is time for the government to step in and bust down these people that are become filthy rich at the expense of the poor and needy. America is truly a capitalist society but when it gets to people turning their back on the sick and other situations because they are so greedy they can only see the money in it for them, it is time for somebody to shake this Country and get it back on the right track.

Willie Means Well

One hundred years from now, someone will read of this incident and will say, *"The world saw America for its' weakness and the people of America were no longer looked upon as being the land of righteousness!"* A Marine, of all the Services whom mission is to protect America, *foreign and domestic,* returned home from a deployment was photographed with legs wrapped around, arms graping, and a big kiss being administered to the lover waiting at the airport for the Marine's return. The catch? Both parties were male!

America has truly gotten sick and this entire sickness head straight to the Democratic Party because the Democratic Party has lower its' standard to obtain the votes the Party needs to defeat the now self-righteous and greedy republican party. Many have forgotten that the Republican Party was the support of the *Negro* way back there in the past. I will only look back as far as the *Regan Administration* and the so-called *'triggle-down effect'*. Who in their right mind would believe that people being so rich would share the overflow of their richness with the less fortunate person? The snowball got to rolling and by the time it came to the bottom of the hill, so many American factories were closed. So many American jobs had been sent overseas because the rich owners did not want to pay a decent salary so people could keep up with the *cost-of-living.* America needs to levy such a heavy import tax on those companies, who sent *American Jobs* elsewhere, that the tax would make up for the unemployment benefit's the government is stuck with trying to make sure people have the funds to buy food to eat.

America has really gotten sick People and it is going to get lots worst before it began to get even a little better. By the time you are reading a copy of this book, see if the gas prices have gone over five dollars a gallon.

Another time, several years later, I went back to the building where Helen uses to live to see m y daughter. A crowd of people was gathered around the apartment door where Helen had lived. A woman was crying and I heard her say to two policemen standing at the door to the apartment, *"Please don't let my son die. Please call the ambulance and take him to the hospital."* The two police officers laughed and looked into the apartment. I peeped between the two policemen and a guy was lying on the floor with a knife sticking in his chest. One policeman told the other, *"it want be long now."* I looked towards a project a block away and I could see the *Paddy wagon* just sitting. I looked back in the apartment just as the guy with the knife in his chest convulsed and shivered then lay still. The lady began to say and cry *"No! No! No!"* Would you believe one of the policemen then called on his radio and the paddy wagon came to get the body? That is why when I was growing up on the West Side we learned to run when we heard a car speed up behind us. The police cars had something called a *three-in-one gear* in the rear end and it made a distinctive sound when the police pressed the accelerator. We all ran in different directions because we knew it was better if they caught one instead of all of us.

Willie Means Well

MARY, MARY

I'll be back...

Mary, Mary so dark yet so bright.
You stayed with me and protected me each night.
Joyce and Dot we had a fight.
While in high school, no girl was right.
Every girl I met, they ran right off.
To get a girl pregnant, my education would be lost.
I would be the first to graduate high school.
No girl was going to get me and play me for a fool.

I was two weeks from my eighteenth birthday when Helen came over one evening. I had been walking on eggs, so to speak, around Joyce and Dot. When Helen came over, I took her to my bedroom because Joyce and Dot had told me they were going to get her. Helen and I just talked and I was trying to get her to have sex with me but I did not know how to go about it. Helen refused my advances as usual and then told me she was going home because she did not want me mad at her too. I walked Helen across the street from her building and returned home. I was

Willie Means Well

walking through the living room when one of my sisters called Helen a whore. I started to stop but kept going. Then I heard the word bitch and I turned and asked them why they were acting like that. I was told, *"That little bitch was not going to stop me from graduating high school."* I told them they needed to leave Helen alone and nobody was going to stop me from graduating. I went to the sink to get some water and when I walked by Joyce I accidentally bumped into her. Joyce was on me like a cat! Scratching, yelling, and trying to kick me, I was holding Joyce hands so she could not scratch my face. Dot jumped on my back and then ran and got momma out of her room. Momma had always told me never to h it a girl. She grabbed me and asked me what was wrong with me. I tried to explain what had happened but she told me I needed to leave and cool off.

I'LL BE BACK

MARCH 12, 2012

I cannot help but wonder why someone has not brought Clint Eastwood's 'Breezy' back to the 'Big Screen'.
I believe it would be a great hit with the "Younger Generation"!

- - -

I also wonder these days, why did those people who sponsored the Female Sorority 'Step Show Contest', take the money from that 'White Sorority' if they did not want a White Sorority to win the first prize.

- - -

After great moments of thoughtfulness, I have determined that people are crooked regardless of what is their Race!

Willie Means Well

MARCH 16, 2012
(Evening)

Was on the road this morning at 5:10. Missed my intended departure by ten minutes. I had to do a little, watered-down *'nite-quil'* to get back to sleep last night. Had to repeat the procedure again tonight after taking a much-needed nap after returning from Atlanta to see another specialist about my shoulder. It seems this specialist was in agreement with me that both doctors who performed surgery on my shoulder lied and *'Workers Compensation'* was more than glad to accept their lies to get out of taking care of my damaged shoulder. I really, really wish someone would take interest in West Central Georgia Regional Hospital and bring a lawsuit against the former directors of all the units. I will always remember a nurse coming to me and informing me that the director of the adult unit ten put the question to the nurses *"how come he always get hurt and have to go to the emergency room?"* Then I had this male nurse come to me, place his arm across my shoulder, and then tell me I needed to start taking a *'goody powder'*, like him, and keep working. I wanted to remind him that his salary was three times the amount they were paying me.

Anyway, I want to begin wrapping this up. According to my calculation, as explained to me by a former dispatcher and friend of mine from my taxi driving days, our income tax check should be here this weekend and I will have the initial payment to get off to get the publication of this book underway. I still have 40 pages I want to add but I do not believe I will get there. I so want to get this book out to try to get some votes for the President. They are laughing and joking about the republican candidates but they are going to let them slip in and take this election.

Willie Means Well

MARCH 25, 2012
(Death is here)

I have said it repeatedly, *"When death comes to your family, death will not leave until it gets somebody."* The last two weeks I have been waking all hours of the night, getting my Bible, going down on my knees, and Praying. When the feelings hit me, I know that someone is going to die but I just do not know how, or I should say, *"I am not bold enough to dabble and find out who it is."* It is not hard but my heart still is not where it should be and I am a prime candidate to be scared to death. The baby girl on the Johnson's side of the Family has died. My Sister Roxanne informed me of this when I called to tell her I saw Momma in the nursing home and Momma's breathing was very rapid. I have asked the LORD JESUS for 100 years for my Mother along with her being healthy. I so wish I could get my Mother to recall the passage in PSALMS 103 about *"So that Your Youth is renewed like the Eagles'"*.

Willie Means Well

GOD BLESS !!!
MARY, MARY

I walked out the door and was waiting on the elevator. When the elevator door opened, I stepped in and pushed the door close button. I saw this lady out the corner of my eye and I hit the door open button. I turned and no one was there. I simply said, *"Come on then."* When I got down stairs this young lady who lived on the first floor just stared at me. I spoke to her and walked out the building. My sister Roxanne lived in the *'Row Houses'* and I went to her house. Big Sister was working two full-time jobs and a part-time job. She told me she wanted her children to have what the other kids had. She was in bed as usual and my brother-in-law was with her. Since they were up stairs, I went down stairs and got into my brother-in-law's alcohol. I did not know what I was doing, but I do remember drinking out of at least six different bottles. I stumbled up the stairs and told my sister and brother-in-law good night. My brother-in-law offered to take me home but I told him I wanted to walk. On my way back home, I seemed to have tunnel vision. I knew where home was and I just kept putting one foot in front of the other foot. I do remember people walking out of the way and looking at me. When I got to my building, the guys looked and faded away. I got to the elevator and some people waiting were staring at me too. When the elevator came, no one got on the elevator but me. I just looked at them. When I got home, I had to pass my mother bedroom to go into mine. I knew better than to go by without saying goodnight. I mumbled a goodnight to Momma and I remember she was reading the Bible in bed. She looked at me over the top of her glasses but did not say anything. The next morning Momma was in the kitchen making breakfast and I was getting ready to go to *'Junior Bowling'* at *Marana's Miami Bowl* out near *Pulaski* and *Archer,* out *South.* Momma wiped her hands on her apron and said, *"I saw how red your eyes were last night so I know you was down your sister's house drinking. I will talk to Roxanne about that later. But what I want to tell you is that when you* went into your bedroom last night, a lady went right in there behind you." I just stared at Momma. I did not sleep in my room for a week.

The Ouija Board

I would love to tell you my friend's name that started me messing with the Ouija board. Then many would know who my teacher was. One day in school, my friend asked me how my studies with her mother were going. I told her I believe I had touched something and it was hard to deny when you see stuff with your own eyes. My friend was such a beautiful young lady. My friend on the track team knew how much I cared about her and another guy name James knew I cared about her. She, on the other hand, would travel the world with me and never suspect a thing because she knew how close her boyfriend and I were to each other. I remember the cat almost got out the bag when he became a little jealous and started telling everyone that I would be taking her to the Senior Prom. Sounded great to me but I knew she would had gotten her heart broken to show up at the prom and see him with another girl. I know I did not go to the senior prom and I believe she did not go either. She and I had been talking about reincarnation and she was telling me of a session when one of her brothers were being *'regressed'* and after turning into two people he had been in previous lives, of a sudden, a very large female Caucasian was sitting in the chair and her head dropped off. My friend said she had seen many things since she joined the psychic band with her mother, but that was too much. She said she took a leap trying to get out the door and landed on her mother's wooden stereo. The stereo could not hold her weight and the legs collapsed. She said her mother kept the stereo but did not repair it so it would be a reminder to my friend of what is real.

  We had been laughing and talking when my friend said, *"Momma got an Ouija board."* I looked at her and asked her did those things really work. I told her I had been playing with that ball, I think iot is called *'kabala'*, and she told me that was kids' stuff compared to an Ouija board. She told me if I came over to her house, she would show me how it worked.

I did not go to track practice but caught the bus with my friend and went to her house. No one was there when we got there so my friend went to her mother's room and came back with, what I first thought was a game, *'the Ouija board'*. My friend was neat and pretty as always and I tried to sneak a peep under her skirt when she sat down on the floor in front of me. She simply said, *"Stop it Willie"*, and that was the end of that. I was looking at the box top while she positioned the planchette on the board. I looked at the lettering and the way the board was arranged and she told me to put my hands slightly on the pancetta. When I reached for it, it moved away from me. I remember I pulled my hands back and looked at my friend who was laughing. She made the statement, *"that's not nice. Willie is my friend."* She told me to touch it again and this time I was allowed to touch it. We then commenced to asking different questions and the thing was actually spelling out answers for us. Then my friend told me to take my hands away and watch this. She sat there and worked the board by herself. She then told me her mother said it could be very dangerous to do it by yourself because the spirit of the board could turn evil. My friend and I heard her mother come in and she quickly put the board away. I told her I would like to try to get the board to work for me. She told me her momma would not let it out of the house and she would get upset if she knew I had been introduced to the board. My friend told me when I leave come back in the gangway and she would hand it to me out the window.

  I was ready to go now. I was determined to make the board work for me as it did for my friend. Her mother was not surprised when we came out of my friend's room. She told her daughter she knew it was I because she had picked up my aura. Then she asked me how my studies were going with *Mr. Manning*. I told her I was really enjoying the book and it seems things were beginning to happen that I could not explain. She told me to remember to look for the light if I got lost and remember to try to stay awake while doing the *Center* exercise. I said goodbye and left. Then I doubled back into the gangway and my friend handed me the Ouija out the window. I put it in my track bag and went home.

CENTER start

WHAT IS REAL

Ouija II

Ouija, Ouija you are no game.
I bet you have driven many insane.
Innocent boys and girls pull you out.
With a squeal of delight, they have no fright.
Poor little angels looking to have fun.
They need a little warning, they need to run.
They ask the questions, giggling all the time.
They soon find out, something have their minds.

CENTER end

    I remember that ride home on the bus. I had to

come from fifty-six hundred West on Washington Boulevard to the five hundred block West on Division. We lived at 1159 North Cleveland on the Ninth floor. *"Hmmm! Just made me think of the movie 'The Ninth Gate'."* What I want to tell you is that I had a great fright that someone was going to take the thing from me. People were always getting stuck-up on the buses and trains in Chicago. It was after seven o'clock when I got home. I spoke to everyone but went right into my room. I locked the door and began to play with the Ouija. Nothing happened. I must have played with that Ouija at least three hours before I came out of my room to get me something to eat. When I returned, I put the Ouija aside and practiced my meditation to relieve my frustration. After reaching the *'Crown Center'*, I spoke my desire for help with the Ouija. I remember feeling light headed and I remember something softly touching my out stretched hands. I got a feeling that the room was spinning and then I realized I had fallen asleep. I got frighten because my light was off and I did not recall turning it off. I placed the Ouija on my bed and then got down on my knees and began to concentrate on putting some energy into the pancetta. I remember asking was the spirit of the board there. The thing moved over and covered yes. I got chills and wanted to take my hands away but I did not. I cannot remember exactly what I did but I remember it was around two in the morning before I finally put the Ouija away. I guess that even then the LORD JESUS had his arm of protection around me. I fear to think what would had happened had I reached the three o'clock hour. All these years later I have found out that, three in the morning is really the wicked hour. With no telling how much killing that had gone on in the building we lived in, there probably would had been something drastic happened both spiritually and physically.

    I had three statues of *Mother Mary* that I would set out spaced apart on my dresser. I spaced them out, left my light on, and went to sleep. Next morning I got up and the statues had been put back together. I did not think anything of it. I was working at Sears through Cooperative Education and I worked from seven twenty until eleven twenty Monday through Friday. I then went to school and track practice after school. Well I had gotten to school when the student helper from the office came to my class and told the teacher I was wanted in the office. When we got in the hallway, the girl told me I had a telephone call. When I got to the office, it was my mother on the telephone and she asked me did I have a key to my room. I reminded Momma that the lock was broken and they had put in a work order to repair the lock. My mother told me the door was locked. She had sent Joyce to get my clothes so she could wash them and Joyce said something pushed her out the room and slammed the door. I did not answer right away and my mother asked me was I still there. I told her yes and I would be home after school. I assured the people in the office that everything was all right and returned to class. I saw my friend and she asked me how it went with the Ouija board. I explained to her what happened and she, like her mother, reminded me to find the light if I get lost.

Willie Means Well

I missed another day of track practice and went home after school. Momma was cooking dinner when I came in and she once again asked me did I have the key to the door. We were walking up the hall and I told her once again, *"Momma the door lock is broken."* I grasped the doorknob, turned it, and the door opened. I remember my mother said, *"Well I declare. Now how can that be?"*

Over the next week, I spent hours with that Ouija and I recall those three words I told you about earlier: *Clairvoyance, Clairaudience, and Clairsentience,* were really acting up. I mean to the tune they were sharpened. I would tell my sisters who was on the telephone before they would answer. It got to the point I would go blocks out the way because I would get the feeling that something was going to happen the way I normally walked home. However, what really got my attention was one day I was meditating and while I was still in the lower centers, something whispered to me, *"I am here."* I was a very soft voice, but very clear and it had to be in my head. I was trying to step up the flame and channel the energy from the lower centers through the solar plexus region to the higher centers when the voice said, *"Open your eyes, I am sitting on the bed."* I opened my eyes and the indentation of someone sitting was clearly outlined on the edge of the bed. I did not panic, but I just sat and stared and then it was gone. I slept with the light on but I remember I kept having one of those dreams where you be dreaming you have turned the light on but when you open your eyes it is still dark in the room. Next day in school I saw my friend and she told me, *Willie, Momma knows you got her Ouija board and she wants you to bring it home."* I told my friend I would bring it home that evening because we were not going to have track practice that day. She once again told me, *"You bring that board home Willie. Momma done had things tearing up the house looking for the board."* I asked her what she meant by tearing up the house? *"Momma can somehow get her spirits to search for things she is missing and it woke me up last night when I woke up with stuff turning over in my room."* I thought for a few seconds and then I realized that is what her boyfriend was telling me when he said, *"Means, Helona knows you and Naomi took her Ouija board out that house and man I can't go over there right now because all kinds of crazy things are happening over there."*

Well I went home and told my mother that I needed to go out to my friend's house and I would be back later. Well guess what?

Mr. Ouija and Me

Ouija, Ouija it is time to go home.
Your master summons you she knows you've been on a roam.
I've gotten comfortable with you and now must get my own.
Perhaps you'll come to my board and leave hers alone.

I got the Ouija, put it in my track bag, and

headed for the elevator. When the door opened, my bag got light. When I looked in the bag, the Ouija was gone. I returned to my room and the Ouija was sitting back on my nightstand. I put the Ouija back into the bag and this time I got downstairs with it. I stepped off the elevator and the bag was light again. I returned to my room and the Ouija was on my nightstand. I just looked at it and then went and telephoned my friend. Do you know she did not even say hello. She simply said, *"You can't get it out of your room can you?"* I asked her how did she know this and she said the Ouija had been attached to me. *"You're going to have to come get me and I will have to get it from your room."*

    I got my sister Joyce to ride out West with me and get my friend. Then we rode back to the North side where I lived and my friend walked up to the Ouija laughing and told it, it was time to come home. She put it in my track back and we rode the bus back to my friend's house. Her mother, and my teacher, was very cordial to my sister Joyce and them she told Joyce she had to talk to her daughter and me. She told us never does that again and she told me I was not ready for an Ouija. She told me I needed to develop my spiritual band of protectors first because there were evil that would try to trap you to the Ouija. Well guess what? That movie *"The Exorcist"* came out and I never wanted to have anything else to do with an Ouija board. I guess you can say it scared me straight.

While I am still thinking of Mary, Pic, and Pete, I want to tell you of the last time I know they came to me as a trio.

Here's to Reality

As I told you, I was raised Sanctified. We believe the Bible from Genesis to Revelation. We believe in Spiritual Gifts, which includes *'Prophesying'*. We had moved back to Lexington and we lived over a church. When you Prophesy, a group of people sit in a circle in a darken room with their hands stretched out on their thighs. (It is not like having a séance.) You began to tell whatever comes into your mind. You have someone there who can tell you what you are seeing. We were gathered together and I was really in a relaxed state of mind when mother spoke.

"You're welcome here; Peace!"

Everything was quiet and I continued to relax my mind. Then I heard my mother say, *"You're welcome here. No one is going to hurt Willie Earl."*

I eased my eyes open and saw that my mother was staring in my direction. I got cold chills. Someone asked my mother what did she see and my mother told someone to turn on the lights because they were gone now. Everybody was a little shaken and the service was ended. When we were alone, my mother told me there were three people standing around my chair and they were staring at her. She told me there were a lady and two men. She said what got her attention they had turban like the one the one wraps on their heads and they all had on white robes like the Egyptian Scholars used to wear. I knew she had seen Mary, Pic, and Pete. I myself

Willie Means Well

have never fully seen them. Even now, sometimes I wonder did I dream it all until I get with people and they began to ask me about those times. Like I explained earlier when I was coming home on the highway and I had to be dozing off and on. I am sure it was the hand of my guardian Angel that kept me from missing my exit and running off the road. I figure I let the *Exorcist* scare me away from my studies but throughout my life I have always had that helping hand when I did not know where I was going to get help from.

By the way! I have had two chances to win the lottery here but I did not know how to use the information when it was given to me. I will give you a few more of my poems from *Poetry.com* and maybe I will elaborate and explain them. It is the day after Christmas 2008 and I know that *"The Sixth Sense"* is very much alive.

CENTER start
"YOU ABANDONED ME"
CENTER end

You know sometimes I hear the words *"YOU ABANDONED ME!"* shouted at me in my head. At this time, I become like Mother Mary when the Bible explained how Mary *"pondered these words in her heart"* when the Angel Gabriel informed her that she would be Mother of Our Lord and Savior JESUS CHRIST. If you recall, I spoke a lot about *Mary* but nothing that pointed particularly at *Pic* and *Pete*. I cannot explain this. Perhaps their help were channeled through Mary. As I said, the movie *"The Exorcist"* scared me away from the Ouija and my periods of meditations. Sometimes when I hear those words in my head, I wonder if the three are still with me and I somehow abandoned them back on that higher plane. Mary, however, I believe still comes to me when I am troubled about something. Sometimes I even wonder if the lady I saw that night looking in at me in my taxi on Britt Avenue in Columbus possibly could had been Mary. I also believe Mary, somehow, held the bond between me and my friend, who taught me how to use the Ouija, together through the years. There have been times I have experienced trouble enough physically. However, at those times, even when I sleep I am assailed by evil and I find myself running and getting nowhere until my friend comes to me in my dreams or I just hear her voice reminding me to *"look for the light Willie!"* When this happen I normally find my eyes open and I am staring at the ceiling wherever I have fallen asleep at. I am going to share this with you and allow you to be the judge.

While stationed in Friedberg, West Germany in 1978, I decided to take 30 days leave. The guys in the Section with me, and a few of the guys *'FDC' (Fire Direction Center)* allowed to hang with them, threw me a little going away party. I remember in Germany, when I got there in July 1977, we had beer machines in the barracks and soldiers were allowed two beers with their lunch. Needless to say, the guys in the Battery who depended on little benefits like this to get through the day stretched that benefit. The machines in the barracks had American brand beer in them. However, many of the guys would go to this little pizza place outside the gate and get German *'double-bock beer.'* So what is different you say? Two of those German beers equaled a six-pack of American beer. I think it was later in the year, when it turned cold and so many guys in the Brigade were wrecking their cars at lunchtime, that they removed the beer machines and killed those two beers with your lunch policy.

Anyway, the guys were giving me a little going away party and a lot of them were saying how they wish they could go to Chicago with me. I laughed and told them they were not missing anything and that I would probably be down South in Reform, Alabama with my father by Friday. It was Wednesday I was scheduled to leave. The laughed, joked, and said no way would they take some little place in Alabama over Chicago.

When I got home, my welcome back to the 'WORLD' (which is what we called the States) was a taxi driver giving me an early morning tour of the North Side, the downtown area, a shot through the Loop and the South Side, then finally where I wanted to go which was 2842 West Lexington on the West

Side. That was in 1978 and all that riding only came a little over twenty-three dollars. I drove a taxicab in Columbus, Georgia from February 1986 until December 2001. Even with the old fare that rides would have easily cost forty dollars. I guess every city have guys who try to get a little extra rather than be honest with the customer. I remember in Columbus the drivers who owned their taxi normally were retired military and you always got complaints from the military of drivers padding the fares. You will always have that selected few that will give all the others a bad reputation. In Columbus, the only time people look on taxi drivers with favor is during the Christmas and New Year holiday season. There is a program called *'Safety Cab'* sponsored mostly by Saint Francis Hospital that give people who have drank too much free rides home. Other than that, you hear taxi drivers called every despicable name you can think of. I gave that driver a twenty and told him he used up his tip. He attempted to argue and I told him I know the fare was between fifteen and sixteen dollars. He could take the twenty or I could call the police and tell them how you just gave me a tour of the city instead of bringing me straight home. The guy was angry but he left.

It was Wednesday morning and I cannot remember who came and got me but I remember everywhere I went, someone put a beer in my hand. Out of courtesy, I drank the beers and it was not long before I was drunk. I had only been gone less than three years since I moved south to my father. I had learned to drink but normally I drank *'Jack Daniel'* or *'Bacardi Rum'*. I guess everyone was trying to show they were glad to see me. However, all they had to do was remember my track and field days and they would realize I did not care for that stuff. I remember a teammate when I was a senior yelling that everyone were going to meet in *Gym 12* and smoke some *'pot'*. I looked at the guy and asked him was he crazy. Coach had said if you want to make it in sports, it was nice to hold a girl's hand and steal a kiss every occasionally but never start messing with drugs. The guy told me I had to be the biggest 'square' in the high school. That was fine with me.

Anyway, I got to my sister's house and she lived on the 14th floor in those same Cabrini Green Housing Projects. There were some children jumping *'double-dutch rope'* and they asked me did I want to take a turn. I laughed and told them maybe later. I recall days when Johnny and I taught ourselves to jump double-dutch and we sometimes out jumped the girls. The girls would get into arguments as to who have to have us on their teams.

I was lucky enough to catch one of the elevators working and I rode to the 15th floor and walked downstairs to my sister's apartment. Man, everybody was glad to see me. In addition, guess what? Somebody stuck a beer in my hand and one of my sister's friend put a *'joint'* in my hand. I looked at the damn thing and tried to stuff it in my pocket to throw away later. The job I had in the military required a type of clearance that had you *'pee'* in a bottle every occasionally. Even though I was going to be home for 30 days, I did not want to take a chance of having anything illegal come up on a *'piss-test'*. Before I could put the thing in my pocket,

Willie Means Well

the guy took it back and lit it. He took a deep drag and then passed it to me and I, like a fool, smoked it. I had smoked the damn thing, drank at least two sixteen ounce beers, and was sitting at the kitchen table. This child's voice asked me was I ready to take my turn jumping rope. I turned and I could swear the children were outside the window asking me to come out and play. I do recall, as you probably are saying right now, but you are on the 14th floor, opening the window and had one leg outside the window when the telephone rang. The children looked at me and I told them to hold up and let me answer the telephone. I got my leg back in and walked over and picked up the telephone. Without saying hello, how are you doing? Alternatively, may I speak to Willie? The voice on the telephone simply asked, *"Willie, what do you think you are doing?"* The voice on the telephone was my friend Naomi. I said, *"Naomi?"* My sister walked from the back and wanted to know whom I was calling. I told her I did not call anyone but Naomi was on the telephone. My sister said, *"What! Boy, let me speak to her."* She took the telephone, said hello a couple of times, then looked at me, and told me no one was on the telephone. She put it up to my ear and there was a dial tone. She hung the telephone up and then looked at the open window and said, *"try not to open this window that wide because I do not want a bird to fly in here."* Without speaking, I eased over to the window and looked down. The children and some more people were staring up at the window. I looked at my sister and told her I needed a ride to the bus station. Believe you me I was glad to get on that bus and get out of Chicago. I had searched for Naomi for years and I think it was 2005 and I was a member of *'Classmates.com'*. I had recently made contact with an old English teacher of mine, Ms. Helen Lundergan. Ms. Lundergan said she took pride in telling people about one of the few students she ever gave an *'A'* to. I expressed to Ms. Lundergan how I was the godfather of Naomi and Cherry's child but I had not been in touch with her for years. I knew Cherry had been murdered in the early *'80s'* and the child should be grown. It was about a week after I spoke to Ms. Lundergan that Naomi popped up on 'Classmates'.

CENTER start

MY ROSE BLOOMED ANEW

(Dedication for Naomi)

It was 30 years ago following a misunderstanding,
The words were dumped on him "the rose is dead"
Such a thing as this should not have caused such dread,
However, the love he had for her was so demanding
A miracle it had to be he knew,
For the rose had lived the days numbered twenty and two
The wisdom of a mother was shown quite plain
His love so steady and strong left her so drained
To his best friend, she surely belonged
He loved her just the same like she were his own
As the sun brings life to a rose at dawn
Her love he cherished and it made him calm
The knowledge he knew brought him turbulence and

Willie Means Well

guilt
The bond between them his friend surely felt
With skirts riding high and showing so much thigh
His friend fought bravely but gave in with a sigh
Years went by; his friend went home on High
He longed for her but his love had to be denied
He found her again but they were no longer kids
The feelings they had for each other they kept them well hid
A love so rare, the rose is still there
CENTER end

My Rose is very dear to me. I have told you some things of her but I try not to bother her. My Rose went through many things herself. When we were seniors in high school, she probably knew, but I did not, that she was carrying Kevin's baby. I remember her sitting in that hospital bed on the Southside of Chicago and saying to me, *"Willie, I don't know how, but I will be walking with our Class when it's time to walk across that stage."* My friend James Scott had gone with me to see her that night. We both braved the possibility of getting beat up or even killed to go on the Southside and see My Rose. A Blues singer called *'The Ghettos "nothing but concrete reservations."* Many times, I look back at situations that almost cost me my life on the streets and realize the Blues singer was correct in calling them concrete reservations. If you did not have a store bought gun, you simply broke off antennae; shaped you a piece of wood to hold the antennae, tape the antennae to the wood and you got a quick *'zip-gun'*. I guess they called it such because it o only fired one round at a time. When my friend Wilfred almost drowned at *Social Center*, it set off a war between the Vice Lords and the Mts... I was in my English class at Manley when *'Grim'* walked in and told me he needed the firing pin from my zip gun. Remember now, I told you I was not in the Vice Lords but all of my friends were. What they did, they taught me too. That day, Grim and I both had the zip guns but no firing pins. I had planned to make the firing pins in workshop that afternoon. Grim had just left when several Mts came in and jumped a guy I later found out was an *'Unknown Vice Lord'*. It was three Mts but that guy held his own. That afternoon the school was locked down and the police called because the Vice Lords were on one side of the school and the Mts were on the other side. Both gangs left and we left school.

Anyway, that night when James and I left the hospital seeing My Rose, these guys near the train station started whistling and James and I got on the train just as the guys came running up the stairs probably to rob us and even to hurt us. We dodged a bullet so to say but we were ready to do it all over again the next night but My Rose was discharged from the hospital. Love is a strong *'PUSHER'* and it blinds you to things when it is right in front of your eyes. My Rose did walk with us at graduation and I believe had her baby in September or October 1973. I was the child's God Father but really never had anything to do with the child. Even today, I regret not planning my life better and remaining in My Rose's life. My friend Kevin got killed I think in 1980 and I sure wish I had been there for My Rose.

Willie Means Well

Well! Here's to another day in the life of Willie Means

Today is the day before New Year's Eve. The ending of 2008 and the coming of 2009. I am in one of my moods this morning. Sometimes I want to share with you what you would probably consider *'little things'* and of no great significance. My mind is looking back on many moments that have shaped and guided me so far through our, *"Oh so mixed up world."* When I get like this, I simply say I am going into a *'Peak Period'* and I really do not know what to expect when I go into one of these thing. If you have not figured it out yet, for lack of a better name for something I cannot name, I simply call it a *'Thing'* or something that can be anything. From my military days in Public Affairs, I picked up the term *'Stuff'* from some of the Senior Officers I worked with. Just like, if I have not done it so far, making a statement that will send certain groups of people in a *'tailspin'*.

Willie Means Well

While in Artillery, I was a *'Fire Direction Specialist'* *(FDC)*. *FDC, the brains of the Artillery.* Guess what? Really thought I was something plotting data for our guns to send steel down range and cover a target called in by the *'The Eyes of the Artillery'*, *the Forward Observers.* Sometimes when we put metal-on-metal, an Observer would lose his cool and forget he is talking on the radio over an open line and we would hear something like, *"GOD DAMN FDC! YOU BLEW THE SHIT...Ooops!"* Then they regain their military composure and get back to proper radio etiquette. Something like, *Yankee five-inner (Y59) this is Zulu Four-two (Z42) tanks in the open on fire, goo shooting Yankee five-inner out."*

You know, I remember going to Germany in July 1977 and we enjoyed going to the firing ranges. We were allowed to use live ammunition and you have to see real damage that your weapons could do. However, the people had just elected a Democratic President back home and it was not long that we in the Unit I was in and probably the rest of the military saw and felt the results. My crew served weapon was a *'M203' Grenade Launcher.* It was a built-up *'M-16' Rifle* with a grenade launcher that fired a *40mm* type round. I really enjoyed having that weapon. I remember hitting 40 out of 40 with the M-16 on the Qualification Range. When I had to use the grenade launcher, on area targets you could see the round going down range and you got pure satisfaction when you got a hit of metal-on-metal. Fire jumped everywhere.

    Well guess what? The election of that Democratic President took care of that. Where as we did live fire missions with our big guns and fired live ammunition on the ranges, we were reduced to doing *'dry'* fire missions and when we went to the ranges to fire our crew served weapons, we used blanks and dummy ammunitions. However, let me tell you this! We had so much food in our *'Chow-halls'* that everybody in the entire Military probably picked up a lot of poundage. You would have to eat the food to understand picking up weight eating chow-hall food. The food is nutritious and full of protein and filling when you eat. However, you never gained weight with the physical training you did. Now, you had three difference kinds of meats on the serving ling, you get out in the eating area, and you had additional meats like roast beef and other foodstuff. I pitied those poor guys in the *'Armor'*. They had to remain slim and trim to get in those tanks. Speaking of the Armor, I was on the Kasern and ate in the chow-hall of the Unit that Mr. Elvis Presley was in during his tour of duty in the Army.

    I do not understand why when we change Presidents someone has not come up with a concrete plan that would give the *Department of Defense* the total budget it needs to oversee the safety of this Country. Group anything that has anything to do with protecting this Country under the Department of Defense. Then you take what is left and you take care all the Social Programs. I did not see it personally, but I heard so many people talking about our Elderly buying cat and dog food for their own consumption because they could not afford to buy *'People Food'*. Now of a sudden, it seems we have found ourselves back into those kinds of days again.

Willie Means Well

You know, from my Sociology Classes, you learn there is no reason for there to be one hungry person in this Country. However, greed has taken over, the Rich really is getting richer and the Poor, and the *Working Poor* is starving to death.

Well, are you still with me? I told you I felt like, as Louis L'Amour once wrote, *'Youndering'*. I will get back on tract but I am fifty-three years old and scheduled for fifty-four on Saint Valentine's Day. I feel I am truly blessed to have seen the changes in Society from the late fifties through now. There need to be lots of *'ME'* out there with stories to tell of what has happened to the *'Little Man or the Little People'* in our Society that *mores* have rolled over and left struggling to survive. I am going to hit you with another one of my poems right now and I might even explain it. However, more likely than not, I will talk of it later.

CENTER start
ACTUALITY!
Here's to Reality

Willie Means Well

CENTER end

    Today is April 8, 2012 and I am now 57 years of age. Currently, about the only good thing I can say about our Society, *"the people are making it."* The Country is still trying to recover from 16 years of Republicans taking care of the rich and wealthy. The Democratic President we have had for the last four years has been doing his best to try to pull the Country back together and Unite Us as one. I truthfully believe you replace this President with a White President, and the Country would get together and began solving all these social issues. However, since Mr. Obama is African American, and the new *klu Klux Klan* is calling themselves *'The Tea Party'*, the rich and the wealthy are doing all they can to keep the Country struggling and in a depression. These days you hear the media talking of the *'Middle Class'*. I do not know where they are getting there information from. I only see *The Poor, the Working Poor, and the Rich.* Who, by the way, have sent so many of our jobs to these other Countries; it is really hard to keep gas in your vehicle and food on the

Willie Means Well

table. When you talk of living paycheck-to-paycheck, it is not a good thing for us. When you are constantly worrying how to take care of your family, it brings your health down. The President tried to help all Americans by getting a *Healthcare Bill* that provided care for everyone. The new *Ku Klux Klan* along with some, plain and simple, *dumb people*, have been doing everything to get the Bill kicked out. Our Society has gotten so poor. Some talk of another *Civil War* in America. What is so sad about this is people would rather go into slavery than give all people a chance to live decent and healthy. If the *KKK* stop and think, they will go into slavery with everyone else because you can damn well bet that one of or former enemies, if not all of them, will declare War on America, move in, and take over while the fools are congratulating each other for hurting minorities.

    The *'mores'* in this Nation have been shattered and now it is time to reshape how the *"I'm White, so I'm Right"* generation have had this Nation. It is time to empty the prisons and get the ones that can be reformed back into society as productive citizens. It is time to clean *"death row"* of the ones that have taken others' lives. It is time to look at the World as a whole and let the one percent, rich and wealthy, of every Country know that their time is up and the *Poor and the Working Poor,* whose backs the Countries are supported on, be given their chance to live comfortable and healthy lives.

    I read where this television preacher recently celebrated having the one millionth born again Christian signed on as supporter of *'Christians United For Israel (CUFI).* I recall a verse in the Bible that tells you *"Pride goes before destruction".* GOD has been watching over Israel since forming them back when. When Israel got out of line, GOD punished them. If you read in *The Book of Joshua,* you will see where GOD punished Israel for the sins of *one greedy person.* GOD is awesome, powerful, and a very jealous GOD. GOD does not need any human helping HIM out.

    It is so ironic that the republicans were trying to punish the NAACP for trying to muster votes for the President. Yet, you have those mega churches, especially in Texas, trying to be smart and tell their congregation to vote republican. What a bunch of hypocrites.

CENTER start

LITTLE SPIDER

Do you want it, she asked of me!
She was only eight or nine, ten maybe.
Do I want what, I asked, looking into her eyes.
The coy look on her face made it clear and I gave a heavy sigh.
Oh, little child, where is your mother?
As I looked all around me, I thought, why even bother.
A web of intrigue tightly woven.
Strands set out, waiting to be broken.
When the prey is captured, and the door is locked,
Who will be next once the web is rocked?
All these eyes and hungry mouths to feed.
We've come to this now; we use the children for the seed.

Willie Means Well

CENTER end

This happened on a hot, summer day in Columbus, Georgia. It was during my taxi driving days and I had gone on a call to this housing project named *'Baker Village'*. Driver was already paranoid from these Projects because we had a driver killed in those Projects. As I was striving up this street, I saw these children running back and forward across the street so I slowed down. A truck from the housing authority backed into the road and I had to stop. As I was waiting for the truck to clear, that is when the child came up to the car and propositioned me. The dear, had on a dress that hung off her shoulder and her hair was loose and thick. As I looked into her eyes, I saw wonderment as if she was giving me a promise of pleasure. There were some adults sitting on a porch and I realized they were watching the whole situation... It really saddens me to realize that those adults knew what that child was doing. So many times, you hear and read about people who have sold even babies to drug dealers just to get drugs. *"Vengeance is mine"* is attributed to GOD in the Bible, I think. I can see why such a thing is not trusted into the hands of the likes of me. I would go throughout the World and really punish people who I knew even fantasized such thoughts in their heads. That particular day I would have did something to all of those adults sitting on that porch. So many times, I hear the cries of children in my head and it makes me want to weep to know that somewhere at any given time, some child is being abused physically and sexually.

I will share something else with you also. The male gender must forever be on their guard when dealing with the female gender. A lot of interaction between female children and males is pure and innocent. However, the feelings they can sometime convey to the male have sexual overtone to them. They tend to grow up faster than their male counterparts do. When I was eight years old, we loved it when Momma went with friends on overnight fishing trips. Normally the children would be left at our house and we played games, sang songs, and enjoyed ourselves before going to bed. At eight years old, I wanted to have sex or so I thought until one night Cynthia and her brother, *Duke,* were left at our house. It was a year earlier when my best friend, *American Best People,* that was really his name, had taught me, at seven years old, how to *masturbate.* Lord knows I did not know what I was doing but it sure felt good and I do believe by the time I was ten, I probably already had been gifted with what most guys got nowhere near until they were in their twenties.

    Cynthia was nine or ten and she followed me everywhere that night. I really ate up all that attention. Cynthia was pretty as all get out, with a head full of thick hair. All while we were singing and playing games, she stayed by me and we did everything together. We were all young so at bedtime Roxanne allowed all the children to pile into one bed. I do not know how Cynthia wound up next to me but I do remember the feel of her hand on my penis. This scared the dickens out of me but at the same time, my body responded to her touch. I jumped up and told Roxanne I was going to make me a *pallet* on the floor because I could not sleep in the bed with the other children. Ms., little, Cynthia chipped in her share, *"Yeah! I and Willie Earl can't sleep with all these children."* I got down on the *pallet* and so did she. I do not know what that young lady had planned for me, but I guess my sister noticed my fear and made the boys go to the back room to sleep and the girls stayed in the front room. I remember Cynthia stood in the door with her arms crossed as if she was trying to still figure out a way to get in that bed with me. My question? Where did she learn to do such a thing at such an early age? I always wondered later, what she had been exposed to by her mother.

Well, today is January 16, 2009 and I guess the time must be moving back into one of the Aquarius time.

I have so much I still wish to share with the world but I really want to wrap this book up and get on to another book. I will get back to the poems I have written but I want to say something about the first African American President. Yes, I voted for him because I too saw that the Republican Party is so wealthy that they had begun to flaunt their wrongdoing in front of the Nation and their attitude was *"SO WHAT! YOU CAN'T DO ANYTHING ABOUT IT!* I you disagree with this, look back on the years 2004 through 2008, then look in the mirror, and continue to tell yourself that lie. Anyway, just want to say, I am a Veteran. I voted for change but I will never forget him turning his back on the symbol of our Great Nation, *'Ole Glory'*.

What I want to share with you on this cold January morning of the day after the inauguration is the ability of the body to adapt to its environment. While stationed with the *197th Brigade (Mechanize) (Heavy) (Separate)* in 1984, we went to Fort Drum, New York for *'Winter Environmental Training'*. The first two days the uniform of the day was cold weather parker and Mickey Mouse Boots. We were not allowed to ride anywhere and the temperature averaged minus 13 degrees. After two days of walking and shoveling coal, we begged that the uniform of the day be changed to field jacket and overshoes. Would you believe the temperature rose to ten degrees and we were outside playing football in the snow in tee shirts. You would come in from outside and you would immediately start sweating as if someone had poured water on you.

I remember I was sending photos back to my garrison for the newspaper that showed us in snow blizzards while the people back in Georgia was enjoying eighty-plus degree weather. I captured the front page of the Post newspaper for the entire month in April 1984. I wanted to share this with you because I still find it funny that people believe we crawled out of the sea... *IDIOTS!!!* The body is such a complex piece of work that it had to take someone with a vast superior intelligence to put us together.

Something else I wish to share with you is the death of a fellow soldier. It has been a quarter of a century ago but the incident still lies heavy with me.

CENTER start
A Ride in the Snow

Willie Means Well

CENTER end

When the Brigade Training Officer (S-3) contacted me and told me the Brigade Commander wanted me to go with him and take photos of him in the field with the troops, I was a good soldier as usual, went, and got my field gear and my assigned Canon F-5. I loved that camera. You could do some neat stuff with it. As a matter of fact, later that year while training at Fort Irwin's National Training Center (NTC), I had the Post Training and Audio Visual people upset and trying to get me in trouble because they thought I had used the camera to take sexy photos of one of my soldiers. My Captain did not accuse me but he was upset after the Post Public Affairs Officer (PAO) chewed him out. My Captain told me the *PAO* said I was still a *'loose cannon'* and someone needed to control my activities. You see, my first assignment as a photojournalist was at Fort Irwin in September 1980 and I did what I had to as a Sergeant E-5 to get m y mission accomplished. I had to establish contact with the local media and the town of Barstow was thirty-eight miles away. I asked for a typewriter and the reply I got was what I needed with a typewriter when I could share one with someone else. (The Defense Department was just reopening the Post and there were all kinds of new equipment sitting in boxes not being used). I asked for a vehicle to get into town so I could introduce myself to the local media and make contact with the Public Affairs at the Marine Corp Logistic Base, and I was told all the vehicles was for senior people and no way was I getting a vehicle. In Public Affairs School, the one thing they taught us over-and-over was if people got in the way of our mission, contact the Public Affairs all the way up the chain-of-command to the Pentagon if we had to so someone could help us. After several days of trying to get things accomplished on the telephone, I waited until everyone went home for the day and called Office of the Chief of Public Affairs at Forces Command (*FORSCOM*). I remember I talked to a Colonel (Full Bird) David and filled him in on what I was going through.

    The next morning I had to report to the

Director of Personnel and Community Activities (*DPCA*), and I must admit... the Lieutenant Colonel (Light-bird) was very patient with me. As I told you, I was just a Sergeant E-5. Everybody I was dealing with held the rank of Senior Noncommissioned Officer or Field Grade Commissioned Officer. I made my Sergeant Rank while in Artillery. The highest-ranking officer I ever saw while in Artillery was the Division Commander, Colonel Tanzer. He was a Full-Bird. My first assignment as a Public Affairs Specialist at fort Irwin, there were so many General Officers and other Field Grade officers, I felt intimidated at first and tried not to draw any attention to myself. Look like everybody my rank was picked for any detail that came up. Those first two days I was caught up in those details but after I talked to the Colonel at *FORSCOM*, everything changed. There were two particular Light-birds that I seem to taint the very air they breathe when I came into their presence. However, even they became cordial to me after the *DPCA* spread the word that the Colonel at *FORSCOM* had talked to the Post

Commander, which was a *Brigadier General,* and the General had gave the command to assist me in whatever I needed to get the word out to the public about Fort Irwin. The guys at the motor pool assigned me a *CJ-5* that was painted red, white, and blue and had been used in some parade that was held to celebrate America's two hundredth birthday. That little jeep and I have to be known all over the Post and the City of Barstow.

    Anyway, that is how the *PAO* knew me and many times when I was told I could not have something, I would go to the General. Public Affairs were on the Commander's *Special Staff* and I had an open door to the General at anytime, I never got to the General of course. The General had a Chief-of-Staff, which was a Full-Bird, and a *general-aide-to-camp, which* was a *First Lieutenant*. The top noncommissioned officer was a *Command Sergeant Major* and between the three of them, they were my *'shakers and movers'* when I needed something. They eventually had this *Light-bird* come *TDY* (temporary duty) and run the Public

Affairs until they got a *PAO* assigned. The very first morning after he had been briefed by the command, he eased into our office, closed the door, looked at me, and said, *"Sergeant Means. You called Colonel David?"* I told him yes sir I did. He repeated the question again. *"Sergeant Means. You really called Colonel David?"* I explained to him I could not even get a typewriter and everybody wanted to know why I needed to go into town and not use the telephone. He told me calling Colonel David was like calling God. He had me promise him that if he was doing something wrong; I would talk to him rather than call *FORSCOM.*

With the Colonel to run interference for me, I have to write news stories and take many photos. The one thing I did not like about being a photojournalist was the 247th Medical Evaluation (*MEDAC*) Unit was next door. This was a mobile medical evaluation unit that flew helicopters. Many times, I had to fly out, strap myself in, lean out the door, and take photos. I must admit that this scared the hell out of me but I did not want the *flyboys* to know how much they were scaring me. When that Light-bird got ready to return to Fort Hood, he told me that he would love to have me work with his staff at *13th COSCOM.* That really made me feel good and I missed him dearly. Especially after the Major, I got in, as *PAO* was very disgruntled and did not like me at all. He proved it to me by giving me a seventy-three on my first Enlisted Evaluation Report *(EER)* when the lowest score we are supposed to get as a noncommissioned officer is 121.

    To get back to my Captain getting upset with me, he told me the *PAO* told him many good things about me but he also said I was a radical. My Captain told me he was going to give me a chance to explain why I was shooting photos of female soldiers' legs when I was supposed to be training my soldiers. I laughed and that made him mad. He told me I could be in serious trouble and the Major asked that I be given an *Article 15* (a punishment given to military people to try to keep them in line). The Captain and I walked into the back office at the Public Affairs Building and I showed him a picture of a group shot posted on the wall behind a desk. I asked him to look at the picture, he told me he did not have time to be going through this, and if I did not have a good explanation, he was going to have to put me in for the *Article 15*. I pointed to a young lady in the picture sitting with her legs crossed... I told the Captain that was the photo. He just looked at me. I reminded him he told me I was to take every opportunity I have to train the soldiers and I used the picture to explain how to use the extension rings on the *F-5*. He then lightened up and began laughing. I thought to myself, *"yeah, he is laughing now but he was ready to burn my ass."*

Back to Fort Drum and the ride in the snow. We flew out to one of the training units and it took forty-five minutes to get to the unit by air. After following the Commander around and shooting some photos, the training officer with the Unit asked the Commander if I could stay and take photos of the soldiers training. The Commander looked at me and asked, *"You don't mind, do you Babe?"* I did not realize just how well the Commander knew me but I was told by my boss that the Commander really like the job I was doing. So when h e called me *'Babe'*, there was no way I could tell him no. I will admit my heart sure did want to be back o n that helicopter going back to garrison.

The Major at the training unit explained he wanted me to ride with him on his track and take photos of the soldiers training. As we got on the track and pulled out, it began to snow. The Major was sitting on the track hatch and I was standing in the track commander *(TC)* hole. After we visited two positions, it really began to snow hard and the wind began to whistle and howl it was blowing so hard. We crested a hill and the Major told the driver to stop. We scanned the area in front of us but saw no movement. The snow was deep and still coming down very hard when we took off again h headed for a tree line. Of a sudden, I thought I heard someone scream. The Major yelled to me did I hear someone scream. I motioned I could not hear with the wind blowing so hard. The Major told the driver to stop and asked did the driver hear anything. The driver said he really could not hear anything with the driving helmet on. The Major stood on top of the track and looked around but visibility was down to a few feet. The Major told the driver to go on and we headed back to the operation center set up in the woods. The Major thanked me and then had me get on the back of a chow truck headed back to garrison. I do not exaggerate when I say it took that truck three hours to get back to garrison. I do not know about the other soldiers on the back of that truck with me but I practically almost froze.

What I remember most about that entire day was it was around three in the morning and I had just gotten warm lying in the bed when someone knocked on my door. When I asked who it was, the *Charge-of-Quarters (CQ),* explained they needed me at the operation center. I asked what was wrong and the *CQ* told me they just had a call in from the field and they found a soldier dead. I told him to tell them I did not have any more film and they needed to get Post personnel to help them. I had no intentions of going back into that cold and loosing the rest of my sleep after just getting warm.

The next morning I reported to the operation center and they were having an emergency meeting about the soldier found dead. They discussed the area where the soldier was found and I looked at the Major whose track I was on. I will always remember that Major giving me a brief sign of silence. He caught my eye a couple of times but looked away. After the meeting, I went over to the Post photo lab and the guys were looking at the photos take. That track had sliced off h half that soldier's face and pushed that *M-60* Machine Gun back into his chest cavity. You want to talk about residual fall out. When we returned to Georgia, one of the guys in the soldier's section was cleaning his *M-16 Rifle* and the report we got was he put the barrel in his mouth and pulled the trigger. Everyone wanted to know where he got the rounds for the weapon. Less than a week later, another guy from the same section went to the *CQ* desk and the *CQ* told me the guy talked about the other two guys and began to cry. The *CQ* said he did not know where the soldier got the weapon from but the guy had an *M-1911A1, put it in his mouth,* and pulled the trigger.

Perhaps I have it wrong, but that Brigade too so many soldiers' life. Many of you do not know the purpose of the *National Training Center (NTC)*. However, it trains our military in certain tactics. That Brigade holds the distinguished honor of being the first to defeat the *OPFOR (Opposing Forces)* at the National Training Center. When this happened, we all knew the Brigade Commander would be receiving his first start of generalship. That was a great honor for the Brigade but it got seven soldiers killed during the training. They also got their butts beat like all the other units who came out there to train in 1980 and 1981. When they claimed the honors of being the first to defeat the *OPFOR*, they got four more soldiers killed. Many Veterans will say that is part of the training they signed up for. However, I want to say this is not the Warsaw Pact Countries. During my artillery days, we were always reminded that the Russians normally lost thousands during training because their training is so realistic. I want to remind everyone this is not Russia.

I am going to tell you two more things here and then try to keep my military stuff for another book. Thanksgiving Day 1983, my Major I invited me to come over and watch football with him. I told him he knows he would be spending Thanksgiving with his family. He told me not so. His wife had planned for her and the children to be at her mother because he would probably be in the field training. As he explained to me, the Brigade had a policy that the Brigade would be training most holidays because that was the best time to get good, *TOUGH, TACTICAL, TRAINING (TTT)*! During the holidays, the trainees normally go on pass. If they were on pass, the Brigade did not have to worry about them being in the way out in the training areas. In addition, many might be shaking their heads about my credentials. I was only a Sergeant E-5 but I was working in an E-7 slot. We got in an E-7 and the Captain was discussing with him his assignment to the Brigade. The Captain went to Brigade and discussed the situation with the command then came back and began to beat around the bush about the E-7 being assigned to the Brigade. The E-7 did not seem to understand what was being offered so I spoke up and said, *"What the Captain is saying if you want to be here you will but if you want to go to main post we could make that happen too."* My Captain looked at me and told me I had just gotten a *'D'* for tact. I did not see why he was beating around the bush with the man. The E-7 decided to go to main post. The Captain closed the door and told me the command wanted to know what they needed with an E-7 when they had Sergeant Means. This should have made me feel good and it did. However, I needed that E-7 so I could relinquish my position and return to *The Defense Information School (DINFOS)* for more training. You see we went through a lot and soldiers and other military people go through even more today with these conflicts going on. Next time you see a military person in uniform, if the situation allows it, shake the person's hand, or give them a hug.

Willie Means Well

New Years 2009

I know I am jumping around but for those of you this book is geared towards, this jumping will only fuel your desire for more.

New Years Day while driving into Columbus to my day job, my mind is on the happiness I heard in the lady's voice at the publishing house. I shall simply call her Ms. 'K'. I am quite sure Ms. 'K' knows who she is.

Sometimes I head down that single roadway and my thoughts lean towards the old ways and I want to think of everything as a man may think. Then I look at my track and field days, my college days (seems I have been in college forever. Pre-calculus Algebra away from a bachelor of science in psychology with Troy University), and of course my military days, then I simply remind people *"girls have locker room talk too!"*

So! How many of you have had similar situations where you cross pass with someone and the lyrics come to mind *"Oh, it's sad to belong to someone else when the right one comes along."* There is something in Ms. 'K's voice that make me want to go to the end of the world, if need be, in order to be in her physical presence.

I normally keep my radio on a Christian Station but this morning I was scanning and came across the song *"Blinded by the Light."* As I listen, I was taken back to my days with Dad in Reform, Alabama. I worked at Georgia Pacific (GP) in Belk, Alabama and my Pontiac T-37 and I used to get around those hills in the early morning hours headed to *GP*. Look like I could not drive to work in the morning without hearing that song. It was so beautiful, yet so lonely, the route I took through those hills. Sometimes, I wanted to pull to the side of the road, turn the car off, let the window down some, and just become one with the environment. I never did however, because that road I took had the reputation of being one of those roads where you might get hitchhikers. Even though you may not stop, sometimes the hiker wound up riding with you anyway. Know what I mean? Many children growing up in the South have heard of such going on. They probably heard of *"The Crossroads"* in Mississippi or travel across country and I understand a similar highway can be found in the California Desert. So many things that is not explainable.

CENTER start

OH BY THE WAY

(My life in a nutshell)

Oh by the way, it's ok what they say.
I am an ordinary guy. Sometimes I even cry.
Born in 1955. I was a Negro and glad to be alive.
In 1966, a move to Chicago, we did not fit.
Three boys, three girls and a Momma too.
The man meant well but we made him blue.
Now we're on an odyssey, an adventure, off to roam.
My mother took care of her family, for us she found a new home.
Here, there, almost anywhere.
There was always someone, to help us out.
Concord Pentecostal Missionary Baptist Church.

Willie Means Well

I met Reverend Clark, into my life came hurt.
I loved that man, a father figure for me.
One lesson on the organ, the piano too, even a Junior Deacon, I was happy.
Then came the command to play for the choir, I became frighten and had to flee.
It was my fork in the road, track and field, over Church.
Many times, I look back wanting to mend the hurt.
Off on a roam, trying to find my way.
So many stops in life. I still search for a place.
Married now, three boys, a girl, and one I don't know.
I still look to the future, for there lays my hope.

Just a Chance

All they needed was just a chance
Not all this brutality, but a helping hand
They are so innocent, young, and expectant
When parents hurt them, they do not understand it
That child is your flesh, your blood, your life
Do not abuse it because you are full of strife

Willie Means Well

This one has a black eye, but why won't it cry
The fear I see I n that little face makes me want to die
They tag along trying to keep up
However, the pace you set is excessively tough
When the child falls down it wants no help
You have taught it well to fear your belt
There is one in the cold in shabby clothes
The parent wastes the money on crack I am told
These are the future, learning today
Without a little chance, someday we will pay
What will they grow to be, watch as they play?
The games are full of violence, there is no escape
Give the children a chance, help them grow up
If we don't help them now, their bodies will go to dust
CENTER start

It is my intentions someday to have a complete city of this caliber. I intend to take children from all over the world and give them *"Just a Chance"*.

Thanks!

CENTER start

Willie Means Well

The End

(I am a Fucking Dinosaur)

CENTER end

I have concluded that I am a fucking dinosaur. If I have not cursed before now, oh well, what the hell. I am going to end this for now. Finish it off and let the editors straighten it out! Sounds familiar? *"Le Mercy'! Cry Havoc and let slip the Dogs of War!"* In other words, *"Kill Them All and Let God Sort them Out."*

I have been blessed to see many things come to pass these last fifty years. So many do not even understand what they have been a part of. I remember our Country being so innocent. Television and life was so simple and pleasurable the late '50s and early '60s. Cartoons and Westerns ruled primetime television. *The Deputies, Laramie, Man without A Gun, Gray Coats (*a show about Confederate Calvary-and I am Black), *Wagon Train.....etc. The Flintstones, Bugs Bunny, The Jetsons, The Little Rascals on Cousin Cliff.....etc.*

Willie Means Well

Many of you are shaking your heads and saying things like *"Hidden Racism" and "Oppression"*. Some maybe but it was not for everyone. I too am glad for many changes but our Society is headed for a great let down. You have always had that group that claimed television does not influence people. With all the gore on television and the movies, you had better rethink your thoughts. You will be shocked if you knew what was going on behind many closed doors. Two young four-year-old females died in a house fire. Someone made the statement, *"I do not understand! Was there no adults to try and get them out?"* Earlier that morning there had been a drug bust in that area. Did someone perhaps use this as retaliation? See what I mean? I have moments to regret. I love my wife and sons and would not give them up for the world. However, had I seen the movie *"Somewhere In time"* in 1980, I guess I would be happily deceased. I would had gone with Elizabeth to Myrtle Beach and gladly be hung for mixing Races just to share her love for a while. When I do *"Willie's Girls"*, she will be there leading things off. I am angry now! I will see you all later.

GOOD DAY! (Bilbo2Shire)

I hope that if you are reading this, you will go out and is your part to help President Obama reelected. If you need to give someone a ride to the polls, do so. This is America, Land of the Free. With the election of our first Black as President, you have so many who have shown that they will lie and do everything else to make every dollar any way they can but they care nothing for the less fortunate. Regardless to what any of you say, the Republican Party has shown its true side and they are everything that is wrong for Minorities to get an even chance to make a good living.

Momma named me Willie Earl Means. I have a ton of nick-names: Buster, Scatter-Brain, Scatter-teeth (all from uncles I am told); Mean-mo (track and field and early days with the guys on Lexington); then, of course, Heartbreaker, given to

Willie Means Well

me by some of the older girls and guys from Lexington after an embarrassing accident one night talking to Black Man and one of the pretty girls in the neighborhood, *Janice 'Pap' Smith.* We were discussing the "birds and the bees" and it was getting intense to the tune of getting aroused. Of a sudden, I felt this breeze down below, and the young lady must have noticed the look on my face because she followed my eyes down, and I do not know how, but my penis was sticking out the front of my pants.

"Got damn! That is big!" shouted the young lady. At her shout, Black Man looked down and yelled, *"damn, Mean-mo!"* Me, I am trying to get my penis back in and zipping up my pants without getting the damn thing caught in the zipper.

The young lady ran out the yard and Black Man, damn fucker, ran out yelling, *"Buster's dick came out his pants!"*

CENTER start

February 13, 2011

(Last night to be 55 and still alive)

CENTER end

    My mind is on Hazelnut tonight my first wife. Driving to the store to get me some blackberry cobbler, I was radio surfing and settled on 92.3 FM WLWI out of Montgomery, Alabama: Country and Western Music. They played a song by Vern Gosdin and it took me to another song by him I recalled listening to on my way back from Korea in September 1983: *"I wonder where we'd be tonight".*

Willie Means Well

www.ingramcontent.com/pod-product-compliance
Lightning Source LLC
Chambersburg PA
CBHW051415290426
44109CB00016B/1309